TULISA
JUDGEMENT

Love, Trials and Tribulations

CW01496268

First published in the UK in 2025 by Blink Publishing
An imprint of Bonnier Books UK
5th Floor, HYLO, 105 Bunhill Row,
London, EC1Y 8LZ

A CIP catalogue record for this book is available from the British Library.

Hardback ISBN: 9781785128592

Also available as an ebook and an audiobook

1 3 5 7 9 10 8 6 4 2

Design and Typeset by Envy Design Ltd
Printed and bound in Great Britain by Clays Ltd, Elcograf S.p.A.

The authorised representative in the EEA is
Bonnier Books UK (Ireland) Limited.
Registered office address: Floor 3, Block 3, Miesian Plaza,
Dublin 2, D02 Y754, Ireland
compliance@bonnierbooks.ie

www.bonnierbooks.co.uk

by now you would assume
d loose faith in my spiritual
ourney and realise that life
simply a box of chocolates.
On the contrary, looking back,
he years that felt like the wo
ears of my life at the time, la
n made me the person I am today
iving me lessons, values and moral
aking me a better, stronger per
nd sharing it with others, which
spired thousands of people and
ffect, changed lifes. nothing I belie
s more powerful than that, being
ble to change peoples lives, for
etter. This year is no different f
he rest, maybe the lessons to be le
re different and the effects, and
ts tougher than the rest but its a
ike the lessons before were trainin
though   her   f

For Byron and Plato Contostavlos

CONTENTS

PROLOGUE

MY NAME IS Tula Paulinea Contostavlos, better known as Tulisa. I am 34 years old. I am a singer-songwriter, popstar, TV personality, one-third of the dynamite trio N-Dubz, former *X Factor* judge, brand owner, and dabbling actress. Since I was a child, all I'd ever wanted was to be rich and successful, in that order. And through a lot of hard work and determination, I had managed to live that dream.

In the United Kingdom I'm classed as 'famous' and a 'celebrity'. And in 2013, when I started writing this book at the age of 24, I was the kind of famous where people actually forget what you do for a living. The sort where you're just famous for being famous, because people and the media are more interested in your personal life than the things you achieved to get there.

* * *

I stared down at the large handful of pills I held in my hand and the almost-empty bottle of vodka in front of me, as I sat with my back against the bathtub on my bathroom floor, drunk and disorientated. *I can't do this anymore,* I thought, *not another six months of this. I just about got through the first six, but I'm not built for this. Why is this happening to me? What's the point in being alive just to be miserable? How am I ever going to find happiness after this? Even if I'm found innocent, I'll be empty inside by the time I get to the end of it, and my life will be ruined.* I stared back down at the pills, feeling more defeated than I'd ever felt in my life. I didn't even know what these pills did, but their name rang a bell and I knew they were strong. They were all I could find when I looked through my drawer of medication. I tried to Google the name on the packet, to find out whether or not they would kill me, but the wi-fi wouldn't reach through the locked door of my en-suite.

I didn't like the thought of slitting my wrists and being found covered in blood, I thought about how disturbing that would be for my loved ones. I hesitated for a moment.

Well, fuck it, if it's meant to be then it's meant to be, I thought. I necked back the pills two by two with the leftover vodka. I hoped they would kill me. I'd rather die than feel this way anymore.

Chapter 1:

THE SET-UP

IT WAS APRIL 2013 and I was in LA to meet my new acting agent and take a shot at some of my first Hollywood film auditions. I had dabbled in acting before but never plunged in at the deep end. I was now ready to take a leap of faith.

The British press was well aware and had already publicised the bold career move I was making so the pressure was on. Gareth Varey (my friend and PA) had received a call from a female casting director who worked for 21st Century Fox. She wanted to put me in touch with some bigtime Bollywood film producers who were trying to get hold of me for a role in their first Hollywood/ Bollywood production. She had reached out through the 21st Century Fox Twitter account originally and then put Gareth in touch with one of the producer's personal assistants, a woman called Nish, who said they were very interested in me for a role and wanted to fly me to Las Vegas for a meeting.

I agreed, excited, and so Gareth, me and my friend Michelle who I'd taken to LA with me, were booked on to a first-class flight to Las Vegas by Nish. Once in Vegas, we were picked up in a limousine and taken to the Venetian Hotel, where Nish greeted us in person.

She was a very friendly, sweet and petite Indian woman, with the most beautiful piercing green eyes. She showed us to our two hotel suites and told us she would be back to collect us for the meal that had been planned for later on.

Later that night, while heading up to the producers' suite, I was buzzing with nerves and excitement. I couldn't believe I'd bagged an opportunity this big so soon. Luckily, once I sat down the nerves began to dissipate as I fell into work mode and my alter ego (The Female Boss) kicked in.

One of the producers was a small, well-spoken British Indian man named Samir Khan, and the other was his taller cousin, a man named Rahul, who spoke with a slight Indian accent. The producers spent the entire dinner being super-friendly and getting to know us. It was fun, there was a lot of casual chit-chat, and they were constantly trying to banter with us and convince us to party with them over the next few days. Eventually, after the meal, we all sat down with them in the sofa area, so they could tell me more about the role.

It honestly sounded like a dream come true. It was

going to be the first ever Bollywood film starring an urban British lead, hopefully sparking a whole new genre. They talked about wanting to win an Oscar and said I would star alongside Leonardo DiCaprio if I won the role. He was my ultimate childhood crush at the time (like every other girl my age), and I would be paid millions for the job if I got it. They mentioned then that they were looking for a 'bad girl' to play the part, and how they thought I was perfect for it because of my 'past'. They wanted someone that 'didn't have to act', so to speak, because she *was* the character, a bad girl, from a rough council estate in London. *I can do that*, I thought, *piece of cake. I can convince these guys that I'm the girl in the role, no problem.* Because, in some ways, I *had* been her. If it meant moving closer to everything I'd dreamed of, I could stretch the truth a little.

My trip to the US came at a time when I was at odds with my career as an *X Factor* judge, a role I'd had for the previous two years. Since my ex-boyfriend 'he who has no name' released our private sex tape, nothing had felt the same. I'd felt this huge turn in public perception, and a dark change from the press. There was so much judgement and hatred towards me everywhere I went. Every expression on my face, every word that came out of my mouth, every place I went to, every person I was seen with, every outfit I put on, what I weighed, what I ate, how I wore my hair, how I did my make-up, any mood or emotion I was feeling that accidentally showed was scrutinised under a microscope. Every day felt like I was the subject of a witch-hunt, and every time I stepped out onto a stage I could feel it. The 'Evil Eyes were on me', as my Greek Granny (my Yia Yia) used to say.

I had come to hate my life. I was miserable. I had spent almost every day of my younger years fighting for this success and to be in this position, like my life depended on it because, at the time, it literally had. This was all supposed to be an escape from the pain and restraints of my past. But now every day was another battle, trying to keep up with the multiple versions of myself that I had to portray. Meanwhile, I had to hide my real self, as I was now too guarded and fearful to show any softness or vulnerability. It felt like my back was up against the wall. I had created the Female Boss persona to inspire women and give them strength, but now I was trapped in my own defence mechanism – a beast of a character that I had created to prevent anyone hurting me again. I had to remain detached and unbothered. More than that, I felt I had to be cocky with it too, just to survive. I appeared like the definition of a ruthless egotistical bitch But, deep down, I was just a 22-year-old girl who had been searching for love and validation. Unfortunately, I had looked for it through success, and I had ended up with ten times more hatred and confidence kicks than I'd had before I'd set myself on this path in the first place.

I had started to feel desperate for an escape, so when I was approached about this film it was as if all my dreams had come true. In my mind I went as far as to say the opportunity was a blessing from above to take away this pain and emptiness. It was exactly what I had been praying for. Who I was wouldn't matter anymore, because now I would just be pretending to be someone else, and it would be my job to do so. I could do acting roles and then disappear into the background. I wouldn't have to be at the forefront anymore, being fed to the wolves like I was every night on *The X Factor*. This was it – my escape to a new life, to happiness.

My trip to Vegas lasted three days, and at the end of my stay I was told that I pretty much had the job. After all the media and public pressure of the past two years, I was ecstatic. I really needed this new start for the sake of my mental health. But I still knew better than anyone that, until I signed the deal, nothing was set in stone. And lo and behold, when I got back to England, to my dismay they went quiet for a week. This made me extremely nervous as I had so many hopes tied up in this. When we finally received a phone call, they told us they were thinking about getting someone else to play the role, but there was still a possibility I could get it. Gareth and I were hanging on the other end of the phone by a thread – we both knew how much I needed this.

They kept ringing, and Gareth and Nish were back and forth over email for about four tortuous months. At least there was still hope.

They kept us hanging on, still indecisive over whether they should give the role to a more established actress, or someone like me that was more similar to the actual character. They kept asking for evidence to show exactly how similar I was, wanting footage of me being a bit of a bad girl in real life. Clips of me kicking off at contestants on *The X Factor* or arguing with Dappy and Fazer on our docuseries *Being N-Dubz*. Even personal footage of me being a bit of a rebel if they could get it. I got the gist. The more of a bad girl they thought I was, the more likely it was that they would give me the role, but what more did I have to do to prove it? I felt like I was being teased. All I wanted was to get this job, to the point that I was ignoring every other possibility. I began burning bridges with *The X Factor* because I just couldn't face the job there anymore, not with the possibility of this enormous change being dangled in front of me. In my heart I felt it was meant to be. It was going to happen, it had to happen. I refused to believe it wouldn't, and I couldn't face the idea that I would have to do another year on the show. An inside source had told me that the team at *The X Factor* could see what kind of place I was in. If I wanted my job as a judge next year I'd have to reach out and fight for it, show certain people that I wanted it, that I was focused.

The truth was, if I didn't get the acting job I *would* need the show. I'd just put a half a million-pound deposit on my house. I had serious bills to pay. But at the same time, I'd always had this sense that everything would work out in my life for the better, no matter what I was going through. I always followed the signs: I was and still am a very spiritual person. The way that this acting job had come about, the timing, the role, I felt like there were too many signs. I believed it was all heaven-sent. It would all work out exactly the way it was supposed to. So, I didn't pick up the phone or reach out to *The X Factor*. My sole focus was now on this movie role and proving to these producers that I was right for it.

By now, my relationship with my footballer boyfriend Danny Simpson was getting a lot of press interest and – through the drama that came with all the publicity – it had really started to deteriorate. The level of negative attention the relationship brought to both of us was unlike anything I had experienced before. There were constant lies being made up about us, both individually and as a couple. Every week there was a new story about some non-existent interaction I'd had, or he'd had, or we'd had with an individual that neither of us had ever met or remembered meeting.

I was once out, minding my own business, when I was approached by a random female who viciously elbowed me in the ribs out of the blue, just to get a reaction. She didn't receive one because she'd elbowed me so hard she'd winded me, so I could barely breathe let alone react. But she still proceeded to sell a story to the papers, saying I had tried to attack her for attempting to speak to Danny, or something along those lines.

Dan had once had to retrieve CCTV footage from a club just to prove to me that his story of the week had been made up. He was constantly being approached by honey trappers, and not just chancers. Sometimes women who actually worked for newspapers would seek him out in clubs to try and lure him into cheating on me for a story.

It felt like people really hated both of us, and hated us even more for being together. It was like our coming together very much attracted 'The Evil Eye' as my Yia Yia used to call it. Every week it was a different drama and slowly but surely it had begun to chip away at us. It was becoming exhausting. I didn't feel like we were in a place where I could talk to him about how I felt, and I had become just as defensive with him as I was with the public and the media. He was uncertain of his own career at the time, being in between contracts and dealing with the added press pressure. It was starting to affect his work. Even football clubs and managers get agitated by the press and drama that comes with being in the spotlight. He was going through his own shit, and he seemed just as miserable as I did. I felt like I was to blame, like none of this would be happening to him if it wasn't for me.

Just weeks before, he'd been coming home from a night out and stopped at a kebab shop. Someone in the shop began making derogatory comments about me to him, bringing up the sex tape. He was drunk and alone but still stood up to the person and tried to defend me. Long story short, two large bouncers somehow got involved and one of them ended up punching a very drunk Danny very hard in the face, knocking him unconscious and leaving him on the pavement with blood dripping from his mouth. Instead of getting him help, all the onlookers just began filming him and taking pictures that they later sold to *The Sun*. The paper in turn decided to put his bloodied unconscious face on their front page, all because he was my boyfriend. Needless to say, I didn't feel like the ideal girlfriend of the year.

He started going out more and partying all the time. And with me being in peak Female Boss mode, I decided that for every night he went out, I would go out too, and I would make sure I always got home later than him. We spent seven days straight arguing with hardly any proper communication, with silent sleeps side by side, and a massive ego battle to see who would break down first. He finally asked me to go for drinks, to talk and spend some time with him, but I was too far gone, swallowed up by insecurity and fear. So I did what I always do if my heart feels like it's in danger – RUN!

I responded by telling him it was over in a text message, packing up my stuff, and leaving his apartment in Manchester. I was really sad. I didn't want to do it, but at the time I found it too hard to believe that someone could love me enough to get through all this. Dan had always said it was me and him against the world, and he didn't give a shit about what anyone else had to say because he loved me. But everyone in my life so far that had told me they loved me had always let me down eventually, and I thought he would do the same one day. *He's not going to put up with this for long, he's going to leave you*, whispered the sceptical and untrusting little voice in my head. So I decided it was much better for me to leave him first.

Not long after, Gareth got a call from Nish saying they wanted to meet with me again in London. Apparently, they were thinking of hiring Keira Knightley for the job now, but I was still in the mix. Nish told Gareth that she thought Keira could never play the role as well as I could. After all, I was a real ghetto girl, wasn't I? She said all I had to do was show them that I was the girl in the role, that no one could play it better. This time, there was going to be a third person coming to the meeting, that I needed to convince, one of the financial directors.

Apparently, Samir and Rahul were leaning more towards giving it to me at his point, but this third guy, the financial director, was still dead set on Keira Knightley. I was going to have to go all out on the night to convince them all that I was right for the part. So, on 10th May 2013, I went to the Metropolitan Hotel in Old Park Lane in London to meet Samir, Rahul, Nish and the financial director, taking Gareth and Michelle with me. Nish had said my friend Michelle should join us again for this meeting because the producers really liked her the first time, they thought that she brought great energy.

When we arrived, they had my autobiography, *Honest*, waiting on the table, which I'd only just published the year before. Samir immediately picked it up and began using it to refer to my 'bad girl past', explaining my 'urban roots' to the financial director. Anytime I mentioned anything that sounded remotely 'ghetto', like the fights I got into when I was younger, and how I used to smoke weed, his eyes would light up as if it had got him excited. He'd look at me like I was the real deal. So, of course, I began to play up to it. I've always been a great saleswoman, and I specialised in selling an idea of myself. I felt like I knew how this business worked. After all, I'd managed to convince Simon Cowell to make me an *X Factor* judge, so I felt I could definitely convince this guy to give me this role. I tried to make myself sound really gritty while still trying to be as honest as possible. But by the time it got to dinner, I realised it clearly wasn't enough.

Nish took me aside in the toilets for a little pep talk. She looked me in the eye and held my hand like a loving mother. I'd liked Nish from the beginning, she seemed different from the slimy producer Samir, who had just been laughing and joking about celebrity prostitutes for the past half an hour. Nish told me she was a mother, and her daughter was one of my biggest fans. She said she knew all about my very turbulent childhood and all the hurt I'd been through with my mother, who has schizoaffective disorder. She said that she understood how hard it must have been. She was rooting for me, and she wanted me to get this job. She said she was also spiritual, like me, and told me it was all meant to be. This was all happening for a reason, and I deserved this, she said. She also said they were going to give me millions for the role, and all I had to do was get out there and be the rebel they wanted me to be, do whatever they asked, and play along.

This was all I wanted – it was my ticket to a new life. So I did exactly what she said. I went out there and turned it up one hundred notches. I went from being a council estate girl that was a bit rough around the edges and liked a bit of weed to an ex-crack dealer that currently knew more gangsters than Samir had eaten hot dinners. I was spitting out bollocks left, right and centre. I don't even remember half the shit I came out with, but it kept coming, like verbal vomit.

At one point I slipped up, and Samir nearly caught me out. I had said that my ex-boyfriend Adam was a massive cocaine dealer, and I'd just finished exaggerating the story of a court case that we were involved in many years ago. Samir had brought it up in conversation, referring to my book again, and questioned me about it. The truth is that we were basically attacked by a group of men, and Adam had crashed his car into the group in retaliation, then came out of the car swinging a baseball bat. Since I was now upping my game, the story seemed like a good basis from which to expand my ridiculous tales about the character I was now portraying to them. This led me to drag Adam into it, also turning him into a bad guy.

It was all going swimmingly, I thought, until they suddenly asked if he could get them some cocaine for that night...*shit*. They'd already mentioned coke to Michelle and she'd clearly stated to them that I didn't do drugs, nor did I approve of them.

I didn't feel like I was coming across as much of a bad girl right now.

I tried to change the story and say Adam was an ex-dealer actually and not currently selling, but Samir persisted. My lies had got me into a trap. Did he actually want coke? Or was this some kind of weird test for the role? Either way, I rang up Adam in front of him so he could see me press 'call' and then I turned down the volume on the phone. I mentioned something about 'white sweets' to try and sell it. I had never tried cocaine in my life, but it sounded like a fun code name. People call it all sorts, don't they? I was finding it all rather comical, making it up as I went along. *This guy doesn't have a clue about the streets*, I thought. *He'd literally believe anything.*

Adam then said something along the lines of 'what the fuck are you on about, call me when you're sober' and hung up on me. When I came off the phone, I told the producer that Adam couldn't do anything for him because he said his phone was being tapped. I remember thinking what a bloody idiot I was as soon as I said it. What drug dealer admits that he sells drugs but can't right now because his phone's being tapped, on the same phone that he thinks is being tapped?!

It was just the first thing that came into my head, and if it didn't blow my cover, this guy was stupider than I thought. Luckily, Samir seemed to buy it, and I continued to make up excuses as to why the many so-called 'drug dealers' I knew weren't around to sort him out. They continued to ply the three of us with alcohol. Drink after drink after drink. Both Gareth and Michelle were beginning to look and sound extremely drunk, absolutely steaming in fact, especially Michelle. She wasn't herself, she seemed kind of wired almost, like she was on something. But I had no time to deal with Michelle, I had to get this movie role.

I was trying to keep myself sober, but Samir kept insisting I drink more. 'Come on, Tulisa, I thought you were a party girl? I thought you could drink us under the table? I'm disappointed,' he kept saying. I kept thinking what an absolute knob he was, and at one point I even felt his hand rest on my leg. I pushed it off immediately but continued to talk as normal, not wanting to create a bad vibe and risk losing everything I'd worked for.

As the night went on and it got past midnight, Nish told Gareth that he should leave me to go upstairs with the producers alone to their hotel room to talk privately. Gareth immediately pulled me aside and said the same thing I was thinking. I thought back to the dinner when there was mention of famous girls that were also prostitutes for big bucks. Did Samir think I was going to sleep with him for the role? Gareth and I immediately agreed that he wouldn't leave my side.

Once we got up to their hotel room, Nish said her goodbyes, and everyone except the producers seemed to deteriorate. Michelle was in a right state and had locked herself in the bathroom. I wanted this job, but I was still worried about my friend, so I excused myself and went to check on her. I managed to get the door open with a coin and found her passed out on the floor.

I'd never seen her so drunk. How the hell had she managed to get herself in this state? And of all the times to do so? I checked her breathing and gave her a little shake. *Bladdered*, I thought. But as long as she was safe, she'd just have to sleep it off while I continued with the meeting. I had to focus on this film. I was thinking of a way to subtly let the producers know that I wasn't going to sleep with them, but I was still right for the role. That's how desperate I was for this fresh start.

Samir later mentioned something about me and Danny being a power couple. But he said it in a way that implied I was with Danny because he was a footballer and because he looked flashy by my side. He clearly thought I was only with Danny to further my career. Nothing could have been further from the truth. It felt like our relationship was destroying my career at this point.

Mahmood then argued that Danny might hold me back from my acting career. He even asked what would I choose if faced with the choice, Danny or my career? This worried me. It was as if he saw Danny as a possible problem. I knew I wouldn't choose my career over Dan, I would just find a way to make it work. But I was going to tell Mahmood whatever he wanted to hear.

Since I'd split with Danny, he had still been messaging me and trying to make amends. He was messaging me that night, in fact. But Danny wasn't a 'grab the bull by the horns' kind of guy when it came to romantic conflict, he was more of a 'tiptoe his way back in' type. Sure, he would do big gestures like flowers and presents, but verbally he was a little restrained. When I split up with him, a part of me had hoped that he would open up, with huge words of affirmation like 'I can't live without you, I need you, you are the air I breathe'. I was a bit of an extremist and that was what I was used to in my past relationships, extremity and chaos.

Instead, I was getting 'how are you today? I miss you,

when are you coming up so we can talk?'. This chilled approach had me nibbling at my fingernails like Twiglets. I was angry, very angry. I will be the first to admit that when it comes to romance, I have high expectations all round, and especially when it comes to confessions of undying love. Love bombing isn't just normal to me, it's a must. When someone isn't pouring their heart out, something feels wrong, and I can become either passive-aggressive or seemingly very detached.

If I have any thoughts, real or imagined, that my partner isn't as invested as I am or that he's not doing enough to show me he cares, I will keep it inside, pretend everything is normal and let it build up until one day I eventually explode in a fit of anger. Or I will shut down emotionally and leave over something really small, and I will not reveal the source of the anger or my true reason for abandoning them. I certainly have a deep fear of vulnerability. I think the psychological term is 'avoidant'.

So, taking into account my current frustration, and the fact that I now felt like I literally needed to convince Mahmood that I didn't really care about Danny so he would believe that Danny would never get in the way of this job, I told them we had split up. I began ranting about Danny, taking anything small I could think of – and dramatising it. I also began using him in conversation to make them aware of my morals and values, so they'd put any thought of prostitution out of their minds, while letting out some of that pent-up anger. I said I'd had to break up with Danny because he was so shallow and stupid.

'Emotionally unintelligent' was the phrase I think I used. This was code for 'I want him to verbally sauté his heart with a sprinkle of oregano and serve it to me with a side of dauphinoise potatoes and he's not doing it because he doesn't understand why I left him in the first place or what I am expecting him to do now to correct it', which, in female code, makes him stupid.

Then I went on to say I didn't need his money, I had my own. And I wasn't interested in the glitz and glamour or added success that might come from being with him. I was a good girl who wanted to settle down with one person and get married, but I still had a dream, and I was willing to work my bollocks off for it. Meaning I wasn't the type of girl that would be into prostitution. I was contradicting myself so much now, trying to let them know I wasn't a bad girl in that way and definitely wouldn't be sleeping with anyone for anything other than love... but I *was* a bad girl in the way that was needed for the role. It was a hard line to walk, and there I was unfortunately dragging Danny through the mud at the same time because I needed to convince Mahmood that my relationship with Danny wouldn't affect my work. I was also angry and feeling intoxicated, so I was letting rip.

Eventually the meeting came to an end, and I was so relieved. Samir tried to insist that Michelle stayed in their room until the morning to 'sleep it off', but I instantly refused. I didn't trust him as far as I could throw him. God knows what he might do to her, he seemed like a perverted slimeball. They then insisted that we use their driver to get home, saying they would be offended if we didn't. So the three of us jumped in the car they provided and headed back to mine.

What I can remember from the journey is that Michelle was still passed out, but at some point she woke up and had a massive argument with Gareth. Everyone was an absolute mess. I also remember getting emotional myself. I clearly recall having a conversation about someone I knew that was on drugs and how much it upset me. Gareth told me that person was using again, and I responded by saying how badly I wanted them to get clean, and that I didn't ever want any drug dealers coming anywhere near me or my home when that person was around.

The next thing I remember is waking up hungover at home, next to my indoor swimming pool, with little recollection of how the night had ended in the hotel room, and massive gaps when recalling the night before. The next day all three of us said that we felt as if we'd been spiked. After the meeting the phone calls from Nish continued, except now Samir wanted direct contact with me. This made me uneasy, but I had little choice.

Once we were put directly in touch, I had a few phone calls with him consisting of general chit-chat – he was always trying to have a good gossip and get more personal, but not much other than that. Eventually, they set up a meeting with Gareth and my accountant Chris to talk money and the legal side of things, which I wasn't asked to attend. They brought a lawyer and showed my accountant a contract. They also tested the waters with some offshore accounts talk, which my accountant quickly shot down. All the big shots are usually dodgy in some way, so either way it was still positive, and I had high hopes. I felt like I'd done it. I needed change, and the future was looking bright.

I had no idea what was coming.

On 1st June 2013, Gareth received a call from my press manager, Simon Jones. He said the next day, *The Sun on Sunday* newspaper was running a story that I was a cocaine dealer. The headline read 'TULISA'S COCAINE DEAL SHAME'. There was no movie role. There would be no three million pounds. The whole thing had been an elaborate example of entrapment. A sting, by a man called Mazher Mahmood and *The Sun*.

Mazher Mahmood, who'd played the role of the top Hollywood/Bollywood movie producer Samir Khan, was actually a renowned British journalist, Reporter of the Year Award winner and undercover investigator. He'd spent twenty years working for *The News of the World* before the phone hacking scandal shut it down. During his tenure there, he'd been responsible for many investigations, ninety-four of which led to criminal convictions, with many more cases still pending. All the other people involved, Rahul (real name Rizvi), Nish (real name Conny), the driver that took us home from the hotel (Alan Smith), the lawyer, the financial director and the rest were actors who worked alongside Mr Mahmood. The only thing we couldn't figure out was the woman from 21st Century Fox. She actually did work there, so we assumed she'd been paid off. The realisation was crushing.

All the crazy and derogatory things I had said about myself and others during my night at the Metropolitan Hotel were blasted all over the papers, along with footage and voice recordings. It was all over the internet, with absolutely no mention of the entrapment or why I had said those things. As far as the papers were concerned, I had just randomly said those things to an undercover journalist because that was who I was, and I'd slipped up. My 'true colours' had been exposed.

But it didn't stop there.

Weeks after the night at the Metropolitan Hotel, Mahmood had called to say he was in London and he'd asked me if I knew anyone that would supply him with cocaine. He also wanted to know if I had any places for him to go for a night out, preferably a strip club, knowing that my ex-boyfriend Adam currently worked in one.

Within 24 hours of the call, he had cocaine delivered to his hotel. Trying to keep him on my side, I'd given him a telephone number for someone I knew who might know someone – he wasn't actually a drug dealer himself. After the story dropped, I was arrested on suspicion of being concerned in the supply of class A drugs, which in the UK has a maximum prison sentence of up to eight years. For ten days solid I had a huge crowd of people outside my house, from live news crews to police, paparazzi, journalists and onlookers. I think there was even a helicopter at one point. I was pasted across the front pages of every newspaper and news channel as a drug dealer, someone who had verbally confessed to criminal activity and being affiliated with criminals and gangsters.

The headlines only got worse as the days went by. My public image plummeted as more and more newspapers, online media and social networks went over and over the story. Everyone was talking about it. I lost all my endorsement deals and couldn't make the completion mortgage payment on my home. I was now going to lose half a million pounds of my savings that I'd put down on it as a deposit. I was also, more than likely, going to have to spend as much money, if not more, on legal bills fighting my case. My life was, quite simply, destroyed overnight. I had no job, no income, a tarnished reputation, and right now – no matter what the outcome – I had no chance of ever working or earning in the entertainment industry again.

Most of the British public thought I was a disgrace, and even people I had known all my life now wanted nothing to do with me. I had recently been to see Danny and we were in the midst of rekindling our relationship. He had already organised flowers to be sent to my house while he was away working and I felt like I needed him more than ever. I just wanted to feel his arms around me and to hear him tell me everything was going to be alright. I knew in my heart with something this serious he'd be by my side as soon as he could. But then the next headline hit. *The Sun* released another part of the elaborate sting – my drunken rant to Mahmood about Danny while I was trying to convince Mahmood that I could never be with a man for money, especially not in the way I'd felt Mazher Mahmood possibly wanted me to be, and that I didn't care enough about Danny to compromise with my career for him. Which wasn't true but I had run with it because Mahmood had insinuated it could be a problem.

I had also had way too much to drink by that point, after Mahmood had repeatedly ordered me drinks and shots, as well as whatever may have been put in those drinks. All the while, I was in level one hundred Female Boss mode, trying to play up to the 'bad girl' role, and boy, did I rip Danny a new one.

I had said things like 'he's unintelligent, an idiot', but I had also called him 'fake and materialistic'. Which was just projection. I had never felt like I belonged in the celebrity world. I wasn't into fashion and I was terrible at playing the game. Dan, however, was a lot better at it all than me. He dressed well and had better knowledge of the finer things in life. Sometimes it made me feel like we were a bit chalk and cheese. Which that night I translated as shallow and materialistic. I was just dramatising to impress Samir and his friends.

I also called Dan a stalker, which actually derived from one of the things I loved most about him. The fact that when he was growing up, I was his celebrity crush and he had even claimed to people that he would marry me one day. When he became successful himself, he had gone out of his way to do just that and came after me through a friend. I found it all very romantic. It was exactly what I wanted in a man, someone that knows exactly what they want... ME. But that night it unfortunately translated as 'Stalker'.

I said I didn't respect him, that I'd never really liked him that much, and that we had nothing in common. Which also wasn't true, but that night.... You get the gist.

They were all unforgivable things to say. Things that change the way someone looks at you. I had been an outright bitch, and to a complete stranger. Yes, I was smashed, and I was playing a game to get the role, but that wasn't an excuse. You don't speak about people you care about like that, under any circumstances. I knew I could do way better, I felt ashamed. To top it off, now the whole of the UK could read about it. Danny was mortified at my words and felt betrayed and humiliated. Not surprisingly.

I didn't even try to explain to him how it had happened. How could I? It was all so twisted. I didn't think he'd even believe me. My head was so gone with it all that day, I'm not sure if I even messaged to apologise.

Either way, he cancelled his plans to come to London.

So there I was, sitting on the bathroom floor in my big white mansion that I knew would no longer be mine, feeling completely alone. I had literally lost everything. I felt like I was finally what the rest of the world had always seen me as – the chav from Camden that'd just got lucky – and now they could prove it. She'd eventually lost it all and now she was back where she belonged. A number of people had made sure of it.

The only thing left that I could think of doing was to press record on my laptop. Miraculously, somewhere deep down inside, I still had a lot of fight left in me. Maybe even more so because I was under attack like never before. I now planned to fight these bastards to the death in every way, shape and form. Not just because it was the only option I had left. But because I was built for it. Maybe, just maybe, my whole life still meant something, and all the pain and stress had been leading up to this moment.

This time these assholes had fucked with the wrong person.

Either way, I told myself I would survive this horrific stage in my life, and I was going to film and document it while I did. Then one day, when it was all over, I was going to show people what really happened, who I really was, my truth, my story.

So, as well as filming every moment of every day, I began to write a diary, jotting down all the events that had occurred and what continued to occur, as well as all my feelings and thoughts during this harrowing and fascinating period of my life. A diary that I would later turn into a story, in the form of a book. The book that you now read. This, ladies and gentleman, is how the story goes...

Chapter 2:

YOU ARE TU BE CHARGED

I WAS AWOKEN by a tapping on my shoulder and the strong smell of coffee. The realisation of what day it was and where I had to go began to sink in. It was a Monday in June 2013, and I was off to the police station to be charged.

Unfortunately, I was very tipsy when I'd found out my fate at 11pm the Friday before. Gareth did warn my lawyer to wait until the next day to tell me, but he called and informed me anyway. After nearly six months of waiting in limbo since my arrest and being re-bailed three times, the CPS had finally decided that I was going to be charged. As soon as I got the call, I locked myself in the bathroom with a litre bottle of vodka and told everyone in my house that I was having some quiet time. Gareth continued to knock on the door and check on me, but when I stopped responding he used a coin to open the lock on the bathroom door. He found me passed out on the floor, surrounded by empty packets of sleeping pills. The resolve and resilience I'd had when I first hit record on my laptop all those months ago had been beaten out of me.

When the ambulance arrived, I was beginning to come around, as everyone had kept trying to wake me up. I was told by the paramedics that they needed to take me to the hospital to check my organs and make sure there wasn't any chance of liver failure. I refused and sat grumpily in my bed, being forced to stay awake. The paramedics couldn't force me to go to the hospital, so they stayed until they thought it was safe to leave me, and told my family and friends to keep a constant watch on me for the next 24 hours for my health and safety. So, it was safe to say that I'd had a shit weekend, and the day wasn't about to get any better.

'The documentary crew are in the living room and Elena's waiting to do your hair. I tried to wake you half an hour ago, but you weren't moving, so I made sure you were still breathing and gave you an extra half hour. I take it you didn't sleep?' said Gareth, peering at me and placing a steaming hot mug of coffee on the side table next to my bed. I grabbed the covers and pulled them over my head.

'Ohhhhhhhhhhh! Fuck my life! Please, Lord, I can't take much more of this!' I whined.

Gareth and I were as real with each other as two people could possibly get. We were like a 90-year-old couple without the sex. In five years, three of which we'd spent

26

living together, we'd seen each other in every possible light, warts and all. There was no bullshit, and we were beyond comforting each other with words of advice, consoling each other was like consoling ourselves. In some ways it was a bizarre relationship, but ultimately one of the most important I'd ever had as I had learned a lot from it. I peeked one eye through the covers and looked up at him. The light from the skylight beamed behind him, leaving the front of him in shadow. I could just about make out his slim frame and tousled mousy brown hair. I slowly wriggled out from under the covers and sat upright in my bed. I was absolutely shattered. I'd had two hours' sleep at most.

Gareth, aka G, or GG, stepped closer to my bedside out of the beaming light. I could see him clearly now. His piercing green eyes glistened.

'Let's get this bullshit day over and done with and get you back into bed. You'll be watching Disney movies before you know it,' he smiled.

I dropped my bottom lip and put on a whining baby voice. 'I can't tell you how good that sounds right now, I don't wanna play today.' I pretended to cry and throw a childlike tantrum.

G shook his head and tutted at me.

'Come on, Madame, we gotta get you up and out!' he said in a fake American accent.

I sparked a cigarette and sipped my coffee, my morning ritual. Eventually I dragged myself out of bed to have a shower and get dressed, then headed into the living room.

I paused to compose myself before I entered the room. I was in a foul mood, but that was no one else's fault. *Be polite and smile*, I thought. *Your problems are your own.* I entered with a forced half-smile on my face, and my attention was drawn straight to Jonathan Levi, the man producing the documentary about my life during the aftermath of the sting. Since filming my experience myself during my ordeal, I had been approached by the BBC to do a documentary throughout the legal process. Luckily for them, it had been the first thing I'd thought of, so I already had recordings going as far back as the moment I found out. The con was that I wouldn't get paid because it was based around possible criminal activity.

At first I was wary of Jonathan and everyone else involved. I'd been warned that I'd have no control over the documentary, and they could portray me in any way they saw fit, based on the footage. They could have had it in for me, for all I knew, so I decided to tread carefully around them. Eventually though, my emotions got the better of me with Jonathan. I genuinely liked him, and I couldn't help but believe he genuinely liked me. I could feel his empathy towards my situation, like he gave a shit. So, I concluded that I would give him my trust, and if he stabbed me in the back, he'd be another one for the black book. No matter how many people fucked me over, I still couldn't seem to give up on trust, or on human beings. I still liked to believe I knew a good soul when I met one. A wise man once told me 'When people show you who they are, believe them'. Jonathan was a good 'un.

I smiled at him as he sat on the sofa. He smiled back, and I saw the familiar facial expression that a lot of people seemed to give me these days, the 'man, I can see what a shit time you're having, but not sure if you want me to bring it up'. I reciprocated with my 'I've had enough of life face', and he got up and gave me a big warm hug.

'How are you feeling? Stupid question really, how did you cope over the weekend?' he asked.

'Oh, you know, drank a lot of vodka, necked some pills, chilled with the ambulance crew, as you do.' I smiled sarcastically.

'Oh no, has it got that bad?' He frowned.

'I'm in a bad way, Jonny. I was all strong and ready to rumble, but I just didn't expect this. I don't think I can take another six months, I'm already on my last legs,' I sighed.

'I'm so sorry, I don't know what to say, it's fucking outrageous.' He shook his head.

'I give up, I don't know what the fuck's going on anymore,' I shrugged.

'Well, please don't kill yourself. It would make great television, but I'd miss you too much,' he grinned. I loved that he already got my dark banter, and I chuckled.

'We will keep it as short as possible today,' he said with a warm smile.

I pretty much mumbled my way through the interview. I felt like crap and I didn't know what to say anymore. The same old questions – 'How are you feeling...?'

I wanted to scream at the camera at the top of my lungs, 'How the fuck do you think I'm feeling, my life is fucking over?' But of course I couldn't do that, so I mumbled polite answers instead.

I sat in the car miserably en route to the police station. Not only could I now be going to jail, but I might have to wait up to another nine months to find out if I was. I could make a whole human in that time and give birth to it... Maybe that would be a good idea? The jury might show me some mercy... At least I still had a sense of humour. I sat staring out of the car window, watching all the people go about their daily business. Off to work probably, going home to their families later, living a normal life. *They don't know how good they've got it*, I thought. *I'd do anything to have my life back.* Now that it was gone, I realised I should have appreciated it more. I had forgotten how blessed I was, always stressing about what was wrong, instead of thinking about what was right, always wanting more and thinking things could be better, instead of just being present and realising how lucky I was. It was a lesson learned, the biggest one so far.

I arrived at the police station, where thankfully there were no paparazzi. Gareth's little trick of tipping them off that I'd gone to another station had worked. I got out of the car and walked towards the doors, instantly registering that I could barely walk in my massive heels. I felt the anger and stress rising up in me once again, over the smallest things. I hadn't been able to face picking out an outfit on what felt like the worst day of my life, but couldn't help thinking, *who the fuck picked these shoes out for me anyway?* What a stupid fucking idea! And more to the point, who decided to attach stilts to shoes and make women think they look their best when walking like a baby giraffe on steroids? I'm going to be charged, not walk a fucking red carpet! I exhaled. *Just calm down, T, pull yourself together, this is no time for getting emotional.* When I got inside, I was greeted by my lawyer Ben Rose, a tall, handsome and friendly middle-aged man. He explained what was going to happen as we walked down the stairs to where I'd be charged.

'Are they going to put me in a cell again today, Ben?' I asked.

'The woman sorting it seems quite nice, I don't think they want to draw any more attention to the situation. They just want to get you in and out, so hopefully you won't have to.'

Once we got down to the charging area, Ben gestured for me to sit and wait while he spoke to an officer. I stared around at the so-called criminals, drunks and drug addicts, feeling numb. How the hell did I end up here? What was happening? I watched as some of the officers talked amongst themselves about my being there as if I didn't exist. One of them looked sympathetic. Another looked as if she found it all very amusing, glancing at me and chuckling to her colleague. *Fucking bitch*, I thought. Suddenly I saw a man sat to the right of me pull out his phone and pretend to use it while attempting to take a picture. I quickly turned my back to him and looked down at the floor. I felt sad now. No anger anymore, just sadness.

Ben reappeared and plonked himself in the chair next to me.

'Good news, T! No cell today! You can wait here with me until they're ready for you.'

'Thanks, Ben,' I said quietly.

We sat there for what felt like a decade. I felt like a lion in a zoo, sensing everyone's eyes on me. Eventually, the moment arrived. No matter what happened now, my life was going to change forever. I walked over to the raised desk with three police officers stood behind it. I recognised the officer who was there when I was first arrested. I don't know why he always stood out to me, but his was the face I always remembered more than the rest. I think it was because I sensed more emotion from him than the other officers. I wasn't quite sure which emotion yet. They handed me a form, and as I began filling it out, I hesitated when I reached a certain question.

'Ben,' I whispered, 'can I have a minute with you, over there, away from...' I nodded at the feds.

'Of course you can,' he whispered back. 'Sorry, officer, I need a moment with my client,' he said, leading me aside to the corner of the room.

'What's up, T?' he asked.

I looked down at the floor before I answered, feeling ashamed. 'Basically, I don't know how to answer that suicide question, have you made any recent attempts and all that. I fucked up when I found out I was being charged, and an ambulance was called, so I guess that has been registered. What do I do? Do I have to tell them?'

'Did you? Fucking hell, T, that is really bad,' he exclaimed, louder than I expected.

I was taken aback – he never usually swore. He frowned while tapping his foot intensely.

'I'm sorry, T, you have to tell them,' he sighed.

'Do I have to say it? Can't you tell them?' I whispered back.

'If that's what you'd prefer, of course,' he nodded.

I nodded back at him in agreement. Ben cleared his throat as we walked back over to the desk.

'My client is unsure of how to handle one of the questions on the form, so I need to inform you that there was an incident last Friday when she took a number of pills which resulted in an ambulance being called.'

Hearing those words out loud gave me a sinking feeling in my chest, and I felt tears welling up in my eyes. *Don't cry, T, whatever you do don't let them see you cry, you're stronger than this.* I looked around at the officers' faces. I caught a glimpse of the police officer, he put his head down, like he didn't know where to look. Maybe it was a look of guilt on his face, not liking what he was a part of. Or maybe he just felt uncomfortable. I put my own head down and stared at the desk, the tears were coming on strong now. *Don't fucking cry*, I shouted at myself in my head.

'OK, Mr Rose, we will make a note of that,' the head officer said awkwardly.

When it was all finished and I was free to go, I felt the weight of the tears I was holding back lifting. As I turned to leave, the head officer spoke up again.

'Eerm, Miss Contostavlos,' he said. I turned back to face him, wondering what more bad news would come next.

'Yes, sir,' I replied.

'I hope it all goes well for you, good luck in court,' he said with an awkward smile.

'Thanks,' I said with a half-smile.

I was beginning to get the feeling that a lot of the police felt the same way about this case. It wasn't their fault, I suppose, but that didn't mean they wouldn't do everything they could to secure a conviction. They might feel bad about it, but they didn't feel bad enough to put their necks on the line so, as far as I was concerned, they'd chosen their side.

Chapter 3.

TU WAS A MIRACLE

I BREATHED IN deeply as I felt the cool summer evening breeze rushing past my face. *Smells green*, I thought. *This is why I moved out of London.* It was a couple of days since my trip to the police station, and I was in 'fuck it' mode. *What will be, will be.* I was depressed, obviously, but I couldn't live my life just sat at home crying and stewing over it. This was going to be a long road, and this dark feeling in my heart wasn't going anywhere, so I'd better start learning to live with it. I called it 'fuck it', others might have called it denial.

Driving through the streets of Hertfordshire, I caught a glimpse of my reflection in a shop window. There I was, sat in my white R8 with the top down. I looked like I was living the dream, and I knew the reflection was as fake as people's perception when they saw me drive past. *Funny old world*, I thought.

JUDGEMENT

I'd just spent a couple of hours trying to let off some steam at the gym and, as I pulled up at a set of lights, I felt my stomach grumbling away as it always did after a training session. I wanted food, but I wasn't sure what I fancied. I'd seen a random chicken and pasta meal on a friend's Instagram. It was from a cafe called Miracles, around ten minutes from my house. It wasn't the first time I'd heard of it. All the lads were always ranting on about their fry-ups on hangover days, so I thought I'd give it a whirl. As I drove along, a song came on the stereo from my iPod, Rihanna's 'Stay'. I drifted into thinking about my love life... my non-existent love life. My last relationship felt so long ago now. I'd been on a few dates here and there but never got past anything more than a little kiss. Either there wasn't enough chemistry or they turned out to be complete assholes, which was nothing new to me. I was a bit of an asshole magnet.

I wondered to myself, *would I ever find my Mr Right? My Mr Big?* It was beginning to seem less and less likely. The idea that there was someone out there as perfect for me as I was for him, who I could share a love so strong with that it was unbreakable, seemed like a straight-up fantasy. Or, to put it plainly – bullshit. I was bound to meet my future husband someday though, perfect for me or not. I could meet him right now, outside Miracles – HA! Wouldn't that be a revelation? What if right now, when I least expected it, I just bumped into Mr Right? Maybe I would drop something on the floor and he would pick it up, just like in the movies. *Mmmmm, fat fucking chance!*

With that thought, I changed the song to Nicki Minaj's 'Boss Ass Bitch' and continued to drive.

As I pulled up to the car park across from Miracles, I realised I knew the road like the back of my hand, and I'd just never noticed this particular restaurant on it. So, this was the place I'd heard about. It looked pretty average from the outside so no wonder I hadn't, but from what I heard the food was good. Once I'd parked my car, I walked into the restaurant and asked for a menu. I felt funny stood there on my own, awkward even. I wasn't used to being in public places by myself, because I was always accompanied by a friend or security guard, and anything I needed, Gareth or someone else would go and get for me. I didn't walk around like a normal person anymore – and I realised I missed it. Today, I felt I needed to step out of my comfort zone. So I wandered in with no make-up on, in my gym leggings and an oversized hoodie.

The man behind the counter recognised me and smiled. I smiled back at him awkwardly, with some relief. I didn't get out much anymore, and I never knew how people were going to respond to my presence these days. Once I'd found and ordered the meal I'd seen on Instagram, I took a seat and analysed my surroundings. 'One... Two... Three...' I began counting as I scanned the room. I couldn't help but notice at least four couples. *Love! Everywhere today!* Finally, my food was ready. I couldn't sit with these lovebirds any longer, I was getting nauseous. I grabbed my food and headed for the car park.

As I got to my car, I heard a voice beside me, 'Oi, you! What's going on, where the hell have you been?'

I spun around and came face to face with a familiar handsome young man, who was now standing very close to me, almost in my face. I took in his thick dark hair slicked to perfection in a side parting and his olive complexion, along with his deep brown eyes and wide cheeky smile. It took me a couple of seconds to register who it was.

Jacob was in one of the same social circles as me, and I had been around him a fair bit at one time, but I hadn't seen him in ages because I had stepped off the radar for a while due to my situation. I had partied with him in the past, chilled with him, cooked for him and our group of friends, and even had a few deep drunken convos. Jacob was definitely a playboy. Every time I saw him, he'd had a different bird on his arm. In fact, the last time I saw him he had brought his flavour of the month round to mine for a roast dinner. He always went for very pretty girls, the dolly type I would say, though I'm sure he'd had his fair share of variety. He was very wealthy, due to his family business, but from what I'd gathered he wasn't lazy, he worked for his money and did his bit for the company. He was also very ambitious, with many dreams of his own.

I had admired his beautiful Ferrari a few times when it was parked outside my house. What I liked about him was that he wasn't just your average lucky sperm. He was streetwise as well and had life experience, he hadn't always come from money. He was, however, a bit of a cocky little shit at times. He wasn't lacking in confidence, but I had always seen it as more of a bravado. Either way, one thing I knew about Jacob, the birds seemed to flock around him like flies on shit, and he was never complaining.

'Oh, hello you,' I replied, a little less excited than him. I liked Jacob, but he wasn't one of the people I was closest to in our circle. Probably because of the way he swam in and out of it, just like I had.

'Look at you, acting all reserved, like you don't know me,' he laughed, thumping me lightly on the shoulder to break the ice. 'Like we ain't sat in your bathroom together drunk, talking shit?'

I cracked a half-hearted smile and thought back to a house party I'd thrown ages ago. Somehow me and Jacob had ended up sat on the edge of my bathtub talking absolute bollocks for hours. I felt a little bad now. At the time I had always kept my guard up around Jacob because I'd been dating someone else who we both knew, a guy called Trent. He was amazing and he's still a good friend, but he just wasn't for me in that way. That night at my house party was probably the most me and Jacob had spoken, as I had sensed that if I wasn't seeing Trent, he would have tried it on with me. There were more than a few moments when I'd suspected that he liked me, but he had never overstepped the mark or been disrespectful, and I had wanted him to keep it that way. But now here he was, standing way beyond my comfort zone, very much in my face, and I was single.

'Haven't you been getting my messages? I've been trying to get hold of you,' he exclaimed.

I frowned, confused. 'Messages? What messages? Why, what's up?'

He scowled, as if frustrated. 'I told Claire to tell you that I want to take you for dinner. Hasn't she said anything?'

Claire was another one of the friends we had in common, but she was also friends with the other guy I was seeing back then. I looked from side to side as I pulled a confused face.

'What do you mean, take me for dinner? Why?' I asked.

'What do you mean, why?' he laughed. 'You know I had a little thing for you, don't pretend like you couldn't tell.' He smirked.

This was the cocky little shit I knew, I'd just never been on the receiving end of it. He was completely sticking it on me, and for some reason it made me feel on edge. I had always wanted him to treat me as one of the lads because of Trent. He wasn't supposed to look at me in that way. I felt awkward.

'What about Trent?' I asked.

'What about him? That was ages ago, no? It didn't go anywhere and you're not with him anymore, so what's the problem?'

I tilted my head and frowned awkwardly. It was time to snap out of high school mode and get to the point. 'I'm just saying it's a bit disrespectful, no? I'd feel like a bit of slut if I'm honest! I don't think you would like it if it was the other way round,' I said firmly.

'I didn't think it was that serious. I haven't seen him in ages. I'll phone him now and talk to him if you like,' he said, pulling out his phone.

'No, no, no! Don't do that, that's unnecessary!' I snapped. He stared into my eyes longingly with his handsome face, trying to charm me. I'd never looked at Jacob in that way, it'd been a no-go in the past.

'I just don't think it's right,' I said, fiddling with my car keys awkwardly.

'I doubt he's sitting around worrying about what you're doing, I'm sure he'd be fine with it,' he persisted. 'Anyway, if it's not me that takes you out, it will only be someone else. Let me take your number so we can arrange something.' He smiled cheekily.

I paused and looked down at my feet. 'I'm sorry, Jacob, I can't.'

He reached out his hand and pulled up my chin, so my eyes met his. '*Aaaaaw*, you're cute, Tulisa. Very loyal, I like that,' he said patronisingly.

I flinched a little. I was funny about physical contact at this stage, and – as it stood – we were at no stage at all. I also found his little chin grab undermining. I instantly wanted to give him a dead arm, but I contained myself. *This guy thinks he's got serious game,* I thought. If anything, I wasn't mad because deep down the cheek of it made me giggle. He smiled again, this time a smile of admiration. My words didn't seem to deter him. If anything, they seemed to make him want me more. I could tell he was used to getting what he wanted.

'Look, next time I go out with Claire I'm sure I'll see you out. We can hang as friends,' I said.

He smiled with his eyes this time, a knowing smile, like he'd just had a miniature victory. 'OK, Princess, whatever you want, I'll make it happen,' he said.

Rather than leaning towards me, he slipped his arm around my waist and pulled me towards him, and then pressed his lips on my cheek. Woah! He was way too touchy-feely! But I still admired his confidence. Character-wise, he was my kind of guy. I liked confidence a little too much, I had a type that wasn't necessarily good for me, which was why he was exactly the kind of guy I was trying to get away from. As much as I loved the challenge, I was getting too old for this shit. I needed to get my priorities straight.

'Goodbye, Jacob,' I smiled and raised my eyebrows before getting in my car and flicking on the engine.

I watched him walk towards his car, which was blocking the exit. He looked back at me and smiled as he got halfway. I shook my head and laughed. He eventually got into his car and drove approximately two metres before slamming on the brakes and jumping back out. Had he forgotten something? He proceeded to strut towards me. I wound down my window.

'Nah, fuck it, I can't leave it like this. What are you doing right now? Let me take you for dinner?' he said, placing his arm on my car defiantly. At this point I couldn't help but burst out laughing.

'You're a madman! Chill out, I'll see you around

Claire's or something. I'm sorry I just can't,' I said, shaking my head.

'Alright, alright,' he sighed. 'I'm not letting this go, I'll see you soon, Princess.' He pinched my chin again, then walked backwards, still looking at me, until he reached the door of his car. He smiled one last time before he got inside and sped off. If he grabbed my chin one more time I was going to punch him in the leg, or kiss him... *Kiss him? No! No, no, no, Tulisa. Not today, Satan!* He was a right piece of work, that one. Two years ago, he would have been ideal. I used to thrive on the challenge. But I was wiser now, wasn't I?! When I got home, I texted Claire to ask why she hadn't told me about Jacob. She said she'd forgotten and sent me his number, telling me to call him.

But I didn't.

Chapter 4:

IF TU GOES DOWN, YOU GO DOWN

I JUMPED UP from my bed to the sound of loud banging on my front door. I could hear my Staffordshire bull terrier Narla barking ferociously from the kitchen. I rushed to the top of the stairs and looked down at the front door. Gareth was stood peering through the spy hole; he was shaking, with a look of confusion and fear on his face.

'It's the police!' he mouthed silently, eyes wide with fear.

'Hurry up and open the door! We've got a warrant!' they shouted.

They've come for me, I thought. *What have* The Sun *concocted now? Had they managed to find another way to set me up? What if it wasn't even the police outside?* My mind was racing with what felt like a million thoughts a second.

'Ask to see the badge!' I mouthed back to Gareth, feeling the panic rising in me.

'Can I just see your badge?' he asked.

'Open the door, or we're breaking it!' they yelled back.

G peered through the peephole. 'They've got a badge!' he whispered.

'Open the door,' I said, gulping down my nerves.

As the latch turned, five police officers burst through the door. I recognised one of them as the man that had arrested me. *I'm fucked*, I thought. *How the hell had they got me now?*

'Gareth Varey, I'm arresting you on suspicion of being concerned in the selling of class A drugs. You do not have to say anything, but it may harm your defence if you do not mention when questioned something that you later rely on in court. Anything you do say may be given in evidence. We also have a warrant to search the premises. If you have anything, you're better off letting us know now, before we find it.'

What the fuck?

I looked at G helplessly, as a feeling of deep pain pierced my chest. *Not G*, I thought, *it's nothing to do with him, they want me! Take me!* G looked at me in pure horror. I stared down at him with tears filling my eyes. He had never looked so vulnerable. He stood at the bottom of the stairs, trembling in his boxer shorts with his half-naked body exposed. Even his frame seemed smaller and frailer somehow as I watched the colour begin to drain from his face. I knew how he was feeling. I knew G as well as I knew myself. I was usually the one in his position. And for the first time I wondered how often he had felt the same emotions when he'd watched me helplessly in the past.

I could hear the police officers tearing through Gareth's

room downstairs as Narla howled from behind the kitchen door.

'Call Ben, now!' said Gareth, snapping me out of my frozen stance. I ran to my room to get my phone, frantically searched for Ben's number and pressed call.

'Ben! They've got Gareth! They've arrested him! They're searching the house as we speak! They're taking him to the station...hang on...what station are you taking him to?' I shouted. 'Charing Cross! They're taking him to Charing Cross!' I panted anxiously down the phone.

'Just calm down, T, take a deep breath. What are they arresting him for?' he asked.

'Concern in the selling of class A drugs! Same charge as me! We told you, Ben. We told you they would go for him next,' I said.

'Tulisa, take a deep breath and calm down. Put me on the phone to the police officer,' he replied.

I ran down the stairs and handed the officer my phone. 'It's my lawyer, he wants to talk to you.' The officer reached for my phone.

'Hello, Mr Rose.'

I looked around the hallway for G and got a glimpse of him in his room, getting dressed. I noticed I was also shaking now. I looked down at my trembling hands. I could see the hot chocolate stain down the front of my t-shirt from the night before. I looked a state. My skull pounded, with a sharp pain in time with my heartbeat. I'd forgotten that I'd had a few too many glasses of red wine yesterday, and now I realised that I was absolutely hanging, on top of everything else. *Get it together, T! Sort yourself out! You need to be on point for G!*

I was brought back to reality by the sound of the police officer's voice. 'OK, Mr Rose, I'll pass you back to her now,' said the fed as he handed me the phone.

I grabbed it and ran back up the stairs. 'Ben? What's going on?' I asked.

'OK, so I don't know exactly what's going on yet, but we will find out. I'm away, so Ross is going to have to go down to the station instead. I'll be on the other end of the phone all day and you can speak to Ross direct. Try not to freak out, T. I reckon this is just a fishing exercise, so stay calm and stay by the phone, OK?'

'Alright, I'll speak to you in a bit.' I hung up and rushed out of my room and back to the top of the stairs. I saw two of the officers taking Gareth out the front door.

'G! I've spoken to Ben, Ross is meeting you at the station! Just stay calm, everything is going to be OK!' I called to him.

He looked back at me, still vulnerable and terrified. I knew my words meant nothing to him right now, but I still had to say them. The other officers followed out of his bedroom, carrying plastic bags and papers. I turned to the officer that had arrested me, angry now the shock had left me.

'Has Mahmood been up to his old tricks again? This is bullshit, and you know it! I hope you found what you were looking for!' I snapped.

He ignored me completely. *Because he knows!* I thought. As the last officer left the house, the door slammed behind

48

him. I slid down the wall of my landing and curled into a ball on the floor. Silence. For once, I understood the expression 'the silence was so loud'. You could have heard a pin drop. Narla had gone quiet, but I knew she was still behind the kitchen door with her ears up and body tense, waiting to get out.

I pulled myself up from the floor and headed to the kitchen and downstairs living room area. My footsteps seemed to echo throughout the big apartment. It was a bit like a converted church. The upstairs living area had an open balcony, as well as two massive, tall windows that started at the bottom of the apartment and went all the way up to the ceiling of the second floor. You could see the windows and the upstairs balcony from downstairs. It wasn't my white mansion, but it was still a far cry from the one-bedroom council flat I grew up in. I had bought this place with my ex-boyfriend Fazer when we were together and performing in N-Dubz. After we'd broken up, I had bought his share, and rented the place out. But I never thought I'd be moving back in, let alone under such circumstances.

Narla ran out as soon as I opened the door, and I could hear her pelting around, looking for intruders as well as Gareth. She dashed up the stairs to continue her search. The big chandelier that hung from the giant beams on the top floor glistened in the sunlight. Everything was so still and quiet. I slumped to the ground again, sparked up a cigarette, and took a long, deep drag. No wonder I was smoking so much. I felt small and childlike, sat on the floor of this big place in my pyjamas and bare feet.

When I was six years old, I had watched my mother being dragged away by police officers because of her mental health problems. Something about this kind of reminded me of it. This moment had brought back all those emotions. I felt alone, again. I thought about G sat in a cell, confused and scared. I knew all too well how he would be feeling. I looked down at my phone. Who could I call? I don't have that many friends, and there was only one that was local.

I'd known Cat since I was 17 and she said she'd head over as soon as she could. I scanned the room, thinking of my next move. *Right, snap the fuck out of it, T! Let's be logical about this, there's nothing you can do other than wait for news from Ross. In the meantime, the house could do with a clean. Let's get it spotless for when G gets back, candles on, the lot! Even cook him his favourite Shepherd's Pie for when he's home.* I threw on a tracksuit and went to put Narla's lead on for her morning walk. She was all shaken up. She wet herself slightly as I bent down to her.

'Aaaaw, look at you, you poor thing. Don't worry, we're gonna be alright, kiddo,' I said, sitting down on the floor and cradling her heavy body as she quivered in my arms. 'You're way too big and old for all this now.'

I was unsure if I was talking to her or subliminally talking to myself. When I got outside, the breeze was a little chilly and as it hit my face it sent a shiver down my spine. I walked over to the park area outside my apartment, sat on the nearest bench and unclipped the lead to let Narla do her thing. Usually, it was Gareth's job to walk the dog at this time. I was the night owl. I pictured G sitting in a cell again. It all felt so evil and surreal, like a film. He had got dragged into this so they could get to me. Because people out there wanted to take me out and would stop at nothing and no one to do so. I feared for all my friends now, to the point that I wanted to isolate myself.

Sometimes I felt like I was better off alone, that way they couldn't hurt anyone else.

I began racking my brain with all the theories me and Gareth had come up with as to why this had happened. Someone higher up had to be responsible. Maybe I was paranoid, but the overpowering fear that my life could be in danger felt very real. Someone had made this happen.

I could see how the 'Fake Sheikh' Mahmood had made a career out of choosing his victims and selling the results of their entrapment to the papers. I knew that around £300,000 had been spent on my sting, and it wasn't Mahmood's money. People pay him to do what he does. Mazher Mahmood was technically a media assassin. So, the question was, who had hired him, and why?

The most obvious answer would be *The Sun* newspaper. I already had a legal case against them after the 'Home wrecker' headlines they had run about me. It was a few years before, at the height of my *X Factor* fame, and they'd done an interview with Danny's ex and run away with the story, plastering the accusation all over the front page as if it was fact. Danny sued them too, and I have since received a settlement. Could this be why all this had happened? Revenge?

I couldn't help but trust my instincts and think otherwise. Throughout my career I hadn't exactly played the game in any way, shape or form, not in the slightest. Yet throughout it, I'd seen and heard a lot about others, powerful others. When I was coming into the industry, most people seemed to assume that I was a certain type of person, due to my past, my bravado, and the media perception. They were always sorely disappointed to find out that I didn't do drugs, and – aside from the private sex tape an ex-boyfriend sold of me giving him a shitty blowjob (ASSHOLE!) – I had a sex life and drive as dry as a nun's arse. Everyone has skeletons in their closet, but I've always been very open about mine. Anything scandalous I'd ever done was already out there, so no one ever really had anything over me. I couldn't say the same in reverse, as I knew a lot of things about others. I wondered if maybe it was one of those people at the root of all this, on a mission to destroy and discredit me?

There were other things too. I had gone to Dubai a few months before with a few friends, to take a break from the stress, and Gareth and I were immediately approached by an assistant of two Dubai princesses who were supposedly big fans. They knew I was in the country and wanted to 'party' with me. Gareth and me found it all very suspicious but decided to entertain these people anyway, to check them out. Luckily, G has friends in high places in Dubai, and we found out these 'princesses' of course didn't exist. We still have a recorded conversation where their PA is trying to arrange a meeting with Gareth where he says 'so we can TRAP', then realises what he's said and quickly says 'so we can MEET'. We actually knew a real Dubai prince at the time and he informed us that these people were not who they said they were.

If that was a set-up, how easy would it have been for one of the so-called 'princesses' to drop whatever they'd liked into my handbag, for me to be greeted by police moments later because of an 'anonymous tip-off'? With Dubai's strict laws, I might never have seen the light of day again. Of course, during that time it would have been completely illegal for Mazher Mahmood to set up another sting. But that's what happened, and that's how I felt. I'll let you do the math. Though I'd had a lucky escape, I was still left wondering what the plan was for me during this sting. They were fully aware that I was not a drug user, they had undoubtedly established that from their first sting. Yet they were trying to set me up in a country that carried a death sentence for drugs. Did someone want me dead or locked up for life? If so, and if they hadn't taken me out with their attempts so far and they had gone this far, what would be their next step?

The trees and bushes rustled from a big gust of wind, one bush in particular shuddered harder than the rest. I starred at it intently, looking for someone behind it. *It's just the wind*, I said to myself. People hiding in cars and bushes watching me was pretty ordinary now. We'd even found a tracker they'd put under my tour manager Drew's car so they could follow my every move. These people weren't paparazzi, they were surveillance.

But why would someone want to put me under 24-hour

surveillance when I was already on a charge? The damage was done, so what were they looking for? What were they planning? Gareth and me had our ideas.

I watched as a little magpie flew towards me and landed by my feet. 'Hello, Mr Magpie,' I said out loud. I had always seen magpies regularly throughout my life, but never as much as I had this year. It was always one on its own, like it was following me everywhere. 'One for sorrow,' they say, but I didn't see it that way. In fact, I saw it as a good sign, that someone or something was watching over me and had my back.

Many hours later, I was in the kitchen cooking away, sipping on a glass of red. The candles and incense were burning, the bed sheets changed, and it was sparkling clean in every corner. I poured Cat a glass of wine and gave her a nod. We made a good team. 'To my wingman, who saved my ass today. A friend in need is a friend indeed! Cheers!' I said, clinking my glass against hers.

'Feck off, less of the emotional speech,' she chuckled as she took a sip. Cat was never the emotional type, not on the surface. I got it, that's why I liked her. I heard the bell go and rushed to the door, like a nervous housewife whose husband has just got back from a trip abroad.

'He's here!' I squealed to Cat. I waited patiently at the door to the apartment with an open Budweiser in hand for him. I saw him turn the corner of the hall and his facial expression said it all. I was relieved to see that the earlier vulnerable-looking G was long gone. He bowled around the corner towards me with his now 'I'm so over it' face.

'Get me a fucking drink,' he huffed, as he stormed in.

I pulled out the bottle of Budweiser from behind my back and handed it to him. 'Long day at the office, honey?'

'You know me too well,' he smirked.

He got into the kitchen and let out a big deep scream as Narla whimpered around his feet.

'*AAAAARRRRRRGGGGGHHHHHH!* That was fucking vile!' G yelled at the top of his voice.

I slipped into the chair next to Cat and picked up my wine. Both of us sat up like meerkats, all attention, waiting for him to spill the beans. G perched himself on the window ledge and necked half the bottle of beer before sparking a cigarette and puffing away like his life depended on it. He let out a long sarcastic sigh before he spoke, 'So! In a text that I sent to you around the time of the sting, I asked you, "Do they want a lads' night out or a real lads' night out?", obviously meaning a night club or a strip club. They read this as a night fuelled on coke. So, basically, these days if you say you'll sort out a real lads' night out you're a suspected drug dealer and you can be arrested. Pathetic! It's bollocks! This was a fishing exercise to see if they could collect more evidence on you by searching through my stuff and my phones and grilling me in an interview!'

I let out a sigh of relief. 'Well, thank fuck for that! I thought Mazher had pinned some shit on you too and they were gunna try and get you to go against me to make them drop the charge, like we said.'

'I know, right! So did I. We knew either way they'd try and go for me somehow, but they didn't find enough like they'd hoped. But check this, it gets better. If they charge me then I can't be a witness for you in court. You see where I'm going with this?' Gareth exclaimed.

'Holy shit, you're right! The absolute fuckers. Surely they can't charge you over that though?' I asked.

'Well, nothing surprises me anymore, but I guess that's why they took my other phones, to try and find something out to make the charge more solid. The CPS knew from the second they charged you that they would have to make it stick! Without me as a witness it's your word versus his,' he said.

Cat sat bewildered, guzzling her wine and looking at us both. 'I've never seen anything like it, your lives are absolutely mental! It actually makes me appreciate the simplicity of my own,' she said.

'Welcome to the family, Cat,' I replied, raising my glass to her and G, who was still puffing away furiously at his cigarette. He looked at Cat sternly and blew out a puff of smoke. 'Shit just got real, bitch.'

The next day, we were up bright and early to check the media damage. Of course the headline wasn't 'Gareth gets arrested in connection with Tulisa's drug deal'. Instead they made it sound like he got busted for dealing class A drugs on the street on a completely separate occasion.

We, of course, hadn't expected any less.

It was all a load of nonsense and the charges were dropped, rightfully so, but as usual the damage to Gareth's and my reputation remained.

Chapter 5:

OFF TU PROJECT X

A FEW WEEKS later, I was that little bit closer to the big moment of the trial. I was having my fair share of panic attacks and down days, but all in all, I was becoming pretty numb to the situation. I felt as though I was beginning to accept it and the worst possibility of my fate. There wasn't much to do other than train, go to the studio, and pray, and of course have the odd night out to distract myself. The week before, I had gone to my friend Claire's birthday party, which Jacob had also attended. He had phoned me from Claire's phone, telling me he had to leave at nine to go to an important meeting and asking if I could get there earlier so he could see me. When I told him I wouldn't make it in time, he asked if he could see me after his meeting, telling me to take his number from Claire and call him after. But again, I hadn't.

Tonight, I was off out again to a house party that me

and my friends liked to call Project X. It had become an annual do for the past three years at a house occupied by a bunch of girls that a few of my boy mates knew. This was great for me, as I didn't want to be seen out clubbing or get papped because of my fast-approaching trial. It also meant I could turn up in some attire that was truer to my character, a baseball t-shirt and trainers! There were always a lot of, let's say, rather promiscuous ladies turning up to Project X, and that's exactly what the guys going there were looking for, so I felt a lot more comfortable in my comfy, casual clothes. Michelle and I were driving to our mate Daz's house to kick off the night and meet the rest of our group. I also planned to leave my car there to pick up the next day.

The roof was down, and the house tunes were blaring out as we drove from London to Essex. It was those moments that I wanted so badly to enjoy life to the fullest. I was about as happy as I could get, but the thought of the trial always lay heavy over the back of my mind like a thick black cloud.

As we arrived at Daz's door, he greeted us with his usual cheeky grin. 'Oi oi, son! Welcome to the Playboy Mansion!'

'Oi oi, saveloy!' I yelled at him loudly, before I followed him into the living room, where we were greeted by an array of familiar faces. 'Ello, lads! What's crackalackin?' I grinned.

I was welcomed with a big chorus of 'Eeeeeey' in unison, and big smiles in return. As I did the rounds and said hello to everyone individually, I spotted Jacob in the corner with his usual smooth attire and side-sweep do, looking cool, calm and collected. Of course, his arm was draped around an unfamiliar girl. She was a pretty little blonde thing that was all smiles and looking rather ecstatic to be his girl for the night. I wasn't sure if he'd just met her at Daz's or what exactly the deal was, but I knew she wasn't his girlfriend, since Jacob didn't really do girlfriends. The girl may have unintentionally messed up my potential bit of attention for the evening, but I didn't feel any bad blood towards her. She seemed rather sweet actually. I leaned over to give Jacob a peck on the cheek, and he smiled.

'Hello you, you alright?' I said casually, before turning my attention straight to his female companion. 'Nice to meet you, babe,' I said, kissing her on the cheek and quickly moving on to the next person.

I could already feel Jacob's eyes immediately glancing over at me on the sly. I felt sorry for the poor bird already.

After a few drinks we all left the house in a large group. There were designated drivers for each of the five cars, and we all separated and chose a vehicle. Daz had a girl I didn't know driving him, so me and Michelle jumped in with them. All of the cars followed each other, thumping out various house tunes as we drove out of Daz's apartment complex. The fun had begun. We pulled up in a row outside some shops to get alcohol to take to the party. I wanted rosé, but the first shop didn't have the particular brand I like, so I headed further down across the road to the next shop. Once in the shop, I began scanning the alcohol section when I heard a familiar voice behind me.

'What's going on, Princess? Don't I get a proper hello? Where's my hug?'

I turned my head to look around, but before I could even respond, Jacob had his arms wrapped around me and was pecking away at the side of my face with repeated kisses. My body froze up and I became rock-solid, trying to pull myself out of the embrace. I squirmed awkwardly, trying to move my face away from his, like I was being smothered by my grandmother at a family do.

'Woah, easy, tiger,' I said with a half-laugh, half-frown, as I managed to prise myself out of his grip. He pulled me back towards him again with his face even closer this time.

'What's wrong with you? Why do you keep treating me like a stranger and being funny with me? Can't I even give you a hug?' he asked. I pushed him off with force.

'Jacob, in all the time I've known you, you have never tried to hug me like this, so I don't know what you're on about. You're being very touchy-feely today,' I replied, glaring at him.

'What? It's not like I'm doing it in a sexual way, I'm just giving you some affection! I'm an affectionate guy, that's how I express myself and I wanna show you some love. I'm happy to see you, what's the problem?'

'I'm not a very touchy-feely person. It's nothing personal, I just don't like it, it makes me uncomfortable,' I said casually, pushing him away again as he wrapped his arms back around me. As I stood back, I looked at him in the harsh light. His eyes were glazed and he had a slight sway in his stance. He was drunk, really drunk. *This should be fun*, I thought.

'Why didn't you call me, man? Is that how you're going on, yeah? You just pied me?' he laughed, trying to pull me close to him again. By this point I was just pulling his hands off my shoulders every 10 seconds.

'I'm sure I tried to text you, maybe it didn't go through,' I said, trying to hide my sarcasm. He pulled out his phone.

'Give me your number so I can call you. What's the big deal? We can hang out, no biggie. What's with all this acting like you don't know me business?'

'That's the point, Jacob, I *do* know you,' I said.

'Nah, you think you know me, but I want you to get to know me better,' he smiled. I frowned at him, openly sarcastic this time.

'Aaaaw, you're proper cute, man,' he said, grabbing me before I could move, planting another big sloppy smacker on my cheek. He was so patronising and dominating that I now had the urge to give him a slap.

'Jacob! Stop, man! Where has all this come from? Look how long I've known you for, you're never like this with me,' I said, pushing him off again.

'Listen, fuck all that. It's because I like you and I wanna take you out properly. What are you doing tomorrow?' he asked.

'Recovering from my hangover, of course,' I said flatly.

'Well, we can recover together. I'll pick you up at 6, I'll have something special planned.'

'Alright, alright, you can take me out, but don't be thinking you can grab me all night with this touchy-feely business! Keep ya hands to yourself!' I snapped.

'Alright, alright, I promise... You won't regret it!' He grinned.

In my mind there was no way I was going on a date with Jacob, but at least he was off my back, for now.

I'd already got through half a bottle of rosé, dancing around in the back seat, by the time I got to Project X. I wasn't even tipsy yet, but I was nice and bubbly. I felt good, as good as I could feel. As I stepped out of the car, I felt my trainers hit the floor and a look of pure joy spread across my face as I remembered that I was high-heel free and I'd be boogying in flats all night. I did a little victory dance as I skipped towards the large house. I was on a mission. I was going to have fun tonight if it was the last thing I did. I was going to be a carefree 25-year-old, living life as 25-year-olds should.

As I got inside, the place was filling up, drinks were flowing, and the tunes were pumping out. I felt the bass surge through my body as I got closer to the decks. It was a feeling that never got old for me. I love music. Music is my world, and to feel and hear it with all my mates was the ultimate bonus, it was as simple as that. I didn't go out to stand around and look pretty, I just wanted to feel a big dirty bass line and skank the hell out. As I began warming myself up for the night ahead, sipping on my rosé and doing a little two-step, I spotted Jacob with his lady friend. He put an arm around her and whispered something in her ear. I analysed them from a distance. This guy was something else, *what a cheeky little shit.* I laughed to myself at his audacity, then wandered back through the front of the house to go for a cig. I felt a hand grab my arm as I reached the doorway and I spun around.

'Where are you going?' Jacob asked.

'For a cigarette,' I said flatly.

'I'll come with you,' he replied. I ignored him and continued to walk outside while he continued to follow.

'What's wrong with you?' he asked. I sighed and rolled my eyes.

'What? You think you can come here with another bird and try and stick it on me? Are you mad?' I said.

'What, her? She's my driver for the night so I can drink. I'm not with her like that. She knows what it is, that's her choice,' he said. I continued to glare at him in silence. 'Oh come on, Tulisa, you know what it is – I thought you were one of the boys.'

'I *am*. That's why I deserve some respect. I'm not having a bar of it, mate! Don't think you can come around me with another chick and try and chat me up. Just because you're only shagging her doesn't mean you have to take the piss. It's a bit unfair to her, don't you think?'

'Listen, you haven't called me, you haven't let me take you out, you haven't even given me your number until today! Once I take you out, it's a different story. I didn't know you would be here today, did I?' he said, seemingly genuine.

'Hmmmm... bullshit!' I said, staying stern. Of course I

got it, but it was the principle, and he needed to know I wouldn't put up with any shit.

'Come! Let's go chill somewhere quieter and have a little chat,' he said with a warm smile.

'I'm here to smoke. Feel free to join, mate,' I said. This cocky shit was about to get a taste of his own medicine. I found a spot under a nice tree somewhere out front and leaned against it as I sparked a cig.

'So, what's up, kiddo?' I said. He burst out laughing, holding his stomach for added effect.

'You're the bollocks!' he chuckled.

'So I've been told,' I grinned.

'You could be the one, you know – I've got a feeling about you,' he declared.

'Oooooooh, very smooth, Mister! Is that line a regular, or am I getting special treatment?' I said, pursing my lips.

He chuckled again, taking a step closer and leaning over me, resting his arm on the tree above my head. He looked down into my eyes. He was average height, not overly tall, but a fair bit taller than me. I wondered if that would still be the case if I was in high heels. He gazed at me intensely, as if he was looking for something in my eyes.

'I actually *do* reckon you could be the one. They say you just know, don't they? We could end up getting married, for all you know.' He was now undressing me with his eyes.

'Aaaaaw, how romantic, Jacob! Should I take my pants off now, or later?' I said sarcastically.

'Ha! Cheeky little thing, aren't you?' he grinned.

'You're going to have to do way better than that, kid,' I snapped.

We continued to stare at each other for what felt like a decade even though it was probably only about 10 seconds, neither of us breaking our gaze and barely blinking. It was like we were challenging each other, sizing each other up. I broke the silence.

'You don't know what you're getting yourself into, pal, I'll eat you alive,' I said, leaning towards him. He leaned in even closer, unfazed.

'So, you think you can tame the beast? Come on then, little girl, show me what you've got,' he said with no smile this time, looking at me sternly.

'Now, now, Jacob, play nice. You wouldn't be trying to intimidate me now, would you?' I grinned back at him playfully to lighten the mood.

With our egos, we could have done this all day, but I was intrigued now, and I wanted to dig a little deeper under the façade. Amid all the darkness in my life, I needed to have a little fun right now. In that moment, the rosé daze lifted and it suddenly dawned on me what was happening. This was Jacob, the whole thing felt weird.

'Aaaaaaw, is that your way of backing down? You're too cute! Good girl, Tulisa, you're learning already,' he smirked.

I rolled my eyes at him and chuckled. Proper 24-carat asshole, this one.

'I knew this would happen one day, it was only a matter of time,' he smiled.

'You sound like you've been thinking about this for a rather long time,' I said.

'Do you know when I knew? When you cooked that Greek roast dinner at your house for everyone, the lamb with the lemon potatoes. Don't tell my gran, but it was the best roast dinner I'd ever tasted!' He grinned.

'Didn't you turn around to your bird at the time and say "why don't you learn to cook like this?"' I laughed.

'Yeah, I did,' he chuckled. 'She wasn't my bird though, I was just seeing her.' I raised my eyebrows and nodded. He leaned in a little closer and softened his stare.

'I watched you that day. It was the first time I saw the other side of you, behind all that Female Boss shit. I realised it was all a front,' he said.

'Trust me, it isn't a front. I admit I have a soft side, but it is still very much a part of my character,' I said, kissing my teeth at him dismissively.

'Yeah, yeah! It's a front! But you've been through some serious shit, so you have every right to be like that. You just need to be taken care of, and you'll drop that guard.'

I looked at him and laughed, a big, exaggerated laugh.

'Oh, Jacob, are you trying to break me down? Many have tried and failed, sweetheart. It'll take more than a few wines and some reverse psychology,' I said.

'I don't need to try. If it's meant to be, it's meant to be – we will know all in good time,' he said.

'I thought you knew in the kitchen when I cooked the Greek lamb?' I smirked.

'I did. I thought, she's with me. Maybe not now, but one day when the time is right, she's with me,' he said.

I nodded sarcastically in silence.

'Don't act like you didn't feel something,' he snapped.

'Not really... It wasn't the right circumstances, was it?' I replied.

'You're lying, I know. Come on, you felt something. Just admit it, you're honestly gunna stand there and say you felt absolutely nothing?' he said, searching my eyes for reassurance.

I paused for a moment, thinking before I spoke. 'Maybe one time I looked at you and felt something a little deeper, when we were at Daniel's house and we were alone in the living room and had that conversation about your mum? That you grew up as her carer, the same way I did for mine. I was pretty shocked, but a lot made sense about you. I think we're a lot more similar than you think. Maybe you have a little front of your own going on,' I said.

'Don't we all?' he said, nonchalant.

'Some more than others,' I said softly, staring into his eyes.

He shrugged it off, breaking away from the stare and taking a drag on his cigarette. 'Anyway! Forget this place, I'm only here because of you. I need to go home, I've got my mate's car keys and I need to meet him. Come back with me and chill,' he said, exhaling a big puff of smoke out of his mouth as if imitating a character out of *Scarface*.

'Are you taking the piss? You've got a bloody bird

with you! You've got some bloody front, I tell ya!' I said, shaking my head.

'Forget her, I'll tell her to go home! Come on, man, I wanna chill with you. I like spending time with you,' he said, stomping out his cigarette and placing his hands in his pockets.

'You're going to sack off some vagina so you can sit and have in-depth conversations with me all night?'

'Yeah, why not? I can have vagina any time! This is much more interesting!'

'You wanna see me, you call me in the morning and arrange a reasonable time and do things properly.'

'You're just doing this out of principle, and I'm not going to look at you any different if you come and chill with me now or tomorrow.'

'You just don't take no for an answer, do you? What's your star sign?' I asked inquisitively.

'Give me the last half of that cigarette and I'll tell you,' he said.

'You just had one, and no one tells me what to do. How about I give you your own cigarette, and you tell me your star sign?'

'How about you come home with me, and I'll tell you then?' he grinned.

'Who do you think you are?' I bellowed.

'The boss!' he said, with a raised voice.

'I'm the fucking boss, mate. Are you intimidated by strong women, Jacob? Is that it?' I said, raising my voice louder than his.

'I could never be intimidated by a woman because she will never be stronger than me. I'm the boss and that's how it has to be,' he said sternly.

'Well then, you're pursuing the wrong woman. What kind of idiot that wants to be the boss tries to pursue The Female Boss? Where's the logic in that? I will settle for nothing less than a man that sees me as his absolute equal, and believe me, I will never back down! So, take your egotistical arrogant attitude and shove it up your ass, because it won't wash with me, mate!' I said, throwing down my cigarette and folding my arms with a glare that could have killed.

He stood in front of me with exactly the same stance and the exact same look on his face as me. 'Oh, go on then, why don't you storm off like all the other little girls to prove a point?'

'I'm not your other little girls and this is my spot, so if you don't like what I have to say, piss off. I'm not going anywhere,' I said.

He began laughing, with his familiar high-pitched, patronising cackle. But as I stood there watching him laugh, my glare began to crack. I tried so hard to keep a stern face, but I couldn't hold it in any longer. I burst out laughing with him. The two of us stood there laughing hysterically. Every time one of us managed to stop, the other would start again and set the other off. Eventually we managed to pull ourselves together.

'We are either going to end up absolutely hating each other or getting married, I'm telling you! I can see it already, we're dangerous,' he said, still chuckling and shaking his head.

'Play your cards right and I'll be the best and worst thing that ever happened to you,' I grinned cheekily.

'I prefer the best, just don't let me down,' he smiled.

'Vice versa,' I said, smiling back.

'Come on, come here, you. Let's hug it out before I go or is that too touchy-feely for you?' he said, approaching me with arms wide, pretending to be cautious, like I might smack him one. He pulled me into his arms swiftly and gripped me to his chest. I patted him on the back like a baby. He pulled his head back to look at me as if to say *don't even go there*, and we both laughed again.

'So, are you going to let me take you out tomorrow, yes or no?' he asked.

'We will see,' I smiled.

'Come, I'll take you inside,' he said, resting his arm over my shoulders and leading me back towards the house. I felt as though he annoyed me but entertained me at the same time. I didn't completely fancy him yet, but there was something there, something strange that I could honestly say I'd never felt before. It was like I could see myself in him. It was an attraction that went beyond the surface. But he also got on my tits. *Only time will tell*, I thought.

A few hours later, the party was in full swing! The old school garage was blasting out of the speakers as me and my friends danced our little dances we knew all too well in unison. I was having fun, for the first time in a long time – real fun! I smiled to myself, until it hit me again, that dark cloud. I stared into the distance at nothing, as my facial expression changed. I looked down at my drink and necked it back. *There's nothing you can do, T*, I thought. *Just trust in the universe and carry on.*

The next day, needless to say, I was pretty hanging and I didn't rise until the late afternoon when I woke up to a text from Jacob. We continued to text throughout the next couple of days, getting to know each other better. As soon as I mentioned my case in a message to him, it seemed to bring out his softer side. He never avoided it in conversation. In fact he would bring it up, trying to comfort me in any way he could as a friend. I respected him for this. It was a nice distraction, and it couldn't have come at a better time.

Chapter 6.

TULISA'S SURPRISE VISIT

I OPENED MY bedroom door and threw myself face down onto my bed, letting out a high-pitched whimper. I listened to the sound of my heart beating in my chest as I breathed heavily into my pillow. 'Cameras! Cameras everywhere,' I whined. I'd had just done a one-hour interview in the car for the BBC documentary on the way home from the pre-trial court session, which was a day in court to discuss and settle what was going to be put forward in terms of evidence in the trial, before the actual trial. It consisted of just the judge and no jury.

During the pre-trial hearing on 'abuse of process' (my lawyers always referred to it as the 'abuse trial') that was fast approaching, my barrister was going to stress to the judge the level of entrapment involved in my case and how unlawful it was, in the hope of getting the case thrown out of court. It was my last hope before the 'actual trial'. I was as drained and fed up of the long, complicated process as you probably are reading about it. As if going to court and the reason why wasn't bad enough, I had to deal with the usual flood of pap's and the entire day's events being blasted across the country. I knew it came hand in hand with my career, but let's be honest, this situation was far from normal. Celeb or not.

Imagine you're having the worst day ever, feeling and looking like shit, and all you want to do is hide under your bed covers, but there's a load of people that say, 'Hey, we're going to take a picture of your every movement at every angle during this day, and when we can't take pictures, we're going to sit and analyse your every facial expression and your body language. Then we're going to share all of it, along with our opinion of your situation and how you looked physically and emotionally throughout the day.'

Then, when I do finally get a bit of peace, I have to film my own documentary so I can show the world what's really going on. Draining, but necessary. I'm not one for pity parties, but I'm just stressing exactly how crap a day it was. *Please, Lord*, I thought, *Please, Lord, help me. I can't do this on my own, I'm losing my mind. I need help.* The tears began streaming down my eyes before my prayers were interrupted by the loud ringing of the phone next to my head. I sat up and looked at the screen. It was Jacob.

'Hello,' I said softly into the phone, disguising my tears.

'Hello, beautiful, how did it go?' he asked.

I took a deep breath and sighed.

'Stressful, but I'll survive, I always do.'

'I know you do, I can tell. Can I pop over? I'd like to see you,' he said.

My heart jumped at the words. We'd been speaking constantly since Project X but him coming to my house didn't feel very formal, plus I looked like shit.

'Eeeerm, flipping heck, you don't half spring it on a lady! I'm still in my court clothes! And my mate Alex is coming round in an hour.' Alex is one of my close female friends. She's an absolutely stunning firecracker, and also a professional psychic. We hadn't been able to spend a lot of time together recently so I was looking forward to our night in.

'I feel a state, and I'm about to have a girls' night,' I said.

'I don't care how you look, and that's fine, I'll only stay for half an hour. It's a minor, I just want to see you quickly, no biggie,' he said.

'You're killing me! I look like the living dead and I haven't had a chance to tidy up. Why don't we do tomorrow or something?'

'I can see you tomorrow as well! I'll come for five minutes! I'm just going to pass by, I wanna see you! And shut up about how you look. You're beautiful, you idiot! See you soon, I'll be there in ten,' he said, before hanging up the phone.

What the fuck? I thought. *He's actually serious!* I got up and walked towards the mirror. Ten minutes? I hope it's the longest ten minutes of my life. I ran down the stairs to Gareth and knocked on his door hesitantly before opening it.

'Eeeerm, G, just letting you know that Jacob's coming round in about ten minutes,' I said, trying to quickly close the door.

'EEEERRR, T!' he called.

'Yes?' I replied sweetly, popping my head back around.

'Nice try! Why the fuck is Jacob coming round the house? The other day you didn't even want to go on a date with him, and now he's coming round the house?' he glared straight-faced, while I stared at him like a deer in the headlights.

Gareth was always very sternly protective which I wasn't overly fond of, but I would play along most of the time to avoid a debate.

'Well, he called me and he just kind of sprung it on me, and I was caught by surprise and he just kept persisting and I tried to get out of it and he wasn't really having any of it and I didn't know what to say, so he's coming,' I said quickly, trying to close the door again.

'T!' he called.

'Yeah?' I said.

'Fix your face, your mascara's been running,' he said.

'Thanks, bubs,' I said, pulling the handle towards me again.

'Oh, and T!' he called again. Damn it, I cringed as I turned back round.

'Yep,' I replied.

'Just be careful – we can't trust anyone,' said Gareth seriously.

'I know, I know! I already thought of that! Everyone's a

possible set-up! In a bit,' I winked at him before slamming the door.

I looked at the clock. Holy crap! Seven minutes later I had whizzed around the house like Mary Poppins, throwing any visible mess into closets and cupboards, and changed into a simple pair of PJ bottoms and a vest. I didn't want to give the wrong impression. I was still unsure about how I felt about him or if I wanted to start actually dating him. But we'd sparked a weird connection, and I already had a level of trust because I knew him as a friend. He was also a distraction right now, and that was just what I needed. Minutes later, I opened the door to Jacob's familiar big wide grin. It was a very warm smile, seeming so sincere and loving. *I bet he gives that smile to every girl*, I thought.

'Beautiful!' he said, pulling me into his arms, and holding me tight. As I felt his strength wrap around me, my body just went limp. Like I passed all my weight on to him, along with my stress that I had been carrying at court all day. In that moment, I let my guard down for a second and completely relaxed into his embrace and let him hold me. I breathed in his masculine scent and his strong body gave me a feeling of comfort, like I was safe. I was, quite simply, in need of a hug, and it was as if he knew it. Like that was the reason he was even there. All of a sudden, as his thick hair brushed against my cheek, I recognised another smell. It was Head & Shoulders shampoo, the same shampoo my father used when I was a kid. I immediately snapped out of my little trance and pulled myself out of his embrace and back to reality.

'It's alright,' he said softly, 'you're allowed to have a little moment. I told you I got you. You don't need none of that Female Boss shit around me.'

'Oh, good! Shall I have my nervous breakdown on you here in the doorway then, or should we take this upstairs? I see you came prepared, wearing a black t-shirt, considering all this mascara will soon be dripping down it,' I said.

We laughed heartily together.

'See! You needed that, didn't you? I knew, I could sense it! You're glad I came round now, innit?' He grinned.

'Alright, psychic Sid. Let's go upstairs and you can get your crystal ball out and tell me what else you sense,' I replied.

We sat talking for what felt like hours. He even stayed for a while when Alex arrived. Even though I still wasn't sure how I felt about him, I felt as if I was making a new best friend, which was strange, considering how long I'd known him. He reminded me so much of myself at times, it was like looking in the mirror. I'd never really met a guy that I saw so much of myself in, and felt like I understood so well. There was definitely an attraction, but it came second to our mental connection and the friendship we were building. At such a dark time, this newfound connection was helping me. I wasn't even sure how. All I knew was that when he was there, the dark cloud didn't seem as dark, and I no longer felt alone.

Chapter 7:

DATE FOR TU

I STOPPED THE car around the corner from Jacob's house to check my make-up and top up my lippy. *Just breathe*, I thought, as the nerves kicked in and I felt myself slipping out of TFB mode. Just strut up in that bitch like a boss and kick some ass! And try to have fun while you're at it. Jesus, this is meant to be a date, not a boxing match.

I looked at myself in the car mirror. My hair was down and blow-dried with a baseball cap on, and my face was natural with a bit of light beauty make-up and fluffy lashes, topped off with a dash of baby-pink lip gloss. I was dressed very casually and slightly tomboy, with a pair of tight high-waisted jeans, a white crop top and some high-top Jordans. At least my outfit was figure-hugging, so I had a little bit of sex appeal.

Since the sting, I had started exercising like a madwoman for the first time in my life, and it was seriously paying off for both my body and my mind. I could see the difference, and so could everyone else. But I didn't want to give the wrong impression once again. I had been debating all day whether or not I should even go and see Jacob. I hated first dates, but I hoped with our vibe it would feel like we were just two friends having a drink and a laugh, and if romance followed, so be it.

I pulled up at his house and waited for the big black gates to open. *Nice pad, very secure and discreet,* I thought. Perfect for hiding and secret dates, if it goes anywhere. I told Jacob we couldn't go out for our first date because I was too paranoid about getting papped. I drove down the drive towards the house. It was a very modern bachelor-type pad – expensive but understated and sophisticated. I spotted Jacob waiting by the door to greet me. He looked rather smart compared to me. He was wearing a V-neck t-shirt, trousers, and shoes, with his thick dark hair slicked in a side parting as usual. His big, toned arms were bulging out of his top. I pulled up next to his beautiful Ferrari and admired it. Some girls have a thing for shoes and handbags, I love cars.

'Hello, trouble,' I said, strutting towards him.

'Beautiful! Where's my cuddle?' he said, opening his arms wide before pulling me into a lingering embrace.

'She's finally here!' I said, referring to myself in the third person, taking in his now-familiar scent.

'I knew you'd come around. Hard work, ain't ya?' he grinned. I pulled back and looked him up and down while he kept one arm wrapped firmly around my waist.

'You look very smart, you got someone special coming round, or...?' I asked.

'Starting already, are we? Look at her, always ready for a fight!' He laughed.

'Not at all, babe! Just thought you'd let a girl know, since I'm practically still in my gym gear. Didn't realise you were getting all formal on me.'

'Good! I like you dressed like that! You're being yourself, and that's why I like you, you're the bollocks. Fuck all that dolly bird shit, I see enough of that. You look stunning,' he declared.

'Why, thanks for the approval, Mr Grey, you don't look so bad yourself,' I replied.

'Shut up and get inside. I've got the boxing gloves waiting, let's settle this properly,' he grinned.

'Oh, goody!' I squealed, following him inside. As I came through the door, I instantly began studying the layout. 'Do you mind if I take a look around?' I asked.

'Of course, I'll show you,' he said ushering me further in. I followed him around the house, taking note of everything I saw and what it said about him. Jacob paused as he reached a big leather door on the upper floor.

'This is the big boys' room, you shouldn't really be allowed in here. But I know you've been dying to, and I'm feeling nice,' he exclaimed.

'You're on fire today, aren't you?' I said, before stepping into the bedroom and scanning it. 'Oh, so this must be where the magic happens? All two minutes of it?'

'When you're ready, darling, but right now you're all

talk and this is just play, so I'll let you have your moment because eventually shit will get real. You just let me know when you're ready,' he said seriously.

'Yes of course, sir, whatever you say,' I said, saluting him mockingly.

'Yeah, call me sir. I like it when you call me sir, I think you should address me as sir at all times,' he replied. I looked at him and frowned before punching him in the arm.

'You wish, prick!'

As the evening progressed, we slipped out of our ping-pong banter and found our chill. We sat in the kitchen sipping on rosé with a bit of background music and began getting to know each other on a deeper level. We spoke about our past and exper-iences. It was amazing, unravelling all our similarities. From our upbringings to our views and opinions. I couldn't believe I had known him so long yet hadn't really known him. We were like two peas in a pod. The only thing we seemed to disagree on so far was who out of the two of us was the boss.

I was also very surprised to find one of the major things we had in common was how spiritual we both were and how religious both our families were. As the hours passed, we were both becoming increasingly tipsy and the conversation got deeper still. A particular icon of Mother Mary in the kitchen caught my eye. I stood up to inspect it.

'That's beautiful,' I said, making the sign of the cross and leaning over to kiss it.

'It is, isn't it? I got that while I was away in Italy. I'm

surprised at how religious and spiritual you are. You've got an amazing energy about you, to be fair. The more I get to know you, the more I'm starting to understand why I was so drawn to you,' he said.

'Why, thank you, I see it in you too. A little darkness as well though,' I chuckled.

'What darkness? There ain't no darkness around here, I'm a clean spirit,' he declared.

'Hmmm, so you say. Time will tell. I know what I sense, I see these things.'

'Well, if you can see, you will know! You'll see when you know me properly. I already know where this is going anyway. I feel like I've been sent to you right now, with everything you've got going on,' he said.

'Maybe you have, maybe you have been sent to help me and I'm here to teach you something,' I replied.

'I can't actually believe we're having this conversation,' he said, shaking his head. 'I don't ever talk like this with girls, not the way I talk with you. I'm attracted to you, but I feel like I'm talking to one of my mates. You literally are one of the boys, ain't ya? It's good,' he said.

'I think you've been dating the wrong women, mate,' I replied.

'Maybe I just haven't found the right one yet, no?' he said, standing up and moving towards me. I stared at him warily as he approached me.

'I got you,' he said, his face serious now.

He was now stood in front of me with his face next to mine. I could feel his breath touch my cheeks as he exhaled. His eyes trailed down my face to my lips, then back up again until our eyes met. All of a sudden, he raised one of his hands and wrapped it around the back of my neck while quickly slipping the other around my waist. He thrusted himself towards me while pulling me in and pressed his lips hard against mine. I didn't even have time to think. He completely caught me by surprise, which was probably a good thing.

Without thinking, I parted my lips and I began to kiss him back. It was a long, passionate kiss. His body felt tense and overpowering as he held me in his tight grip like he was taking all of me in, as if he had yearned to do so for a long time. A familiar melody began drifting through my ears in the background. It was Duke Dumont's 'I Got U'. It had become one of my favourite songs of all time that year and whenever I heard it, it always brought me feelings of happiness and warmth. It really heightened the moment. *My song is playing*, I thought. *How strange, and the words, I got you, he'd said moments before.* Very strange, and so fucking cool. This was still weird though. *I'm kissing Jacob, what the heck?*

Then, all of a sudden, out of nowhere, Jacob slipped his hands all the way down the back of my trousers and on to my bum cheeks, and squeezed. Moment killed! I immediately grabbed his wrists and pulled them out of my trousers, before pushing him away.

'What the fuck do you think you're doing?' I asked him in shock.

'What?' he said, as if surprised.

'Are you actually taking the piss? No no no, mate! You need to slow yourself down. Did you actually just slip your hands down my pants like that?' I glared at him. He looked at me like a naughty schoolkid that had just been told off, trying to hide his amusement.

'What? We were in the moment! I was just going with the flow! I only felt your arse. Don't be like that, come here,' he said, trying to hug me and laugh it off. I pulled back out of the embrace.

'Now, you listen to me. Just because I kissed you, does not mean that you're allowed to feel my arse or anything else tonight! I don't know what kind of birds you're used to, or what your intentions are, but you are most definitely not getting laid! No funny business! No touchy-feely! Keep your hands above the waist area and away from the chest. I don't know what you thought was going on here, but you were very wrong, so get whatever you assumed way out your head! Got it?' I said sternly, with raised eyebrows.

'Flipping heck! Yeah, I get it! You are fiery, boy! You're like a little Rottweiler! Come here and give me a cuddle. I'm sorry, I promise no more funny business,' he said.

I frowned at him sceptically as he pulled me back into his arms and rested his head on my shoulder. Then I smirked, before clenching my fist and giving him a playful but sharp jab in the ribs. He jumped back and looked at me, shocked.

'Oh, you wanna play, yeah?' he said.

I nodded with a grin, before raising my fists into a

fighter's stance. He raised his fists in turn and we began playfully sparring with each other. We were like two big kids in each other's presence. As we continued to spar, I could see how surprised he was that I could actually fight. At first, he was giggling but after I smacked him a few times he stopped laughing and focused. All of a sudden, he threw a right jab at the same time as I tripped and stumbled towards him. The vodka was clearly kicking in.

SMACK!!!

We both felt the connection.

'Fuck!' I yelled, putting my hands over my face. I could already feel the throbbing in my nose.

'Oh no, please no, why me, please God, no, let me see,' said Jacob. I could hear the panic in his voice. I stood up straight and removed my hand from my face.

'Is it bad?' I asked. His face dropped as he looked at me.

'I am so so sorry, you just tripped and stepped into it. Oh my God, I can't fucking believe it,' he said, raising his hands to his face with a look of horror.

I instantly walked out of the kitchen and into the downstairs bathroom. I looked in the mirror and saw a tiny cut on the top of my nose with a trickle of blood seeping out of it.

'You fucking bastard!' I yelled. 'You actually fucked me up. Literally!' I stormed back into the kitchen, glaring at him.

He stood still, horrified, with his hands up to his face. I couldn't hold it any longer and I burst out laughing. He tried to hold back his own laughter from guilt. When I finally managed to contain myself, I spoke again. 'It's all good! You better watch your back now though, I'm getting you back one way or another,' I declared.

'Just hit me now, please! Go for it, I'll take it, I deserve it,' he said, shaking his head in shame.

'Don't be stupid, that's way too easy.'

'No more play fighting!' he said, pulling me towards him and hugging me.

'Only because you know I'm gunna fuck you up,' I said.

He pulled my face towards his and pecked me on the lips. 'If you say so, Princess,' and it was in that moment, for some reason, after the kiss, the play fighting and the laughs, that I knew I liked him, maybe a lot, and I was definitely attracted to him, in every way... Maybe he'd knocked some sense into me. There was something very charming and alluring about him, along with the fact that he was practically my male twin, which sounds a little narcissistic, I know, but wasn't it also what compatibility was all about? Either way, I decided right there and then, I was definitely going to give him a run for his money.

As the night went on, we both became very drunk and seemed very comfortable while doing so. We went from laughing and joking to emotional chats about our childhoods. We held each other as we spoke and were so busy talking, we didn't even have another kiss. Eventually, daylight started peering through the windows and we headed upstairs to bed. I snuggled my head into Jacob's chest, looking forward to what I knew was going to be a good sleep.

'On a serious note,' he whispered, 'I had the best time tonight, you're the bollocks.' He kissed me on the forehead and I smiled a very contented grin.

'I'm actually glad I came. Good night, babe.'

* * *

The hot sunlight streamed through the half-open curtains on to my face, disturbing me from my slumber. I felt like shit. I rolled over, shutting my eyes again, and sunk my face into the pillow. I felt the strong arms that were wrapped around me give me a tight squeeze before one of them started to wander off down my thigh... Then I felt something else. Huh? I opened one eye and took in my surroundings. It took me a few seconds to register where I was.

'Jacob! No! Hands off,' I moaned. 'Oh man, it's so early and you're starting already! Why don't you have a coffee first or some breakfast? Chill out a bit?' He groaned.

'How about I shove that boner of yours into a hot cup of coffee and you see how that feels?' I replied.

'Honestly? The way I'm feeling right now, sticking it anywhere sounds more appealing than lying here like this. You're killing me!' he said.

'It's only day one! Get that shit under control, mate. You've got a very long way to go.'

'I'm cool, I'm cool! Just early morning urges, it will pass. Just wanted a little feel of the body before you woke up. Feeling good, by the way,' he said, nuzzling his head into my neck and showering the side of my face with kisses.

I embraced the attention, feeling cosy and content.

It had been so long since I'd felt affection from anyone other than my dog. I rested my head on his chest and stared at the ceiling while he stroked my arm. After a few minutes, it dawned on me that the first moment I woke up was usually spent remembering I was facing a possible prison sentence, but today it had been different.

'What are you doing today?' asked Jacob.

'I've got a hair appointment and a training session. Life on a drugs charge. Fun fun fun,' I said.

'Cancel it,' he said.

'What?' I said, still groggy.

'Cancel it!' he declared.

'Why?' I asked.

'Because I want to spend the day with you,' he said.

'Haven't you got work?' I asked.

'I'm not going,' he said.

'What? Why?'

'Because the only thing that is important to me today is making you smile. I work every day and I will work tomorrow. Today I want to spend with you,' he said.

'But I need to get new extensions fitted and my roots done today,' I replied.

'So, rebook it. You can do that any day! Look, I'm sending the text, work cancelled! Done!'

'But...'

'Shhhhhh! Just cancel your appointment, your hair looks fine. Though it does smell like vodka and Silk Cut purple! But you can give it a wash later. Let's go for breakfast, where do you want to eat?'

Chapter 8:

I SWEAR TU TELL THE TRUTH

I STARED AT Gareth blankly, trying to make sense of what he was saying. I was zoning out as usual. Any statement that involved the words 'court', 'jail' or 'legal costs' seemed to go straight over my head these days. It was the day before the start of the abuse trial. I had just got home after a meeting with my lawyer and was now sat with Gareth, talking about the week ahead. Even though it was a dark time, I could only hope for the best. We both hoped the judge would see what a set-up this all was and throw the case out before it went to trial.

'They can't possibly let it go to trial once they see the evidence, G. That would be insane! Even a 10-year-old could see this for what it is!' I declared, focusing on the conversation again.

'I know! I just can't see how they would let it go ahead, unless it's a bigger set-up than we thought,' he suggested.

'Well, enough said. We can only hope,' I said.

'Hope is the key word, mate,' he sighed.

'For me and you both, kid,' I sighed back.

We were trying to stay positive. Technically there was a lot to be positive about, but – the way our luck had been going and with what people had managed to do to us so far – we knew anything was possible. I, for one, had a sneaking suspicion that this wasn't going to be over any time soon. My head said 'prepare for the worst', while my heart told me something would give, but not until the last moment. I would have to ride this out till the end. And at the last minute, when I thought it was all over, I would be saved. I don't know why but that was my hunch. I just didn't want to say it out loud. I needed to be hopeful about this abuse trial, but from experience, I always had a big fall before I could rise. And if I was ever going to rise from this, the fall was going to be one hell of a drop.

G's phone went off with a ping. His facial expression changed.

'What now?' I sighed flatly.

'Eeeeerm, lawyer's messaged me, you need to have a sitdown with them next week about the appeal for the assault charge.'

'Oh, Goooooooooood!' I yelled. 'When will it eeeend?!' During the summertime after I had found out about the sting, I had gone to a music festival called V Fest. While I was there, I was socialising with multiple people from the industry that I knew. There was a guy there called Vas. The only experience I had had with Vas was when he and a girl called Chloe Green had attempted to join my table in a club, and because I didn't know them, I asked my security to remove them. Later that night, there was a tweet from Chloe's Twitter, saying something along the lines of, 'you don't know who I am, big mistake'. Down the line I had spoken to Chloe, we had squashed our beef and she'd told me that it was Vas that had tweeted it from her account.

I didn't like his energy, and I just wanted to steer clear of the guy. When I was at V Fest, I had accumulated a large group of associates by the end of the night and we were all heading back to the camper van I had arrived in, to chill. Vas began tagging along because he was hanging with some of the people I was hanging with. Which was fine and I ignored him until I reached my van because, of course, he wouldn't be coming in.

So, I left it to the last moment, when we were about to go in the van, before I proceeded to tell him to fuck off. This led to a heated argument. All six foot of him towered over me, hurling vindictive and spiteful insults, referring to my current situation, saying that I was finished, I was a joke, I was broke, I was nothing. He also said something along the lines of 'you're fucked in the head like your mentally ill mother'.

I don't do well with bitches or in mean girl type scenarios. Where I come from, once it's taken below the belt, it's going to be a physical fight. But, of course, I wasn't 18 anymore and I wasn't in the hood. I was also famous now, so I was trying to adapt to this new world

93

and an industry that, let me tell you, is full of bitches. I may have lost my temper many times with some of the extremely annoying wasp-like species I had come to encounter, but I had never got violent, because I was no longer under the threat of violence I had once been in my younger years. These people were all mouth, but I was having to learn that and manage my reactions, having come from a place where something so verbally heated would most definitely turn into a fight.

Verbal aggression aside, I was doing rather well. Though I may have told him he was a little bitch and I would love to put him in the boot of my car, I kept my hands behind my back while I was yelling. The reason I kept my hands behind my back was because Vas very much gave off snitch energy and I didn't want there to be any dispute as to whether I had threatened him with violence off the back of me waving my hands around. Eventually, I walked off and into my camper van because ultimately it was a waste of my energy.

A few days later, I got a call from the press to say that Vas was claiming I'd hit him. But then I was contacted by the police and brought in for questioning and charged with assault. Was I surprised? I wasn't surprised in terms of how many times could I be set up and fucked over by the justice system in one year.

A friend of his had originally given a statement, saying she had witnessed me hit him, but in court she had changed her story to say that I was waving my hands around frantically and one of them may have accidentally made contact. Funny that, when my hands were behind my back the whole time, to avoid this exact situation.

There was also a random security guard publicly claiming online to have been at V Fest on the night in question and saying that he saw me hit Vas.

He was now also testifying against me in court. However, once on the stand, he told an interesting tale – that from a distance he had seen a female with long dark hair punch Vas, but that he had only realised it was me when someone later 'told him it was me'. Bear in mind at the time of V Fest, my hair was in a very short bob.

Though there was a girl there who was a friend of mine with long dark hair. My tour manager Drew, who was personally infuriated by the injustice against me at the time, had said on the stand that my friend had staggered into the van and claimed that she'd punched him after my interaction with him because she was infuriated by the way he had spoken to me and towered over a young woman in a threatening demeanour. Hypothetically speaking, if I was aware that one of my friends had done this, I would never say that out loud as it goes against personal law of code. So either way my personal opinion or knowledge of that situation is irrelevant.

But the facts are that there were two testimonies pointing towards the same incident. The security guard had to also be warned while going through the court proceedings that he needed to stop posting about me, as he had been posting things about my physical appearance and bringing up the sex tape while inside court and outside of it.

There were also three other celebrities there that I knew, who had witnessed the event. I had initially named and shamed them in this book, but as time has passed, I've become the kind of person that prefers not to seek revenge. I'd much rather leave it to the universe, which seemingly always likes to dish out some guaranteed karma on my behalf.

I had contacted them all and literally begged them to step forward, and they had all responded by saying they didn't want to be involved. Though one of the responses, from a male celebrity, was more down the route of street code and that he didn't want to snitch on anyone.

I can't even begin to tell you how hopeless I felt at this time. It made me feel physically sick. The worst part was that everyone knew I was going through the drugs trial and I had told them that if I was to get done for this assault and then get done on the drugs charge, I would one hundred per cent be going to prison. Still, no one said a thing.

So, excluding the other three celebrities there was Vas and two witnesses against me. Vas claimed I punched him with a closed fist. Another witness who had originally claimed I hit him but changed her story on the stand to I had 'accidentally' hit him while waving my hands around, the other, a security guard who was also an internet troll that had been posting malicious things about me during the court process, claiming he saw a girl with long dark hair hit him, and that he only later came to the conclusion it was me when he was later made aware that I was there and of Vas's story.

On the side of Team Tulisa was Drew, my tour manager, Gareth, a random female bystander who had seen the news and stepped forward, but she had been dismissed as a witness on the stand as an unreliable character to tell the truth, because of a nine-year-old unpaid parking ticket, and Alexandra Burke's brother, who was also present. So that had made it five against three, including myself. All claiming that I undisputably did not hit him, and one claiming it was actually my friend with long dark hair, that the security guard had also seen, that had hit him.

Yet I was still found guilty, at a time when I just so happened to be on another huge and very public trial that was very much of interest to the CPS. Considering how it would look for them if I had been found innocent for both. And I was not given a jury for the assault charge because common assault is only tried in the magistrates' court, but I would have most definitely welcomed a jury.

I mean, do I need to say more? What the hell in the Will Smith *Enemy of the State* was going on? Between the drugs trial and this, it was like a real Hollywood blockbuster. I may not have got to star in one, but I was certainly getting to live one. I was appealing the case, but my lawyer was trying to orchestrate the appeal trial to happen after the drugs trial, to try and minimise the chances of me going to prison.

I was absolutely sick of taking this shit.

In the end the appeal ultimately failed and I had to accept the Magistrate's decision.

Chapter 9:

TU THOUGHTFUL

ME AND G sipped on our coffees in silence, lost in thought. My phone pinged with a text from Jacob. J: Are you at home?

We'd been in constant contact after the two days we'd spent together, during which we'd made an undeniable connection. A deep connection that made me feel as if I'd met him for a reason. He now felt like a true friend, but a very flirty friend with a lot of chemistry. So, I felt no pressure thinking about where it would go and taking it to the next level. He made me feel good, I liked him, and when I was with him, I felt happy and safe. I didn't want to think into it anymore than that, and I didn't need to. Before I could reply, the phone rang and he was calling.

'I'm outside your door, I've got something for you,' he said.

I giggled. 'OK, I'll be down in a ticky.' I looked up at Gareth with a girly smile.

'Oh God, here she goes,' he said.

'I'll be back in a sec! Jacob's brought me a gift,' I grinned.

I dashed down the stairs to open the door to him, where I found him empty-handed but stood with a warm smile. Hmmm, no flowers, I thought.

'Hello, you,' I said.

'Hello, beautiful,' he said, wrapping his arms around me. 'I'm not coming in, I've got a meeting, but I wanted to give you something before tomorrow,' he said in a serious tone.

'What is it?' I asked, highly intrigued. He reached into his pocket and pulled something out, taking my hand and placing the small item inside my palm. I opened my hand to look at it. It was a very small wooden icon carved into a book, with two parts so you could open and close it. I opened it up and squinted at the small pictures. On one side was a picture of what looked like Mother Mary and Jesus, and on the other side was a picture of Jesus holding a prayer scroll in foreign writing.

'It's beautiful,' I said, staring at it in awe.

'It was my grandmother's, she gave it to me before she died. I've held on to it and prayed with it during my own struggles ever since. She's never let me down,' he said.

I looked up into his big brown eyes and felt my ice queen heart literally begin to melt.

'Babe, I don't know what to say, it really is beautiful. I can't tell you how much I appreciate it,' I said, feeling lost for words.

'That icon has never left my side. I've never given it to anyone, but I want you to hold it through your trial, till it's over. Guard it with your life, and don't let it leave your side. I don't know what I'd do if I lost it,' he said.

'You have my word, babe. I won't let go of it, I've got it at all times.'

'And I've got you. If you don't know that after this, then you'll never know,' he said. I leaned forward and kissed him on the lips.

He grabbed my chin. 'You must be very special, I hope I'm right about you,' he said.

I looked deep into his eyes. 'Real recognise real,' I said.

It was an urban saying, meaning 'good people recognise other good people'. He smiled and kissed me once more on the lips. 'Good luck tomorrow, I'll call you after.'

I watched Jacob walk down the hall before staring down at the little icon and clenching it in my hand. I was scared. This time it wasn't because of the trial, but because of Jacob and my feelings for him. This man was either an angel in disguise or the devil himself. I hoped it was the first.

Chapter 10:

TIME TO FACE MAMUSIC

IT WAS JANUARY 2014 and finally the first day of the abuse trial. I woke up feeling rather positive about the situation as I prepared myself for the days ahead. In a way, I was finally going to get the chance to give my side of the story, through my barrister. I'd waited over a year for this moment, sitting in silence, watching and listening to the British media rip me apart, until my reputation and career were left in tatters. Meanwhile the public took it all in, scrutinising and judging me on the account given by one person: Mazher Mahmood.

I did my usual long mirror check before I left the house. I was wearing a pale turquoise suit and white heels, with my hair slicked back in a side parting into a bun.

'I really love this look, G. I can't believe how comfortable I feel in suits, I've finally found my swag! Four years too late, but never mind.'

'I agree, I fucking love it! Gemma is a G!'

Gemma had been my stylist since my first year of *X Factor*, and though we'd parted for a brief period due to management issues we were now back on track. I had always had issues with styling, mostly because I was never into fashion. My clothes always felt like a uniform. 'Just put me in whatever, I don't care,' I'd always say. I just wanted to finish the day and put my trainers back on. A tomboy was a serious task for any glamorous stylist, but Gemma had always been my number one, as a friend and at her job, doing the best she could and coming to a decent compromise.

That had all changed now, because at some point during the past year, and the months I'd been awaiting trial, I'd begun to *like* fashion. I don't know exactly how it happened, but it just did. Now, thanks to Gemma, and amazingly, numerous court appearances, when I stepped into my first suit I had never felt so comfortable. Probably because it balanced fashion and my masculine energy. I loved dresses, heels and more feminine fashion now as well, but when I stepped into a suit, it felt like me. I'd decided to use this hard time in my life to turn around my reputation with fashion, and there was no better time to do so. My court entrances were now my Fashion Week, whether I liked it or not, so if they wanted a show, it was a show they would get. Gemma had always said, 'You will find your inner fashion goddess one day, Tulisa! And I will look back and say I told you so.' And now, she did. I just didn't expect to find it when I was walking into a courtroom.

I sat nervously in the car with the big film camera and a bright light shining in my face for my documentary.

'What's that you've got in your hand, Tulisa?' asked producer Jonathan.

I fiddled with the precious icon Jacob had given me and looked up at the camera.

'It was a gift,' I said sheepishly.

Jonathan could tell I didn't want to go into detail and didn't press me any further.

It was obvious to him that I was seeing someone, but I refused to talk about it on camera and only spoke to Jacob when the cameras were off.

Jacob had already called and had been texting me on the way to court, calming me down and reassuring me. I was truly grateful – somehow through this terrible time he was still managing to make me smile.

I felt nervous, but hopeful. No matter what happened, I had to hang on to hope.

When I arrived, I was greeted by the usual media circus of flashing cameras and busy people outside. I went in and had a short meeting with my lawyers before I was led to the dock. I sat feeling numb while waiting for the judge to come in. There was a loud knock and the words 'all rise' as he entered the room. I stood up quickly, only to sit back down again once he was seated. *The psychological authority effect*, I thought.

I looked around the courtroom at all the press watching me intently, typing and taking notes. The prosecution and police officers were all chatting away, like it was just another day at the office, and then there was the very serious-looking judge with his stern presence. All this for little me? I felt so small and young, compared to all these older people. I was only 25, five foot six inches tall, and I weighed just under eight stone from all the stress. I'd always loved food, it was at the heart of my family life and my friendships. I had so many memories of cooking with my Yia Yia and dinners with friends, but the last few months had robbed me of my appetite and the joy I felt around food. I felt like a little child again. Like I was back in school being bullied. I always thought, when I grew up, I'd never have to feel helpless again. Yet here I was, as a so-called 'adult', feeling more helpless than ever. Why were these people doing this to me? I squeezed the little icon in my hand again.

Don't cry, T, don't let them think you're weak, I told myself, before beginning to pray silently.

As the day progressed, I tried to keep up with the legal verbal vomit coming at me left, right and centre. I didn't know much about law or legal technicalities, but I seemed to get the gist, the more time I spent in court. To cut a long story short, my entire defence could not be used as a defence at all. Unlike in many places in America, entrapment was not illegal in England, even though my defence stated it wasn't just entrapment but a set-up. So, before I'd even had a chance to give my evidence, it was already ruled out as a reason to get the case thrown out. The whole thing was full of technicalities, loopholes and legal bullshit. Everyone could see it was a set-up, see what was really going on.

I didn't realise until I was on the other side of it just how bad the British justice system really was. After lunch, it was time for Mr Mahmood to give his evidence and be questioned on the stand. My heart pumped furiously as I waited for him to appear. I felt ill at the thought of seeing him, the man who had ruined my life. He stepped up to the stand and I saw his face for the first time, as his true self, since all the pain and destruction he had caused. I felt a wave of sickness come over me that made me want to heave. My heart pumped even faster and I began to feel short of breath.

Not a panic attack, T, not now. Control your breathing, stay calm, there's nothing to be afraid of right now.

I took in a deep breath and imagined a beaming ball of light around me. I visualised my uncle's hand touching my shoulder and his soothing voice. 'It's OK, T. Breathe, you're gunna be fine, we've got you,' my Uncle B's voice said. Uncle B was Dappy's dad and he'd always been like a father figure to me, encouraging me throughout every trial and challenge in my life. Uncle B was the best male role model you could ask for. He had sadly passed away from a heart attack when I was 18.

I heard Mahmood's voice as he took the oath and I snapped back to reality.

Look at him, the snake. He can't even look at me. I'm not afraid of him, he's the weakest of the weak.

All the panic left me as I stared him out, waiting for eye contact, but it never came. I sat and listened to him being questioned and all his responses, lie after lie. *How could someone be so evil?* I thought. Eventually, my barrister got onto the subject of missing recordings and footage which I'd been waiting for all day. *Ask him,* I thought, *go on, ask the bastard what he did with the recording in the car that he's claiming doesn't exist! Ask him about when I sat and spoke about being anti-drugs and helping someone I knew get away from drugs!*

My anti-drugs conversation was something his own driver had confirmed in his initial statement to the police. But then he'd changed his statement just before we got to court because he'd apparently 'made a mistake over who actually had the conversation'. He later told the police that it was Michelle who'd had that conversation, and not me. This was a crucial part of my case because what Mahmood had done was only legal if he had a 'source' who could provide evidence proving I was a drug dealer, though he did not have to reveal his source due to a legal loophole called 'journalistic privilege'. If he had been given evidence to suggest otherwise, like the conversation he'd had with his driver, then that evidence would have challenged his source. And without the source, the case would have no standing.

He didn't make a mistake, I thought. *He changed it because you told him to! You lying bastard!* I looked at my barrister as if egging him on to speak aloud the questions in my head.

'Mr Mahmood, considering this was an investigation, did you not record the car journey that you insisted Miss Contostavlos, her friend Miss McKenna and PA Mr Varey should take home with your colleague, who posed as a driver, Mr Smith?'

'No, I did not,' replied Mahmood with no emotion.

How convenient, you liar, I thought.

'Did you not ask Mr Smith what happened during the journey afterwards?' asked my barrister.

'I think he mentioned that they'd had an argument or something like that, but that's about it,' said Mahmood.

'Did Mr Smith not mention to you that Miss Contostavlos had a conversation in the car with her friends, clearly stating that she did not approve of drugs, nor did she take them, let alone sell them, as your driver Mr Smith clearly stated in his original statement?'

'No, he didn't,' Mahmood replied flatly, once again.

'Did you speak to the driver between the time he made his original statement, which stated Miss Contostavlos didn't approve of drugs, and the time he changed his statement?'

'No, I didn't. The last time I spoke to him was around the time that he drove her home,' replied Mahmood.

'So, you didn't speak to him about the statement or ask him to change it?' my barrister asked again.

'Definitely not, no!' said Mahmood.

You LIAR! I screamed in my head. *Please, Lord, help me*, I thought. *Do not let him get away with this.*

I shook my head in disgust and amazement. I felt like I was in a movie. This was insane. I looked to my right and saw the journalists typing away, relaying my every move. *This was sick! You're all sick!* I thought. I felt like an animal in a cage, sat behind the glass for everyone's entertainment.

This wasn't a criminal trial. It was a freak show! And by the looks of things, it was going to be a bloody long one at my expense.

By the time I got through the three days, I was exhausted. Well and truly mentally head-fucked. The judge had postponed the verdict of the abuse trial, so now all I could do was wait and hope that he would throw it out. But with the case under the watchful eye of the press, I doubted he would want the responsibility of dismissing it. I knew under normal circumstances I wouldn't even have been charged in the first place. But because I was a celebrity, and this whole case was being printed as front-page news, it was supposedly in the public interest. It therefore had to be taken as far as it could. I was never going to get a fair trial, not even with a jury.

I was a public figure who was, to say the least, Marmite. People had strong opinions about me. They loved me or hated me. If this went to trial and even a few of the jury members didn't like me, which, due to my general media perception let alone all the recent press, was likely, I was well and truly fucked.

Chapter 11:

FIRST DINNER FOR TU

'WOW, YOU ACTUALLY ate it all. Slow down, cowboy, you'll get indigestion,' I said to Jacob, watching him scoff down the first meal I'd made him one on one. I'd headed straight over to his after court to wind down and cook dinner. Cooking was like meditation to me. It was the thing I enjoyed most, second to music.

'Indigestion? I'm having seconds! Load me up another plate please, babe.'

I looked around at all the candles he'd laid out and how clean and tidy the place was, along with the smart shirt he was wearing, while I made him another plate. I admired his effort. After he'd scoffed down the second plate, we took our glasses of wine and headed upstairs to chill by the bar. Handy that he had one, considering we couldn't go out for dates.

'So how's this book coming along that you told me

you're writing? What's it about again?' Jacob asked.

'It's about everything that's happening every day in my life right now, it makes for one hell of a story. It's going good, I pretty much write every day, keeps me distracted.'

'Writing about everything that's happening keeps you distracted from what's happening?'

'Yeah it does, bizarrely,' I laughed. 'I think it kind of gives it purpose, makes it worth something. All this drama and stress is being turned into something great – art in the form of the book. It's literally turning a negative into a positive, I guess.'

'I get that, you're a warrior,' he nodded. 'You said what happens "every day"? So does that mean that I'm in it?'

'You are actually. Comes with the territory, I'm afraid. Though I've given you a name change,' I chuckled.

'Anyway, enough about me. So, tell me, Jacob, when was your last relationship? If you've actually ever had one?' I asked.

'Mmmm, wouldn't say relationship, but there was someone I was seeing for quite a while but I ended it a few months back. Really good girl, beautiful little thing,' he said.

'Thing?' I chuckled. 'Let me guess, you broke her heart?'

'Nah, not on purpose. I tried to commit, I just got bored. We didn't have enough in common, she didn't get me.'

'You mean she was too nice and didn't keep you on your toes,' I said, raising my brows.

'Hey, there's nothing wrong with being nice. That's exactly what I want, a really nice girl,' he replied. I burst out laughing.

'So you say! But that's not what you need. You clearly need someone with a pair of balls to challenge you or you'll walk all over them. You may not intend to, but you can't help it. It's in your nature!' I declared.

'And how would you know?' he asked.

'I know, because I'm exactly the same. I want a Mr Nice Guy, but for the long run it won't work. I have commitment issues too, but mine usually kick in after six months. With you it happens after the first one, obviously.'

'Hmmm, interesting to know. And are you faithful?' he asked.

'One hundred per cent faithful, that's never an issue,' I replied.

'Well, I can't lie, that's where I struggle. I fell for some-one when I was younger, and they fucked me over, so I don't trust people or fully give myself to them, I suppose.' He shrugged.

'But you let them give themselves to you and still make them believe you can do the same in return,' I said.

He frowned, then smiled and shook his head.

'I can't believe we're having this conversation, why am I telling you this? I keep talking to you like my mate and forgetting...'

'Forgetting what? That you want to shag me?' I interrupted.

'Listen! I can have as much sex as I want, I don't need to waste my time,' he said.

'That was the original goal though, wasn't it? But now you like the mental stimulation and the challenge.'

'Well, I must do, because that's all I'm clearly getting right now. Listen, bighead, I'm committed in every area of my life, I just have a little trouble with women. But at least I can be honest about that with you. Too honest with you,' he chuckled.

'Only because you can't bullshit me 'cause I'll see straight through it.'

'I agree, but I also don't want to bullshit you. Believe me, I can play the game. But you're real, and I like you. It's weird but I feel like you're my mate, like a boy mate even though you're a woman,' he said.

'Yeah, I tend to have that effect.' I smiled cheekily.

'Nah, I don't think you understand the levels. I wanna tell you 'cause I think you'll understand. You might think I'm full of shit and giving you the smooth talk, but I think you might get it.' He paused and sipped on his drink.

'Go on, nothing surprises me, as you know,' I said, waiting for him to continue.

He hesitated before he spoke.

'Alright, I feel like... like I've been sent to protect you. It's like this overpowering feeling that makes me want to take care of you right now, and from my own experiences, the timing of everything, it's like it's meant to be. It's not like a physical voice telling me, but yet something is, it's a feeling. I just really want to protect you and make you happy right now, and that's what I'm gunna do, if you let that bullshit guard down and let me,' he said.

'So, basically, you feel something spiritually is telling you to take care of me right now?' I asked.

'Yeah, I suppose so,' he replied.

'Well then, you're either the biggest wanker I've ever met and desperate to get in my pants, or everything you've just said is true and I can believe it. But it's not that simple either way. I'm not a fun time girl. Nor do I need to be taken care of "right now",' I said.

'What is it you want from me?' he asked.

'What do you want from *me*?' I replied.

'I asked you first. Don't deflect the question smart ass!' he shot back.

I paused and took a sip of my own drink.

'Hmmmm. I don't know what I want. I don't do sex before monogamy, and you're not very good at that. But I enjoy your friendship and we have a connection,' I said.

'It's way more than friendship and you know it, you know where this is going,' he declared.

'Well, no, I don't actually. You don't do relationships and I won't have sex unless I'm in one. Where does that leave us?' I asked.

'I didn't say I don't do relationships, I just haven't met the right person yet,' he said.

'But, as someone that has issues with staying faithful, do you think if you met the right person you truly could?' I asked.

'If I was married, yeah,' he replied flatly.

'YOOOOOUUUU WHAT? Are you taking the piss? If you were married? So you're basically saying to me, we could enter into a relationship but it's unlikely that you would actually stay faithful, and you're asking me to accept that?' I half spat out my drink.

'No! Obviously, I would try if I entered into a relationship. I'm just saying I'm not very good at it. But cheating's not something I'd feel as capable of if I was married and had made a vow to God. What do you want me to say? I'm just being honest, I don't want to lie to you!'

'And I suppose I should feel privileged because you lie to every other woman?' I said.

'How can you be mad at me when I'm being real with you? You're tricking me, I don't know why I'm telling you all this. You're making me feel comfortable and luring me in and then I'm telling you shit and you're vexed! Usually, I would play the game. You think I can't do that? I'm the fucking king at it! I'd have you wrapped around my little finger by now but I'm choosing not to!'

I stood up from my seat, leaning my face towards his, and glared at him.

'Because you can't. I see you! I know exactly what you're like and what you're capable of! I've been raised around the worst men when it comes to how they treat a woman. I've seen everything! I know men better than any woman you've ever met. And you being the clever little cocky shit that you are, see that! You know that trying to bullshit me will get you absolutely nowhere, and that's why you're taking the approach you are. Not because you've had a change of heart and are ready to change.'

I stood back and folded my arms, unimpressed. He paused before clapping his hands slowly.

'Well done, bighead. Clever girl. That's why I like you. But you knowing that doesn't change anything. I still like you and I'm taking this approach for a change. What does that tell you? You of all people should be judging me on how I am with you, not how I've been with other people. There may be certain reasons why I've ended up being this way with you, but it's still real. Games can be fun, but they're tiring and I can only imagine how tiring they'd be with you. I can also see you are more than capable of playing games yourself if the fancy takes you, Miss Innocent. I'm sure you've had men eating right out of the palm of your hand. I can see that because you're like me. So, you're right, we can't bullshit each other!'

I looked at him, trying to hold back a smile.

'Great speech, Jacob for president. I think you should get that in writing and blown up on the wall so it's the first thing people see when they walk in your house,' I smiled sarcastically.

'You are something else, the bollocks, I'll give it to you! Come here, man, give me a cuddle. Why do we love arguing with each other so much?' He grabbed me and tried to pull me into his arms.

'No! Hands off, this isn't resolved yet. Are you mental? What are we doing here? I can't continue to date you, cuddling and kissing you, knowing that if we get together you're basically guaranteed to cheat on me! This is pointless. Let's just keep it as friends, I'm gunna go.' I lifted my bag off the table and put it on my shoulder.

'What? What do you mean you're leaving? Are you taking the piss?' he frowned.

'No, are *you* taking the piss? Because I'm deadly serious. What kind of woman do you think I am? What do you expect?' I snapped.

'What, you're really leaving, yeah? Cool, what can I say? You know where I am if you change your mind, go for it.'

'You're delusional! We're cool, just not when it comes to romance. You're you and I'm me, and you're not for me. I'll get a cab and collect my car in the morning.'

I headed towards the staircase, but suddenly felt his hands slip around my waist and pull me back towards him. He placed himself in front of me with his hand on my shoulders.

'She's actually leaving! Go on, the girl,' he laughed, stunned and amused. 'You're a strong one, I give you that!' He grinned.

'Oh, fuck off, you patronising little shit! Get out of my way!' I snapped, pulling his hands from my shoulders.

'Alright, just chill for a second! We are friends above anything, right?' he asked me now, seemingly calm. We stood with our noses practically touching, our shoulders back and our heads leaning forward as if ready for a fight.

'What do you want from me?' I glared.

'You asked me am I capable of staying faithful? The answer is yes, of course I am. I just haven't met a person that I'm able to do that with yet. Which as you know is the case with most men our age, they just don't say it. But I want to get to know you because for all I know you could be that woman. I promise I won't lie to you and I'll keep it real. And since I've spent time with you, I haven't had any interest whatsoever in other women, and if that changes, I'll let you know. Deal?' he said, softer now, staring meaningfully into my eyes.

I paused and thought to myself for a moment before responding.

'Fair enough, but you fuck with me and I'm out the door, that's my promise,' I glared.

Maybe I was mad. Did I look for trouble? In truth, I couldn't have picked a worse guy to date at this point. But in reality he wasn't any worse than half the other guys I'd dated. The only difference was, he was honest about it. He was admitting to being everything I thought he was and more, and I was taking a strange comfort in it. The more honest he was with me, even admitting to things that could hurt me that I didn't like, the more I warmed to him. Partly because, when it came to romance, I was brutally honest myself about my own commitment issues, which in turn had upset or worried my ex-partners. My point is, I knew that ultimately he was telling the truth, and so was I. Right now, being caught up in such a web of lies, I was craving something real, good or bad. Better the devil I know than the devil I don't.

There will always be people in this world that will fuck you over, whether by choice or unintentionally, and I'm fully aware of that. I tread with caution and weigh up and explore all the possibilities. That doesn't mean I won't open up or give people a chance. I just like to do so keeping in mind all of the possibilities. And in this situation, so far I figured I had pretty much got them all sussed out. I'd also be lying if I didn't say I liked the challenge. I felt safe and in control with my knowledge. So, as usual, forever the little rebel, I decided to take a chance. I would carry on seeing Jacob and assess the situation at a later date. I could only hope it wouldn't end in tears. Either way, right now, it was still the perfect distraction.

That night, we continued to drink, cuddle and talk bollocks about life. Growing closer and getting deeper as the moments passed. My attraction towards him was getting stronger. He would still try it on with me but happily settle for cuddles, and boy, were they good cuddles. I was smiling instead of constantly thinking about the trial. And Jacob was staying true to his word, for now.

Chapter 12:

TULISA'S ON THE RUN

After that night, me and Jacob had become practically inseparable. We'd spent every day together, aside from work, and our bond was progressing way ahead of its time. We were sat in his kitchen getting ready to go out when his phone rang.

'What's going on?... Uh huh... yep... what?... Yes! Say no more, I'll call you in a bit.' He hung up with a big grin on his face

'Babe! I've got a week off! I kept a week free to sort out a business deal and it's gone through on the first day,' he exclaimed, rubbing his hands together frantically, pulling his now-familiar little excited face. 'It's bloody you! Good things keep happening when you're around! You little witch!' he said, grabbing my face and giving me a big exaggerated kiss.

'What kind of witch?' I giggled.

'A good witch, maybe. Or some kind of... What did you say those things are?' he asked.

'Earth angels,' I said.

'That's the one. I don't know what you are, you little spiritual weirdo, but there's something funky going on with you. You'd tell me?' he asked, seemingly serious.

'An alien... from Uranus!' I replied, bursting into a fit of laughter.

'You're a proper dickhead!' he laughed back.

'I'm a spiritual being!' I said, as I sat on the kitchen table and lifted my legs into a yoga position and hummed.

'Whatever you are, it's serious! Now, what the hell am I gunna do this week? I wanna go away, I've been dying to go away,' he moaned.

'Don't talk to me about dying to go away. No one's dying to go away more than me,' I sighed.

'So, what are you doing this week?' he asked.

'Well, I've got my verdict from the abuse trial, duh. So it's a pretty big week. I'd probably rather be anywhere but here when I get it though,' I said.

'Let's go for a weekend then?' he replied.

'Yeah? Fuck it, I'm down! Let's get the fuck outta here then,' I yelled.

'Whaaaaat?! Is that a yeah? Where do you wanna go?' he grinned excitedly.

'Wherever it's hot in Europe right now that isn't a commercial destination. But how the hell are we gunna do this without being caught? There's always a possibility when I book a flight that someone at the airline tips off a pap agency when they see my name come up on the system. We would have to book the tickets just before we fly so they don't have enough time. This is risky stuff, I don't think you understand,' I said.

'Well, fuck it! Do you want to take the risk or not? What's the worst-case scenario?' he asked.

'It's not me I'm worried about, it's you. You don't understand what they will do to you if they find out about us. Everything will change,' I said, looking down at the floor and feeling a wave of sadness come over me at the thought. He raised my chin with his hand.

'Listen, I'm good. I know what I'm getting myself into. I don't wanna be in the fucking papers, but if I have to choose between that and not seeing you, I know what the answer is. Fuck the risk, you can tell me about it on the plane. I got you,' he said, raising his other hand into a fist to spud me. I looked up into his gleaming eyes and warm smile and instantly felt full of excitement and adventure.

'Oh, fuck it, I'm gunna trust my instinct, let's just do it,' I declared. I felt so alive at the thought. We were both such rebels and even more so in each other's presence.

'Oh no, I've just thought. We've got a bigger problem than the press,' I exclaimed as we headed to mine to grab my passport and clothes.

'What's that?' asked Jacob.

'Gareth.'

* * *

I sat on my dressing-room floor surrounded by a pile of clothes, frantically picking out summer outfits and throwing them into my suitcase. Jacob was waiting upstairs in my room, which I thought was safer at this point. Gareth stormed up and down in front of me, like an angry headmaster.

'You're fucking insane! What the fuck are you doing? Everything you've been through – and you still haven't learnt? You're waiting to find out if you're going to trial! The press are on you like flies on shit, and you're swanning off around the Mediterranean with lover boy, who's got a past! Do you know how this fucking looks? Are you actually thick? They want any opportunity to rip you to shreds, and you bloody go and give it to them! We said no trips away till after the case! That's what we agreed!' he shouted.

'Why? Because I can't be seen to be having a good time? Be happy? Actually live my life like a normal person?' I snapped.

'Not when you're on a fucking drugs charge and facing prison! You're Tulisa! No, you can't just carry on as normal and live your life, because the press won't write it like that! You know how it works!' he said angrily.

'Fuck the game, fuck the press, and fuck the justice system! Fuck them all! They won't end me and they will never own me! I haven't done anything wrong! The universe is good and it won't forsake me! With that knowledge I will fight this till the end, mate!' I said with feeling.

'Oh, save the spiritual bullshit and start facing reality!

They're about to finish you off, so you better start playing the game!' he yelled.

'No! I will not play their little devil games! None of this matters! Don't you see? It's all a test! They can judge me how they want on this earth! It's the day I die that matters! I'm not selling my soul to these wankers! They can do one!'

'Yeah, you carry on with your Female Boss attitude! That's why they tried to take you out in the first place! You don't have to sell your fucking soul! Why can't you just be like every other popstar and pretend?' he growled through his teeth, trying to keep his voice down.

'The ones that need to aren't pretending, mate! They're well and truly sold!' I glared at him.

'What's the point? Why do I fucking bother? You don't listen to anyone! You're too fucking headstrong for your own good! What about him? If not for yourself, think of him? They're going to ruin him!'

'They're going to ruin anyone I get with! So, what does that mean? That I should be miserable and alone for the rest of my life? Give them what they want? It's no way to fucking live! I'm a human being with feelings and needs, not public property! And right now, I need some love and a bloody holiday! They're not even gunna find out anyway,' I snapped, continuing to pack.

'Of course they will find out! I fucking miss Danny right now. You had a nice calm lovely boyfriend, and you had to go and fuck it up! At least he agreed with me that you constantly choose to forget who you are. He used to calm you down! You and this one are like two fucking loose cannons! You're fucking yourself and you can't see it! You stupid girl!' he shouted.

'Right, that's it!' I said, rising to my feet, 'Enough! I'm a 25-year-old young woman! I've been alone my whole life, and I've made my own decisions and that's not about to change! I don't wanna hear another word! I'm going, and that's that! You've given your opinion and I'm fully aware of the consequences! If it goes tits up, it's on me!' I yelled sternly.

'Fine! You know how I feel about it! I think you're insane! And as for him, I thought maybe he could be good for you right now. Turns out he's actually a bad influence because he doesn't understand and he clearly has no idea about your life and responsibil...' Gareth paused as Jacob entered the room and nodded his head.

'Gareth, I know you're worried, but I promise you I'll take care of her. She's safe with me, trust me,' he said.

'She's never safe with those vultures out there. Not with you, or me, or anyone else! The sooner you realise that, the better!' Gareth stormed out the dressing room and into his bedroom, slamming the door.

I sighed, looking up at Jacob. 'Told you he'd kick off.'

He shook his head. 'Nothing worthwhile is easy. Hurry up, let's get out of here before something else tries to stop us.'

After running into the car, hiding under a blanket down in the passenger seat and doing our usual roundabout checks to make sure we weren't being followed, we were sat in the Ferrari and headed to Heathrow. I had necked a triple Jack Daniel's before I left for some Dutch courage, and it had hit me like a ton of bricks. We found a song on my iPod that felt quite fitting. It was Beyoncé and Jay-Z 'Part II (On The Run)'. The song blasted through the speakers as we stared at the clear midnight motorway ahead of us. Jacob rested one hand on the wheel and held my hand with the other. We stayed silent, hand in hand, listening to the words.

'Who wants that perfect love story any way, anyway cliché... What about the bad guy goes good, and the missing love that's misunderstood... Baby as long as I'm next to you, and if loving you is a crime, tell me why I bring out the best in you...'

The words rang true and filled me up with emotion. Imagine if I just left right now and never turned back. Just carried on going, leaving all my problems behind and starting a new life. I could open a bar on a quiet island somewhere. No more fighting, surviving or looking over my shoulder, I thought. But that's all it was, just a tipsy thought, not my reality. The next song came on, it was Rick Ross's 'Thug Cry':

I just wanna be the one. I just wanna be the one you love, I just wanna be the one you run to when you're down, I just wanna fly, I'mma show you tonight.

Jacob squeezed my hand, bringing me back to reality. I looked at him and smiled. He smiled back.

'Fuck 'em, babe,' he said.

'Fuck 'em all,' I replied.

He put his foot down and the car kicked as the engine

roared. I turned my head to face the window and my reflection, watching a small teardrop begin to fall from my left eye and down my cheek. I wiped it clean before Jacob could see. We played the two songs back-to-back for the rest of the journey. That night, those two songs became 'our songs'.

We pulled up outside the hotel 45 minutes later.

'This is it! I hope you're ready for this,' I said.

'No going back now,' he sighed. He picked up my sunglasses from my lap and placed them on my face, securing my baseball cap and hoodie firmly over the top.

'There you go, no one would ever know,' he chuckled. I pulled down the passenger mirror and stared at myself.

'I look like a fucking idiot!' I said, trying to keep a straight face before we both burst out laughing.

An hour later, I was sat on the bed anxiously in the hotel room, waiting for Jacob to return. Finally, I heard the door open. He came into the room rubbing his hands together with his excited face.

'Pour me a drink! We've only gone and done it! We're flying in five hours!' He jumped on the bed, tickling me with excitement.

'AAAArrrrrrgh! We're actually doing it! I fucking love this shit! What a buzz!' I squealed. He stopped and looked at me seriously.

'I'm really happy right now, you know.'

I smiled. 'Me too, Jacob. Thank you for all of this, for making me smile again, I really appreciate it,' I said sincerely.

'You're nothing like how I expected you to be, you know,' he said.

I looked up at him and grinned. 'You underestimated how dangerous I am.'

'Nah, that's the stuff I don't like, that attitude of yours. I like Tula, not the Female Boss, so get that out of your head if you think that's what's winning me over,' he said.

'Aaah, so you say, or think. But the two come hand in hand. I wouldn't be me if I wasn't the Female Boss as well, and you know that's the truth,' I smiled.

'Yeah, yeah. I wouldn't tell you even if it was,' he said, before going silent. I could feel him thinking something.

'What's up?' I asked.

'Nothing. I'm great, mate.'

'No, you ain't, I can feel it,' I said.

'Alright, Psychic Cindy. Did your spirit guide tell you that?' he chuckled, though I knew it was forced.

'Seriously, what's up?' I asked again. He took a deep breath and exhaled.

'Talk to me about this whole fame bollocks. What would happen if we got caught?' he asked.

Oh gosh, here we go, I thought. I'd been dreading this conversation. I sighed, twiddling my fingers through his hair, debating how to word it.

'You're scared I'm gunna run away, aren't you?' he said.

I stared at him. 'If you run away, you run away. I'm good, mate. I was good before you came along and I'll be good when you're gone. But either way, I wouldn't blame you,' I said.

'So bloody stern! Go on then, break it down for me,' he said.

'Where do I start?' I sighed, taking a deep breath and exhaling. 'Erm... Basically, if we were to get caught, you're automatically my new boyfriend.'

'Wow, that's intense! You would have to shag me then. I'm not being in a relationship without the sex, that just takes the biscuit,' he chuckled.

'I'm being serious! If we were photographed, you'd be in every paper and magazine across the country. Then they'd drag up your past, every bad thing you've ever done and call you a bad boy and a player...'

'But I'm a businessman, not a thuggish little boy. How the hell can they do that? Isn't that defamatory?' he asked.

'Yes it is, and yes, they can. Then you will get ex-girlfriends or ex-shags coming forward, selling their kiss and tells on you, and if there are any girls you've met or spoken to while you've been around me, they'll probably come forward and say that you're cheating on me with them. You will have paparazzi on your doorstep immediately after that, following you around. The press will go to your friends' houses and your family's houses, including your mum's, asking for quotes and information. Then some of your friends, even family, people you know, will turn on you and sell stories. A few will be true but mostly exaggerated stories and the majority fake. Some will possibly come forward publicly to sell them, but most behind your back, and you will start to question everyone that may have a motive around you. You will be in the papers all the time and become public property, having lies made up about you constantly. Journalists working for top papers will try and honeytrap you every time you have a night out by luring you in with an overly hot woman that will want to take you home to make it look like you cheated on me. You'll get recognised when you're out, sometimes by fans that will just want to take a picture with you 'cause you're my boyfriend, and then sometimes by randoms who don't like me, who will give you abuse and try to start fights with you. Our whole relationship and your life will be documented and spread across the UK and even other parts of the world, without an accurate account of it, and the media will portray you in whatever way they see fit. Your world will be turned upside down and life as you know it will change forever or until people forget your name, if they ever do.'

I sighed, feeling relieved that I'd got the reality of our situation off my chest.

'Wow... Anything else?' he asked.

I took a deep breath and closed my eyes, trying to contain my frustration.

'Yeah, Mahzer Mahmood could try and come for you, to set you up, to get to me.'

Jacob exhaled loudly. 'Anything else?' he asked.

'I've probably missed a few things, but that about sums up the major issues.' I sighed again.

We sat in silence for a moment. But it wasn't long before I had to express my thoughts – as usual.

'You're terrified, aren't you?' I asked.

'No, I'm just taking it all in. I didn't realise it was that bad,' he replied.

'It wasn't always this bad, it's a lot easier when you're on the good side of fame. When the press are onside, work is good, and you're not on a drugs charge with Mahzer Mahmood making it his life's mission to bring your world to an end. Maybe one day I could get back to that place again, if the trial went best-case scenario, but it wouldn't happen for a long time, even if I did.'

Jacob continued to lay there silently.

'What are you thinking?' I asked, unable to bear the suspense.

'Honestly?' he said.

'Go on, I can handle it.'

'I'm thinking about you and your past, everything I know about you that you've told me. Even things I sense you haven't told me, to the life you live now and what you are going through...' He paused before continuing. 'I think you are one of the strongest women I've ever met, strongest person actually. Forget the fact you're a woman. There's not many people I respect on the level that I respect you.'

There was a long silence before I exhaled loudly.

'Thanks,' I said softly, feeling lost for words.

'Don't thank me for stating the truth. Most people I know wouldn't still be standing in your position, but you're actually handling it extremely well. Knowing how soft and emotional you are deep down, I woulda thought you'd be a hell of a lot worse. I'm surprised you're still here

132

and stronger than ever, by the looks of it,' he said, turning his face towards me with a smile. I smiled back.

'I guess the Female Boss side of me comes in pretty handy.'

He frowned. 'I'll let you off with that one,' he said before pulling my face towards him so our eyes met. 'But cut the front. I've got you, I'm not going anywhere.'

Hours later we were on the flight. 'Thank God,' I said out loud as we squeezed each other's hands, looking at each other with relief. We'd gone through the check-in and security process so paranoid that we literally felt like an MI6 couple on a 007 mission. We were acting so dodgy from the paranoia that at one point I thought we were being flagged as possible terrorists when Jacob's bag got searched because he'd left a bottle of water in there.

'It's exciting though, you have to admit it!' He grinned.

'Listen, you've lived five minutes of my life. Believe me, give it six months. Once the heart palpitations kick in with the never-ending drama, it won't be so exciting,' I said.

'True, but I haven't, so right now it's quite fun,' he grinned.

'Famous last words, mate,' I said, while searching for my phone to switch it off. I looked at the screen and saw a text from Gareth with a picture message attached.

G: You've been clocked!

My heart instantly thumped throughout my entire body from my chest and I felt the familiar shortness of breath coming on. I stared down at the photo. It was a picture of me and Jacob in the airport, but a very blurred one. A fan had posted it online with the words 'I've just seen Tulisa in the airport, I'm telling you it's her'.

'Jacob! We've been clocked, look!' I said.

'WHAT?' he said, jumping up right away and grabbing the phone out my hand. 'What the fuck?' His eyes widened.

'It's from a fan. She must have snapped us on the sly in the airport,' I exclaimed.

'It's blurry though. Can you even see us?' he asked.

'That's not the point. If there's a pap or journo searching Twitter for me and they see it, they have connections. They could pay someone off for my flight details. By the time we get to the other end they could be waiting,' I said.

'So, what can we do?' he asked as I felt the plane begin to take off.

'There's nothing we can do. Just pray it goes unnoticed,' I said.

'This will be a fun flight then,' he said.

I grabbed the seat in front of me with one hand and Jacob's leg with the other, wincing as I felt the turbulence kick in as we took off.

'Did I mention I'm terrified of flying?'

Chapter 13:

TAKE ME TU MY BEACH

ME AND JACOB stood on the beach with our feet sinking into the sand as we admired the view. We looked around at the older people and foreign couples. *Perfect!* I thought.

'Woooooow, YES! This is what I've been waiting for! What a moment!' Jacob yelled.

I jumped up and down in my bikini, squealing with excitement. Neither of us had been away for a while.

'We did it, babe! We fucking did it!' We grabbed each other in a warm embrace, feeling the sun beating down on our skin, along with the fresh sea breeze. Luckily there had been no paps at the airport when we landed, so it was more than likely they wouldn't find us.

'Time to do what I've been dying to do all year,' he grinned.

'What's that?' I asked.

He leaned his face towards mine and yelled 'SWIM!'

before running towards the sea and diving in. I followed him, pelting towards the shore, but as my right foot hit the water, I instantly froze.

'It's absolutely freezing,' I yelled. It was still only early spring so the weather was hot, but the sea was still ice-cold.

I'm no chicken shit! I thought, as I continued to strut into the freezing sea until the water reached my waist. I began to tremble as I got deeper. *Hell no, fuck this*, I thought, before spinning around and quickly retreating back towards the shore.

I couldn't believe Jacob was still swimming off into the distance like it was nothing. I went and sat on a rock by the shore and watched him as he swam out further and further. I felt a little defeated. Usually, I was the one trying to drag people into the water. I debated getting back in to prove a point. *Give it a rest, TFB!* I thought. *Just enjoy the moment.*

I watched Jacob and giggled to myself as I noticed that my stance on the rock was identical to a scene in *The Little Mermaid*. I scanned the distance between me and the nearest member of the public before I began singing quietly to myself, 'I wanna be where the people are.' I chuckled and shook my head.

I was brought back to reality when I noticed Jacob strolling back out of the water and, to top it off, out of all the Disney princes he actually looked like Prince Eric. I admired the full extent of how handsome he was and realised I was becoming more and more attracted to him by the day. I looked at the water dripping off his muscles and beautifully tanned skin. His hair was wet and looked jet black as he pulled it back off his face. *He looks gorgeous*, I thought, scanning my eyes down his amazing body... until I got to his shorts.

'Holy crap, babe! Those shorts are horrendous!' I said as he strutted towards me. I couldn't believe I'd only just noticed them. They were bright red and covered in multicoloured flowers – like something you'd get at a Hawaiian hotel if you forgot your swimwear.

'Piss off, you horrible bitch! We were in a rush. Can't you just pretend to like 'em?' he glared.

'Mate, I'm sorry but you can't be serious. You're not walking around with me like that,' I said, shaking my head as we walked over to the deckchairs to find a spot.

'You really are like a guy, taking the piss out of me like you're one of my boys. You need to be more feminine! Act like a girl – you don't have a pair of bollocks, you know,' he said.

'If I did, they'd probably be even bigger than yours, bigger than most men actually,' I chuckled.

'Yeah, that's the problem. No man wants a bird with a pair of bollocks,' he frowned.

'Well, it hasn't scared you off yet, has it?'

'Nah, I don't even see you like that right now. Seriously, it's like hanging out with one of my mates. You're literally like one of the boys, I just like your company. That's why I've stopped trying it on with you. Haven't you noticed?' he asked.

'Oh, that old chestnut! Let me guess, you're not attracted to me anymore because I'm not feminine and sexual with you,' I said flatly.

'Nah, you're an attractive girl, but 'cause of your personality I just stopped thinking about it,' he shrugged.

'Yeah, yeah, keep working your magic. Great reverse psychology, kid,' I replied, rolling my eyes.

'No, I'm just telling you what it is. Take it how you like,' he said, acting deadly serious.

I paused before I leaned towards him, grinning. 'Bollocks!' I said.

'I do bet you're absolutely naughty in the bedroom when you get down to it, though. And I've had the best of the best, mate. Every bird you can imagine, but I bet you would give 'em a run for their money.'

'You are so manipulating and egotistical it's unbelievable,' I yawned.

'Vice versa,' he shot back.

'Well, don't bullshit a bullshitter then. And anyway, don't be comparing me to some of the porn stars you've shagged because you'll be sorely disappointed,' I said.

'Wow, that's the first time I've heard you play yourself down,' he chuckled.

'You want the truth? I can't enjoy sex unless I feel completely secure with someone, hence why I wait till I'm in a relationship. I'm actually rather submissive. I suppose you could say the bedroom is where I'm most feminine,' I admitted.

He looked at me and frowned. 'Really? I find that very

surprising, I expected you to be the opposite. That's good though, maybe I like to dominate,' he smiled sexily.

I rolled my eyes again. 'I'm sure you do, bighead.'

He winked at me seductively before jumping up from his sun lounger. 'I'll go get us some drinks, shall I? We're allowed this time of day, we're on holiday,' he grinned.

'Cool, I'm gunna explore the beach,' I said, standing up and winking back before strutting off down the shore.

I came across a beautiful spot right at the end of the beach. There was a towering cliff on my left stretching far out into the sea, and a massive pointy rock in the water to my right that was the same height as the cliff. I sat directly in between the two, on the sand with my legs in the sea, admiring the view. It looked beautiful, like some kind of gateway. There was something quite spiritual about it.

'Boo!' Jacob crept up behind me with the drinks.

'Come and sit down, babe. Check this spot out,' I said. He handed me a cocktail and sat down next to me, staring out at the sea in between the cliff and the rock.

'Wow,' he said.

'Can you feel it?' I asked.

'Powerful!' he replied.

'Do you know how lucky we are? There's people starving in the world and there's nothing they can do about it and here we are, two young people that can just jet off at the drop of a hat and see the world. I know I could be going to jail and when I come out my career will be fucked, but I've still been blessed, just to live the life I lived so far. Hopefully I'll find a way, I always do. Either way I've lived a great life. I've done things and seen places that most 25-year-olds can only dream of, and so have you. Sometimes we forget how blessed we are,' I said, deep in thought.

'You're right, I agree. But you're not going to jail, I told you I can feel it,' he said.

'I feel good energy about it too, but I have to be realistic,' I answered. I stared out over the sea, wondering if I really wanted to ask my next question.

'Will you come and visit me inside, worst-case scenario?' I asked.

'Don't say that, man. Of course I would, and I'd write every day. But I don't wanna think about that,' he said, shaking his head.

'It's reality though, isn't it?' I sighed.

'Fuck reality. Right here, right now is reality. You can't determine the future. What will be will be, and it's not your path.' He grabbed my arm and pulled me down towards him where he was laying flat on the sand and gave me a slow, passionate kiss that sent tingles down my spine. I pulled back and looked at him. The sunlight glazed over his deep brown eyes, turning them hazel against his tanned skin. My long dark hair fell over the sides of my face and draped over his chest. He stared up at me, looking deep into my eyes.

'Are you falling in love, Tulisa?' he asked.

'Are you, Jacob?'

We gave each other our usual identical smirks.

'You're like the girl version of me,' he said.

'Great minds think alike,' I grinned.

'You are though, don't you think? It's weird. I've never met a girl that was so like me before,' he said.

'And you won't meet another,' I said, before leaning down and kissing him gently on the lips.

'Vice versa,' he said as I pulled back.

'I guess we're two of a kind then, bighead,' I said softly.

'I guess so.'

I smiled and knocked back my drink till it was empty.

'You definitely drink like a man as well,' he said.

'Sorry, does that offend you, sir?' I chuckled.

'No, I love it. It's powerful,' he grinned.

'I better get another round then! Same again?' I said, kissing him on the head before I got up to leave.

'Yeah. Here, take mine. You didn't draw any cash out, in case they don't take cards,' he said, handing me his wallet.

'Cheers, see you in another life. I'm off to the Bahamas,' I said.

'Good luck, mate. I'll hunt you down and find you!' he yelled as I walked off.

'I'll be long gone, pal!' I shouted back as I strutted off to the bar and did my best sexy walk, feeling his eyes on me along the way. I saw a group of guys checking me and I knew Jacob would have noticed. *Hehe,* I thought. While I ordered the drinks, I made a quick phone check. I had a text from my lawyer, asking me to call him asap. *Shit!* I'd been having such a nice time, I'd totally forgotten. I was getting the verdict of the abuse trial today. *This is it*, I thought as I pressed call, staring out at the sea, praying for the best outcome. There was no going back now.

'T?' Ben said, as he answered.

'Yes, Ben, what's the deal?' I replied flatly, trying to numb myself in case of a bad outcome.

'T, I'm really sorry, it's going to trial – the judge didn't throw it out.'

I felt a hard lump rise in my throat as I was over-whelmed with emotion and fear. I couldn't speak.

'T? Are you OK? I'm really sorry, T.' I took a long pause before I spoke.

'Not really,' I choked '...call you in a bit, Ben.' I hung up.

I was shaking from head to toe. I grabbed the drinks and slowly walked back down the beach towards Jacob. I was dizzy, I could feel the emotions building up inside me as I reached him and sat down next to him. He couldn't see me as he was sunbathing with his eyes closed. I pulled my legs into my chest and folded my arms around them, resting my chin on my knees while staring silently at the sea. I felt the salty water begin to stream down my face, I couldn't hold it in any longer. My facial expression didn't change. I just sat there, with tears pouring down, in silence.

'You're back. Make some new friends, did you?' Jacob said, noticing my presence and joking about the group of guys from earlier. I couldn't speak. If I spoke, I'd explode.

'T?...TULA!' He called (my real name). He sat up and manoeuvred himself next to me so he could see my face. 'What's happened?' he said softly, noticing my tears. I took a long pause to compose myself before I spoke, and I just about croaked out the words.

'It's going to trial, I just got the call,' I said. He slowly leaned over, pulling me into his arms and resting my head on his shoulder as my tears dripped down his chest.

'Well, that's it now. It is what it is. You have to prepare yourself for the next stage, you have to be strong now,' he said.

'I know,' I whispered through my tears. 'I'm just having a moment. I need to let it out, then I'll be fine.' I exhaled.

'Just remember everything you were saying a moment ago before the call, about how blessed you are. It still stands.'

All of a sudden, a big wave came crashing onto the shore and surrounded us. I was shocked out of my tears by the freezing-cold water surging over my body. We both scurried backwards until we were out of reach of the water. It was almost as if, in an instant, along with the giant wave, the weather had changed. A moment ago, the sea seemed calm and the sun was still beating down on our skin. I looked up to the sky. I saw big dark clouds now surging across the sun, covering us in shadow, along with a hard cold wind that was now in the air.

'What the fuck?' he exclaimed, pulling me to safety. My tears stopped for a moment as I crawled back up the shore with him. But as soon as the wave retreated, I continued to cry in his arms. Eventually, after staring out at the sea for what felt like a decade, but was probably only around five minutes, Jacob suggested we go back to the hotel room. I stood up and wiped my eyes before heading over to the deckchairs where my stuff was, while he went to wash the sand off his body. I grabbed my towel and looked around for my phone, but I couldn't see it. I felt the panic rise inside me as I searched for it frantically. It was gone. *Had someone taken it? No*, I thought. *I had it with me when the wave...* I ran back over to the place where we'd been sitting. *Fuck!*

'Jacob!' I yelled to him in the water over the sound of the now-crashing waves and wind that was furiously blowing my hair around. 'My phone! The tide took my fucking phone!'

The tears began to stream down my face again. I hadn't backed it up to the Cloud because I was paranoid about being hacked. I had evidence on there to help my case and pieces of my book I hadn't moved onto my laptop yet! How could I be so stupid? Could this day get any worse? Jacob instantly began diving frantically into the sea and hopelessly attempting to search for it through the rough waters.

'It's no use! It's long gone!' I cried. I slumped down into the sand and curled into a ball. I began sobbing my eyes out, it was all too much for one day. I sobbed until Jacob returned – I felt his presence tower over me before I looked up at him from the sand. He was in shadow now and I noticed that the sun had come back out and was beaming behind him. The weather had calmed again. I could see him holding something. He knelt down and stretched out his hand.

'Tula! Look!' he said. I looked down through my tears and my eyes widened. It was my phone... and not only that, but to my amazement... it was still on! I grabbed the soaking mobile from his hand and quickly began drying it with my towel.

'Oh my God! But how did you...? But it's...? What the fuck?' I stuttered.

'I swear to God, it was insane. I gave up, I thought it was long gone, and then I was just swimming on the spot, looking at you crying, and I thought, please, God, give her a break, man. And then the next thing you know, I felt something float into my hand. It literally landed in my hand, and I thought, there's no way that's what I think it is? Then I pulled it out the water and there it was!' he exclaimed.

'But it was in there for about 15 minutes? And the waves? Look at the tide! It's not even possible? And it's still bloody working!' I said, tapping away at the phone, which functioned perfectly. 'It's a miracle!'

'I didn't find it, it found me. It floated into my hand. That was some serious higher power. Someone's watching over you, and the fact that it happened when it did, someone's trying to tell you something. You're gunna be just fine, I know it,' he said.

'I know,' I sobbed. I felt overwhelmed with emotion. How strange was it that moments ago I was in absolute pieces, feeling as if my world was coming to an end over one situation. And then I'd suddenly lost something, something that was already there in that moment of distress, only to find it again and then become overjoyed and not feel anywhere near as upset as I had about the current situation before it went missing. Nothing had actually changed, and yet I felt so happy to get something back that I'd always had. You know what they say... moral of the story and all...

I believe life does guide you, if you believe it can. The signs are all around us, if we take note. If the case ended in my favour, I might feel the same way about my life as I now felt about my phone, as silly as that sounds. I had been miserable, even with my freedom. And now I'd lost it, I knew if I was to get it back, I'd appreciate it a whole lot more.

Sure, a part of me felt broken and helpless inside. But another part of me felt something else – hope! I knew in my heart at that moment I had no choice now but to face this battle with every bit of strength I had left. This was the moment I also knew the battle had officially begun. Was the phone situation simply a coincidence? Or was it a sign of some higher power at work? Each to their own beliefs, I suppose.

Chapter 14:

TU'NIGHT'S THE NIGHT

THAT NIGHT, JACOB and I arrived back at our hotel feeling happy as Larry after an amazing romantic evening at a local fish restaurant on the beach. We sat on the balcony looking at the stars, as always sharing our thoughts on everything from religion and spiritualism to UFOs and aliens. I've always been a little obsessed with the universe and life itself, spending countless hours reading books and watching documentaries about everything from space and time to modern and especially ancient theories about aliens. I've always had a deep interest in the book *The 12th Planet* by Zecharia Sitchin and also *Chariots of the Gods?* by Erich von Däniken, both about ancient history or 'theory' as most would say. Jacob seemed to like listening to me talk about it, and the more I told him, the more intrigued he seemed. We yapped away for a couple of hours until we could no longer fight our exhaustion.

'We should probably go to sleep soon if we want to get a full day in the sun tomorrow, babe. We're on the last flight so let's make a day of it,' said Jacob.

'Yeah, you're right,' I said, swallowing down the hard lump in my throat at the thought of bedtime.

'One more drink and then bed?' he suggested.

'Cool, I'll be back in a ticky, just need the toilet,' I said, before getting up and heading to the bathroom. I looked down at my suitcase and pulled out the black silk nightdress that I had thrown in there on the sly when Gareth wasn't looking. At the time, I'd thought it was for a good tease! Acceptable to sleep in but would have had him wanting more. But it wasn't a game now, I wasn't teasing anymore. I got undressed and slipped it on. I looked at myself in the mirror and let out a deep breath. I noticed my perfectly straightened hair in the mirror. *Too try-hard*, I thought, I flipped my hair over and ruffled it, then flipped it back to one side. There I am. I clenched at the sickness in my stomach. *Oh, get a grip, you pussy! You'll be fine!* But I couldn't shake the feeling. The thought of giving myself to someone again and opening up on that level was making me extremely nervous.

'Tulisa,' Jacob called. 'What the hell are you doing in there? Come on! I'm gunna lay down soon, you're taking ages!'

'I'm coming, just give me a sec,' I replied. I looked back at myself in the mirror, talking to myself in my head. *You can trust him, as much as you can trust a guy at this stage. You can trust him, just relax.* Even though we had talked about sex, I still got the sense that he'd thought I was playing myself down, like he was expecting me to actually be some kind of wild sex goddess when it came down to it, and I was feeling the pressure.

I couldn't help but think about the Tulisa he'd known before he'd met me face to face a couple of years ago, the Tulisa in the press that he'd made assumptions about. The wild child, the confident Female Boss, that also had a sex tape. But the way I was seen in the media just wasn't me. If anything, I was the polar opposite of the person I'd been portrayed as for all these years, and now even more so. From the person I'd become, to how I was being portrayed, I could only hope that in all the time that he'd known me, getting to see me in every light, he now knew me well enough to know the difference.

It's our first time, I thought. *He'll understand that I'm nervous, won't he?* I had poured myself a cheeky drink on the way to the bathroom. I grabbed it and necked it back. *Right! Get a grip! This moment will never get easier! You know what you're like, just get out there! Stop thinking about it and try and enjoy it before you drive yourself mad,* I said to myself, before opening the bathroom door and tiptoeing down the hall. I pulled a cringe face to myself before I hit the corner. I stepped around it, expecting him to see me in my 'I'm ready' attire but he was laying down on the bed with his eyes closed, though he must have still heard me coming.

'Bout bloody time, babe! I'm shattered! Come here and give me a cuddle, let's go sleep,' he said. He obviously wasn't expecting me to be ready for the big moment, which made me even more nervous, because now I'd have to let him know I was ready.

'Jacob, wake up,' I said softly, as he stirred in the bed, half asleep.

'You took ages, I'm shattered. Come and lay down,' he moaned. He still hadn't opened his eyes. Well, this was awkward. *Just my luck! Should I leave it? Is it not meant to be?* I thought. *No! I always follow my gut. I'm ready.*

'Jacob, wake up,' I said. He stirred again and made a moaning noise. I climbed onto the bed and planted a kiss on his lips before whispering in his ear, 'It's not bedtime yet.'

He frowned and opened one of his eyes, taking in the black silk nightdress. 'Oh my God, now she tells me,' he groaned. Every night we'd spent together I'd been wearing his tracksuit bottoms and t-shirts, so he now knew what time it was. He wrapped his arm around my waist and pulled me towards him, kissing me hard and slow. I felt my heart thumping in my chest. *This was it. No going back now.*

He pulled back and smiled at me. 'Now I need the bloody toilet, stay right there,' he said, before getting up and heading to the bathroom. I sat on the bed twiddling my fingers nervously, waiting for him to return. Was he brushing his teeth or washing the sand off his private parts? Either way he needed to hurry the fuck up and stop leaving me in this suspense. I took a deep breath as I heard the bathroom door close. I stared at him nervously as he entered the room, expecting him to come and lay down again. But to my surprise, he walked past the bed and straight over to the chair by the window, picking up his pack of cigarettes before he sat down.

I breathed a sigh of relief. 'I'm really glad you did that, I could really do with a fag right now,' I said, as I grabbed a cigarette from the bedside table and sparked it. He smiled at my actions as he took a drag. I wondered why he was taking his time. Was it possible that he was nervous too? Or was he prolonging it, getting a kick out of my nerves? Or was I just over-thinking? I watched him smoke the cigarette as if he was deep in thought. *What the hell was he thinking about at a time like this? Maybe it was a bigger deal to him than I thought?* I had no idea, but it was only making me more nervous. He stubbed out his cigarette and looked at me as if he could sense my angst.

'Come here,' he said in a calm voice, with an intense stare. I put out my cigarette and paused anxiously before I got up and walked towards him. I could feel his eyes burning into me. I made an attempt at a sexy smile as I reached the chair, but he didn't smile back. His face stayed stern as he continued to stare hard into my eyes. *Eeek, this has all gone a bit* Fifty Shades, I thought, *but at least I don't have to take charge!* As I reached him, he instantly pulled me on top of him and began kissing me hard on the lips. He pulled back and looked me deep in the eyes again.

'How long did you say it's been?' he said, his facial expression still stern. *Oh gosh, he can definitely tell how nervous I am,* I thought, and by the looks of it he was enjoying it. I guess in a way he was finally getting what he wanted, to be the boss. He lifted me up and carried me towards the bed, his big strong arms holding me up effortlessly. He lay me down, still holding his intense gaze, taking all of me in, his eyes trailing down my body and back up again until they reached my own. I instantly looked away. *Someone please turn the fucking lights out*, I thought. He put his hand under my chin and moved my face so my eyes met his again. Then he kissed me passionately. I felt a tingle down my spine as he lifted up my black silk nightdress and began kissing my body seductively, getting lower and lower. I looked up to the ceiling before I closed my eyes. *Fucking my life! There's no going back now*, I thought.

The next day I was woken by the sound of birds tweeting loudly. I felt Jacob stir next to me. His arms were still wrapped around me, in the same position as when we had fallen asleep. He gave a loud yawn and squeezed me tightly.

'Morning, Princess,' he said, placing a lingering kiss on my cheek. In that moment I spotted my nighty on the edge of the bed. *Oh gosh*, I thought, wincing like a giddy schoolgirl as memories of the previous night came flooding back. I pulled the covers over my head and gave a high-pitched moan underneath them. He burst out laughing and tickled me under the sheets.

'Come here, you, too late for that, I've seen it all now! The boundaries have been well and truly broken!' He chuckled. I began to giggle as he grabbed my face and showered it with kisses.

'Eeew, get off! We've got morning breath!' I squealed.

'Fuck morning breath, you knob! Have some of this!' He grabbed my face and blew on it.

'Eeew, you bastard!' I yelled. He chuckled and kissed me once more on the forehead before jumping out of bed and heading to the balcony. He stretched out his arms and looked around. 'Beautiful! Absolutely beautiful!' he said chirpily.

'You seem very happy today,' I smiled.

'I am happy, you're making me happy, I can't even front. Just don't fuck it up,' he said. I winked at him with a wide grin.

'Vice versa, pal.'

He walked over and gave me another kiss before heading to the bathroom. I let my head sink back into the pillow, smiling to myself. All was good.

After we ate our breakfast, we lay down on a canopy bed by the hotel pool, which was built into a cliff looking out over the sea and the stunning landscape. I was in heaven. But as I rested my head against Jacob's chest, feeling content and taking in the view, I noticed a woman walking towards us. *She's definitely British*, I thought, as I sat up anxiously.

'Hi! Sorry to bother you, Tulisa, can I have a photograph?' she asked. I instantly froze. *Holy crap! What do I do?* I couldn't even speak because it would confirm I was, well, me. So I just stared at her, as if I'd seen a ghost. Jacob jumped up and began to chuckle.

'That's so funny! People say that to you all the time,

don't they, babe? You're like the fourth person on this trip!' he said. I looked at him and nodded, trying to crack a smile while slipping my arm with the Female Boss tattoo under my towel.

'Oh, I'm sorry,' said the woman. 'It's just that you really look like her, I was so sure,' I shook my head silently, and smiled as if to apologise. Jacob piped up again.

'Ha! She gets it all the time! I tell her she's much prettier though. I don't see what all the fuss is about with that Tulisa, she's not my cup of tea at all. Wasn't she voted Sexiest Woman in 2012? Absolute madness,' he exclaimed, turning to me and shaking his head. 'Anyway, nice to meet you!' he said, concluding the conversation.

'OK, sorry to bother you, guys. You really do look like her though... Sorry, have a nice trip!' she said, before walking back to the breakfast area. I continued to nod and smile until her back was fully turned before thumping Jacob in the ribs.

'Ouch!' he yelped.

'Not your cup of tea, no? You weren't saying that last night,' I glared at him.

'You're right, I wasn't,' he grinned cheekily. 'That was close, though. I had actually forgot for a moment,' he said.

'Forgot what?' I asked.

'That you're famous. It brought me back to reality,' he said, looking out at the ocean as if in deep thought. 'How is this going to work?' he asked after a long pause.

I frowned at him before I spoke. *We've already had this conversation*, I thought.

'I guess if it continues to go well, then eventually people will find out,' I said slowly.

'Why do they have to find out? I don't want to be famous or in the press,' he said, his demeanour beginning to change as he continued. 'After everything you told me, I don't want to go through all that right now. I have to think about other people too. If the papers drag me through the mud, it could affect the business. We have some big deals coming up and the way these people work, if I'm blasted all over the papers looking like a mug, they could pull out. I can't be responsible for that.'

Jacob worked for his uncle, who ultimately called the shots. I looked at him and shook my head.

'If you want this to go anywhere people will find out eventually, it's impossible for them not to. They always do. We're at risk of that happening right now as much as we will be all the time,' I said.

'They don't have to find out. We could just keep it a secret, no?' he asked.

'Yes, for a while, but not forever. I'm not going to sit here and lie to you to make you feel better. I'm under surveillance. Just because we've managed to duck and dive so far doesn't mean we can do it forever. They will get us eventually,' I said, now slightly agitated by his words. We'd already spoken about this. What the heck was he on about?

'So, what? You're not even willing to try?' he exclaimed.

'I'm not going into this with you under the impression that no one will ever know. It's not realistic. And what are you gunna do if people find out? Run away?' I asked.

'No! I didn't say that! We'll have to deal with that if it comes to it,' he said.

'Deal with it?' I frowned. 'Are you taking the piss? It's reality! What if we were to actually stay together? Then what? Do you think I'm gunna spend the rest of my life hiding with you? You're being ridiculous!' I declared.

'Well, what the fuck do you want me to say? We don't know where this will go. Do you want me to give up my life as I know it and possibly fuck with business as well? I told you, all this fame bollocks is not for me! I'm a business-man, not a celebrity!'

I glared at him, I could feel my blood beginning to boil. He could have told me this before I'd slept with him, no? How dare he?! There were a million things I wanted to say, but I took a deep breath and took the usual Female Boss route instead.

'Cool,' I said flatly, with zero emotion.

'What do you mean, *cool?*' he snapped.

I lay back down and stretched out my body, as if to relax.

'I mean what I said... cool,' I replied, still calm.

'What the fuck does that mean?' he asked.

'What else do you want me to say?' I shrugged.

'I'm asking you how the fuck we're gunna handle this, trying to find a compromise and you're telling me "cool"! Like that's it then, yeah? Done? Just like that?'

I looked at him and sighed. 'Listen, there's no com-promise in this situation. Don't play stupid with me, you knew exactly what you were getting yourself into. You went after a celebrity on a drugs charge, who you also knew damn well was in a bad place. I also made you fully aware of my "no sex before monogamy" rule and you still came after me, giving it the biggen and the whole "I got you, I got you" bollocks. Then you wait till you finally shag me and the next day you pull this shit and try to insult my intelligence on top of everything?' I paused. 'You're full of shit and an absolute wanker if you want me to be honest, but it's cool! I'm good! I was fine before you came along and I'll be fine when you're gone! Let's just leave it now, there's nothing more to say.' I stretched out my arms behind my head and closed my eyes as if to continue sunbathing.

'T,' he said.

'Mmm,' I muttered.

'Just give me a minute, I need to think,' he said.

'Nothing to think about, mate. I told you it's all good.'

'There *is* something to think about! I fucking care about you. You're making it sound like I just wanted to shag you and the joke is it's not actually like that for once,' he declared.

'Whatever, man. I'm cool, seriously. We don't have to go into it,' I said casually.

'Well, I'm in it now, aren't I? What the fuck do you think I'm gunna do? After everything you think I'm gunna sleep with you and fuck off?' he yelled.

'I told you! Do what you like. I can't enter into something with a person that never wants to be in the papers, I'd be setting myself up for a fall! I'm famous, it's my life – I need someone who can accept that. It's never going to be easy for anyone unless I date another famous person, but if I meet someone that isn't, then really for that person, it only comes down to one issue,' I said.

'Oh yeah, and what's that?' he asked.

I sat up and looked at him.

'Am I worth it? That is the question that you need to ask yourself, and not me or anyone else can answer that for you, and I certainly shouldn't have to convince you and nor do I want to.' I shielded my eyes from the sun with my hand as I frowned at him. He looked back at me, then looked away.

'You have a proper way with words, don't you?' he said.

I looked at him, unimpressed. 'So I've been told.'

He turned to face me again. 'It's not that simple though, it's not just about me. If it was only me I was putting at risk then yeah, I do think you're worth it. But I need to speak to my uncle. If he says it's OK and it won't fuck with the business then I'm willing to put myself at risk. But I can't put other people in the shit, not my family – it isn't fair.'

'So, what is it you wanna do, Jacob? I understand where you're coming from. Don't get me wrong, I respect it, but I don't take kindly to feeling like an option, so whatever you need to do, don't sit here discussing it and trying to decide in front of me. Make your decision and let me know! But if you have to think too hard, you're really not the kind of person I wanna be with anyway,' I said.

'I never said I wanted to end it! You did! I said I wanted to keep it a secret and now you've given me an ultimatum.' He got up and ran his fingers through his hair. 'I'll be back in a bit, I'm going to call my uncle,' he said.

'Cool,' I said flatly once again, laying back down and placing my hands behind my head. I waited a moment until he was gone before I exhaled.

I felt the tears stinging around my eyes, trying to push their way through, but I swallowed them down. I felt hurt and stupid, not just over Jacob, but over everything, and to make matters worse, I was hungover. Somewhere deep inside I knew where he was coming from, but what about me and how I felt? I needed a man, or people in general, that could be there for me and handle the bullshit. If he couldn't handle the heat, he shouldn't have set foot in the kitchen. This was just the final kick in the teeth, but I wouldn't show it and I certainly wasn't going to let him see me cry. A while later Jacob returned. I pretended to be asleep.

'Oi! Princess!' he boomed over me.

I stirred sleepily. 'Mmhmm,' I mumbled as I squinted at him in the sunlight.

'Come here,' he said, as he lay down next to me and pulled me into his arms and hugged me. 'We're all good,' he said, kissing my forehead.

I didn't respond. He lay there for a moment breathing into my neck before he broke the silence. 'Babe, I said we're all good. Don't be funny with now. Aren't you happy?' he asked.

'I was happy until you had your bullshit freakout and had to ask someone for permission to be with me,' I said grumpily.

'Listen, I'm sorry, but this is all a big deal for me and

I'm dealing with things as I go along. But you're right, that's not your problem, it's mine. And if being with you means having to deal with all that other bollocks then that's a risk I'm willing to take. What can I say? I've got feelings for you,' he sighed.

I paused for a moment before I spoke. 'What was his reaction when you told him?' I asked, cracking a smile. He looked at me and grinned, shaking his head.

'You little fucker! Light me a cigarette and come for a walk and I'll tell you.'

'Light your own, fuck face,' I smirked. He grabbed me and gave me a playful shake.

'Oi! Look at me!' he yelled.

'What?' I moaned, trying not to smile. He held my face in his hands and stared into my eyes

'Tulisa, I got you.'

Chapter 15:

MANCHESTER MADNESS

THE NIGHT WE got back from our adventurous little getaway, we luckily landed in London safe and sound without being caught. Well, almost.

Literally minutes after the flight took off, the airport had been swarming with British press due to an incident. Nothing like a close shave! A few days later, Jacob and I decided to head to Manchester together for a few days. He had a meeting up there and I had been invited to a couple of events. A few of our London friends were also up there for the weekend, and they had all now got to know my Manchester friends. We could all go out as one big group, and entering hotels and parties with Jacob was now a doddle. It still felt rather strange to me though. Considering one minute I was alone, and the next minute I was with him and we were in each other's pockets. It didn't feel like a bad thing, it was just all quite intense, considering what I was going through. Though my feelings for Jacob were true, I still felt like I was throwing myself into it faster than I normally would, to distract myself from what was really going on, which I was always trying to put at the back of my mind.

On our second night in Manchester, we decided to go out and hit a club with our friends. We had such a great time and were very clearly in our honeymoon period, as we spent the whole night all over each other, like no one else in the room existed. We were tipsy and way past caring about the fact that we were in public.

The club was dark and we were in a VIP area, surrounded by a large group of friends who were trying their best to hide us from the public eye. We smooched, cuddled, danced and flirted. Considering I was on a drugs charge, I couldn't remember the last time I'd felt so happy.

A little later, we headed back to our hotel. The paparazzi outside had left, and me and Jacob had snuck in separately at the start so we hadn't been seen.

It was a hot night so the car roof was down and the tunes were blaring. We pulled up outside the club to speak to Michelle who was still outside, waiting for our other friend. Michelle had a funny look on her face, like she was trying to tell me something. I frowned at her and she leaned in over the car and whispered in my ear, 'Perfect timing, kid,' then she burst out laughing.

I looked behind her over at the smoking area, where my ex, Danny Simpson, stood staring right at us, looking like he'd just been slapped in the face by a wet fish.

I'm not sure what pissed him off more, me being with Jacob or the car we were in. Probably both. Our eyes met for a moment. I could see he was hurt. I would have been hurt – our breakup wasn't that long ago. After he'd recovered from the newspaper shock, he'd been back in touch, saying that he missed me, even though he was still angry. He'd said I was the only girl he'd ever changed and done everything right for, only for me to stab him in the back and humiliate him.

And though my heart could agree with that, my ego couldn't. I'd never had to grovel or beg for a guy. I hated showing any vulnerability and I was also completely consumed by what was happening in my life. I had sheepishly apologised, but not as genuinely as I could have. I admit I didn't really take his emotions on board at the time. I could only comprehend what it meant for me. I could be selfish in romance, but mostly because I was so guarded.

Once we were speaking again, I could feel the resentment and apprehension from him, and with what I was going through, I resented him for not just loving me through it. We'd been in contact and had even met up, but as quickly as it felt like we were getting somewhere, it would just all fall apart again. I felt like he loved me and hated me at the same time, and it hurt. I would lash out by going out and getting papped partying with other guys to wind him up, then he'd do the same. We got stuck in a toxic cycle – winding each other up with jealousy.

After the last fall-out I'd heard he was messing with his baby mother again and I had got involved with a guy called Paul. It turned out Danny knew Paul. He had tried to warn me off him, saying he was bad news, and it just got messy. I still had feelings for Danny but I'd had enough. I felt like he couldn't truly forgive me, and I wasn't going to stick around and be punished for my mistakes any longer, especially during such a difficult time. I responded by telling him I was done with all the toxicity and after a heated phone confrontation, I blocked him.

That same night he retaliated by getting papped kissing Vicky Pattison.

As for Paul, we had met through a friend and had met up a few times after, but nothing physical had ever happened. Not even a kiss. But we spoke all day every day for quite a while on the phone and we had built up a strangely strong bond and became very close very quickly. He was already speaking to me as if I was his girlfriend. It was also very fiery and he was very jealous. There was definitely a very strong spark though, but he always seemed to have an excuse when it came to meeting up face to face and would put it down to the long distance as he was also from up north.

It had got to the point where I sensed something was up, and so I'd given Paul a deadline to come and see me. The day before this deadline I'd had a dream that he was with another woman and I'd found out. That day I went to see an old friend I hadn't seen in ages. She asked me about my love life and when I told her the guy's name and that he was coming to see me the next day, she said she knew his girlfriend and showed me an Instagram picture of them both.

So I waited till Paul had caved in on the deadline and he was en route to London to come and see me. When he was nearly in London, I sent him a picture of him and his girlfriend, followed by the letters 'SNM!' (say no more) and then blocked him. It had turned out Danny was right.

And a week after the Paul saga was when things had started up with Jacob.

Me and Danny held our gaze for a brief moment. This felt strange. One minute you can be going through so much with one person and it feels like they are your whole world, then the next you're sat next to a new person you're going through so much with, staring back at the other person like a stranger.

Though he didn't feel like a stranger to me, I wasn't sure how I felt.

I quickly broke my gaze as Jacob lifted out his arm and stretched it over the back of my seat before driving off.

'You did that on purpose,' I chuckled.

'Did what on purpose?'

'Oh, come on, you saw my ex there.'

'I didn't see your ex, wouldn't even know what he looks like,' he grunted.

'Hmmm, if you say so.'

Around ten minutes later I felt my phone vibrating in my bag and pulled it out. It was a friend of mine and Michelle's called Andy. 'One sec, babe, turn that down so I can take this.... Yo, Andy, what's up?' I said, leaving the phone on loudspeaker.

'MAAAAAATE!' Andy bellowed. 'What have you done to Simmo, you've got him fucked up!' Simmo was Danny's nickname.

'I haven't done anything, mate, just out here minding my business.'

'Check your phone, I'll send you the messages he's just sent me.'

The phone began to ping with multiple messages.

Danny: BLACK FERRARI YEAH!

Danny: WHO THE FUCK IS THIS GUY!!!

PING

PING

PING

As I lowered the phone to put the messages out of sight, I suddenly noticed Jacob's eyes burning into me.

'What can I do, mate? It's Dan being Dan, anyway I've gotta....'

'Oh no, it didn't end there!' Andy interrupted. 'He's just called me now going sick!'

'Oh, just ignore him, Andy. Listen, me and Jacob are heading to the hotel. I've gotta go, speak soon,' I said hastily, hanging up the phone. I sat awkwardly staring straight ahead at the road in silence.

Wait for it, I thought.

'How long ago did you break up with this fucking guy? Why is he still in your life like this and your business? He's clearly still fucking in love with you! That's like the third time I've heard one of your friends tell you he's been on the phone to them ranting about you! What the fuck has anything you're doing got to do with him? Why does he feel like he has a right to speak on what you're doing and who you're with, and to all your friends?! It's like he's in there with everyone you know! Guys don't do that unless they're getting something back!' Jacob snapped.

'I haven't given him anything to go on! I've blocked him! I've dated someone else since him! He's just unfortunately very close to my circle. I can't help what he does!'

'It seems to me like you might still have feelings for him,' he said, staring into my eyes now, trying to gauge my reaction.

I kept my eyes on the road. 'Jacob, I want you, I'm happy with you, I don't care about him anymore!'

'Well, if that's the case tell your friends to stop relaying fucking messages and to tell the guy to mind his fucking business! You think you can sit here taking calls about your ex while you're sat next to me like I'm some dickhead! Tell him to fuck off!'

I sighed and stayed silent for a moment before speaking again, softly.

'I haven't given him anything to go on, Jay. But I get it and I'm sorry, I'll tell them to stop telling me.'

I stared quietly out of the window in deep thought. I had meant what I said: I wanted to be with Jacob, I was locked in. But after seeing Danny and looking into those big brown eyes again and seeing sadness in them, I felt sad too. There was so much emotion between us, there always had been. We didn't separate because we were no longer in love. We had some problems for sure, but ninety per cent of the problems were always outside of us, creeping in. If it hadn't been for the sting, we'd still have been together. It was such a messed-up situation. I couldn't help but ask myself: *Was there maybe a part of me that still had love for Dan?*

* * *

Once we got to the hotel, Jacob was finally over it and we all headed to the smoking area outside the bar with our drinks. Jacob wandered off, talking to one of our mates for a moment, as I sat down on a chair to spark a cigarette. I felt my phone vibrating, so I pulled it out of my bag to have a look. It was a number that I recognised. I squinted my eyes tipsily at the screen. No frigging way! IT WAS PAUL! You can't write this shit! Excuse the pun. How the hell was he getting through to my number? It took me a second to register that it was because I had put my SIM into a new phone when me and Jacob had got back from our trip away. I had bought a new one and transferred everything I needed from the old phone in case it shut down on me after it had ended up in the sea. But I hadn't stored Paul's number on this new phone, let alone blocked it, so he could now get through. As the phone stopped ringing, I saw nine missed calls and a text.

Paul: CALL ME! PLEASE!

I was in his town. I hadn't even thought about it, he'd probably been told I was out with Jacob. I couldn't believe after all this time he was even checking if he could still get through? I looked back at the text. *Call me?* I thought. *What a bloody cheek!* I thought back to what he'd done and how I'd felt at the time. I began tapping away furiously at my phone, pressing 'Ignore' as the phone began ringing again.

T: Fuck off, you horrible slimy bastard! I told you not to call me again! I don't want anything to do with you! You disgust me! You can absolutely do one!
SENT.

I saw it had delivered before the phone began to ring again.

'Who's that?' I jumped as I heard a stern voice boom from behind. I spun around to see Jacob towering over me.

'I've been standing here for a while. I saw you send that text. Who's calling your phone?' he demanded, glaring at me.

'It's that bloody guy I told you about, the one I dated but found out he had a girlfriend.'

'So why the fuck is he still ringing you?' he asked.

'I don't know. It's a new phone. I obviously didn't put his number in and block it, he couldn't contact me on the old one.'

'So, why the hell is he ringing you now, and why are you texting him?' he asked angrily, eyes glazed from all the alcohol.

'I'm not! I just saw the missed calls and a text so I told him to fuck off and not contact me again!' I said, throwing my hands in the air and staring at him as if insulted.

'Don't try and take me for a mug!' he scowled.

'I haven't, I swear! I only sent that one text just now!'

He looked down at me as if disgraced. 'So why the hell would you text him back?! Why not ignore him?'

'It's not like that, let me explain,' I said, rolling my eyes and resting my hand on his arm. He shrugged it off with force.

'We're going upstairs, now,' he snapped, before storming towards the hotel entrance and heading inside. I got up and chased after him. He got to the lifts and bashed at the buttons furiously.

'Jacob! Please listen to...'

'Not another word until we're in the room!' he glared.

I put my hands on my head and sighed sarcastically in frustration. Once we reached the room, he opened the door and waited for me to walk inside. He stepped in after me and slammed it shut. The bang made me jump as I felt the vibration pulse through my body. He began pacing up and down the room.

'You wanna try and mug me off, yeah? I bring you here, I give you all my time, I put my shit on the line, I take care of you and you wanna mug me off? You think I'm some kind of prick! Texting your ex-boyfriend while you're with me?' he yelled furiously.

'Oh, don't be so fucking ridiculous. You're over-reacting! The guys only got through because I've got a new phone! All I did was tell him to fuck off!' The phone began vibrating again on the side of the desk where I'd placed it: it was Paul again.

'Ya see that? Ya see? Still fucking ringing! You know

170

why? Because you fucking texted him! You gave him something to feed off! Made him think you care! While you're supposed to be here with me! If you don't care about him, then why the fuck are you texting him?' he shouted.

'I told him to fuck off!' I yelled.

'Yeah, but you didn't need to tell him anything! You're here with me, you're not supposed to give a fuck about him or be giving him the time of day! It's the principle!' he yelled back.

The phone began to vibrate again, along with another text message.

'I don't give a fuck about him! It was just a reaction! He's ringing down my phone and I'm here with you and I wanted him to fuck off so that's what I told him to do! He means nothing to me! We didn't even kiss in the time we spent together, this is ridiculous!'

'How the fuck would you feel If I was sat here texting an ex-girlfriend abuse while I was here with you?!' he shouted.

The phone started to ring again. I felt like I was about to explode, my heart was racing and a hard lump began to rise in my throat. I couldn't control myself. It was all too much – the arguments, the case, the emotions. All of a sudden, I burst into tears.

'You fucking selfish prick,' I cried. 'You have no fucking idea! No idea what I feel about anything or anyone! I told you why I texted him! What the fuck do you want from me? I'm not a fucking liar! I'm the most honest person you will ever meet! Yet all the time, all people do is fucking accuse me of shit and make me out to be something I'm not. Just like you are right now! You don't even know me, no one does. Fuck you! Stay the fuck away from me and get the fuck out of my life!' I gasped through my sobs.

I was having one hell of an emotional outburst, like everything had been building up for so long and now it was all coming out. I ran into the toilet and slammed the door before locking it. I grabbed a towel and pulled it over me as I curled into a ball on the floor and sobbed underneath it. I heard a knock on the door.

'Baby, let me in, please.' Jacob's tone sounded soft and concerned now.

'Go away! I'm not letting you in! I'll be out in the morning! Get another room or something!' I yelled.

'Babe, I'm not leaving you in there. Please open the door!' he said.

'NO! I'm not fucking coming out! I'm feeling fucking emotional and I'm staying in here! I don't want to see you, I don't want to talk about it, and I certainly don't want a fucking hug! Trust me, I'm not coming out!' I sobbed. I heard him slide his back down the door and sit on the floor.

'I'm sleeping here then,' he sighed.

I buried my head in the towel, trying to cry as silently as possible. How could this possibly be my life right now? I tried to tell myself there must be a bigger meaning behind it all that I just couldn't see in this moment, but the emotions were too much to bear. *Fuck this, fuck him, and fuck the whole world*, I cried in my head.

Five minutes went past without a word. I knew he was still sat behind the door.

'T,' he called to me softly. I didn't reply in the hope that he'd think I'd fallen asleep.

'T!' he said, louder this time. I stayed quiet as I heard him get up.

'Tulisa!' he yelled before twisting the door knob and banging the door, trying to open it.

'Just give up and go away!' I finally cried.

'I can't do that,' he said softly.

'Well then, you're gunna have a long night, aren't you?' I replied, wrapping the towel around me even tighter and closing my eyes. He knocked on the door again.

'I'll make you a deal,' he said.

'Whaaat?' I snivelled.

'I'm going to sit on the other side of the bed, well away from the door. Listen, can you hear I've moved away?' he said. His voice sounded more distant.

'All I'm asking is for you to unlock the door and leave it open just a tiny bit. You can stay in the bathroom and I'll stay on the bed,' he said.

'I'm not going kill myself, you twat,' I mumbled.

'Babe, just do it for me, please,' he sighed. I paused for a moment and yawned through my tears, I was so shattered now.

'Speak, so I can hear where you are,' I mumbled once again.

'I'm here,' he called, sounding further away from the door.

'You promise you'll let me sleep now?' I asked.

'I promise,' he said. I slid over to the door quietly and undid the latch.

'There, now leave me alone,' I said as I curled back into a ball and listened intently for footsteps. But it was silent.

When I was a child, the bathroom was the only room in my house with a lock. I had always locked myself in there in times of distress, whether it was because my parents were going at it like two bulls in a china shop again, or my mentally ill mother was going off the rails. It had always been my place of safety. And twenty years later, here I was: back lying on the bathroom floor. Deep-rooted issues, I suppose. When the sex tape had come out, I had slept on the bathroom floor for five days.

After about ten minutes, I began drifting off to sleep. Just as I nodded off, I felt two big strong arms slip underneath me and lift me into the air, resting me on a firm chest. I woke instantly and squinted my eyes at Jacob. I couldn't see his eyes through the darkness but as soon as I felt his presence, the emotions came flooding back, and I started to cry again. I couldn't handle affection when I was emotional. He carried me to the bed and lay me down. He got in next to me and wrapped his arms around me tightly.

'You're not crying because of the argument, are you?' he whispered. It was a statement, not a question. I shook my head and continued to weep into his chest. He kissed my forehead and began stroking my hair. I nuzzled into him, crying loudly now.

'*Sh sh shhhhh*,' he whispered, almost rocking me in his arms like a baby, 'everything's gunna be alright. I've got you, you're safe.'

I couldn't contain it any longer as I burst into a loud wailing that sounded as if I was mourning a loved one. For some reason I felt such a strong connection with this man that I was able to show him all of me. Never in my life had I cried on a man the way I cried in that moment, and I didn't feel a bit of worry about what he might think or how he might judge me after. I wailed out loud for what felt like hours, clinging on to Jacob for dear life, releasing not just the pain from the set-up, but what felt like my entire life. He continued to stroke my hair and kiss my head, holding me tighter to his chest with his body wrapped around mine. We stayed like that all night. Eventually, I cried myself to sleep.

Chapter 16.

TU WHAT?

ABOUT A MONTH later, after my emotional breakdown on the bathroom floor, I was sat in Jacob's kitchen sipping on my coffee while stroking the giant Rottweiler that was lovingly resting his head on my leg. His name was Prince. Prince was Jacob's dog that had been stolen many years ago when Jacob was 17. He had spoken about him many times during our time together so far, always going on about how much how he had loved him and how he missed him. Jacob had him chipped when he was a puppy but when he was taken from outside a shop, he'd had no luck in finding him. Miraculously, a few days before, he had received a call from a dog home, saying that they had found his missing dog, eight years later. It was only a few days prior to the call that Jacob had said to me how much he wished he could find him and what he would give to have him back right now.

As if by magic, three days later, his dog was found! He was overjoyed and overwhelmed with emotion and disbelief at how this could have happened. As usual, he reverted back to his idea that I was his lucky charm and somehow behind the strange things that continued to happen while we were around each other. We both felt as if these strange happenings had now overstepped the bounds of coincidence and that our coming together was meant to be at this time.

I heard the pot on the cooker start to spit and jumped up to turn down the heat. I was cooking healthy tonight. Once me and Jacob had got our frequently intoxicated whirlwind of a honeymoon period out of the way, we seemed to come to more of an understanding and things had become a lot calmer. We would still have the odd fiery and explosive argument, during which I noticed Jacob loved to play little mind games to make him feel like he was in control. But I always saw through it and always gave as good as I got, if not more. We were currently in a calm patch and had a nice little routine going on where I was very much enjoying playing the role of a sweet little housewife. Keeping the house in check and cooking intricate and fancy dinners every night for him to come home to. We were together all the time and only really parted for work.

It was probably the happiest I'd been since the sting. Don't get me wrong, there was still a massive dark shadow looming over my head and I was still terrified. But, compared to how I'd felt before, thinking about it all day, every day, I now had something else to think about – Jacob. I can only imagine how I would have felt if he hadn't been around, but he was. So, I was enjoying a happier period during this testing time in my life, but as usual for me, trouble was waiting just round the corner. I heard the gates open outside and I did a quick mental check of the house and dinner. Yep, everything was perfect. I looked down at Prince, who was getting excited at the sound of Jacob's car.

'Shit! You're not supposed to be in here. Quick, get in your outhouse!' I ushered Prince into the garden and shut the door. Jacob didn't like him in the house, but when he wasn't home, I of course ignored that. Jacob entered the kitchen in his smart work clothes and opened his arms up wide.

'Beautiful!' he said to me, with a handsome grin. He always called me Beautiful.

'What am I smelling? You're cooking up the bollocks, aren't ya? I already know!' He wrapped his arms around me and placed a kiss on my cheek before lifting the lid off the pot to take a peek at the slow-cooked curried chicken with rice.

'Of course, babe! You know me, I don't mess about.'

After dinner, we went to the upstairs living area to chill. We lay on the sofa curled up and having a chit-chat like we normally did, but something felt a little off that day, like he was on edge for some reason. My suspicions were confirmed when he suddenly interrupted me mid-conversation.

'T, I need to tell you something,' he said sheepishly. I studied his face. Whatever it was, I wasn't going to like it.

'What? What have you done?' I said, as the schoolgirl smile melted off my face.

'I haven't done anything, I just need to tell you something,' he sighed, looking agitated all of a sudden. He began huffing and puffing.

'Jacob, don't freak me out. Whatever it is, I'm cool. You know me, just spit it out.'

He took a deep breath and exhaled. 'OK, cool, listen. There's this girl I was seeing before,' he said hesitantly.

'Yes, go on, you were seeing a few,' I said flatly.

'Well... she's found out that she's pregnant.'

I sighed a big long sigh and put my hands to my head.

'Oh my God, here we go. Go on.'

'Wait! Don't freak, she doesn't want to keep it.'

I looked at him and shook my head. 'Right, and how do you feel about that?' I asked.

'It doesn't matter, it's not even my decision either way,' he sighed heavily.

'OK, so now what?' I asked.

'So now nothing, but...' He paused again.

'But what?' I said sternly.

'But, I went to see her, to talk to her about it, 'cause it was the right thing to do. So I met her, and we talked, but obviously I didn't tell you I was going and I promised you I wouldn't lie to you, so I'm telling you the truth,' he said, staring sheepishly into my eyes.

I paused. 'OK, I respect that,' I said, looking away in thought.

'There's more though, I told her about you,' he said, squinting his eyes a bit, as if wincing at the thought.

'What the hell did you do that for?' I snapped.

'Because she was upset, and I know she still has feelings for me and I didn't want her to get hurt if something came out in the papers. She's not a bad person. I don't want to make her any more upset than she already is.'

I felt my agitation rise over his stupidity and took a deep breath. 'So, what did you say?' I asked sternly.

'I told her I'd been seeing you, and it could come out, but it was just a casual thing.'

My eyes widened at his words 'CASUAL! What do you mean, casual? What the fuck did you say that for?!' I yelled.

'Because I didn't want to hurt her feelings! She's distressed enough as it is, what am I supposed to say? "Oh, OK, I'll see you later, I'm off to see my new bird!"' he exclaimed.

'Well, if you're not going to tell her what it is, then you shouldn't have said anything at all! Do you understand what kind of situation that puts me in? How do you know if she's even pregnant? How do you know she wasn't devastated you stopped seeing her and then found out you were seeing me and she's now lying for attention? Not only does the girl fucking hate me now, but she has the opportunity to go to the papers and make up some bullshit! She can say anything! She can say that she was your girlfriend and that you've been cheating on her with me while she's pregnant! Don't you understand the seriousness of this?'

'She's not that type of girl, she would never do anything like that. She wouldn't want to be dragged into the papers for something like that!'

'Listen to me! Once you enter my world, it's a game changer! People you thought you knew, you don't! You would be surprised what people will do and how they can instantly change their morals for money or fame.'

'No, no way. She doesn't want anyone to know about it as it is, never mind the whole of England. She's just not that kind of person.'

'Well, you seem to have a lot of faith in this bird, so let's hope you're right! It's too bloody late either way now.'

'Trust me, babe, it will all be fine. I know it will.'

'The problem is, Jacob, until you live this shit, you'll never know.'

'Listen, I'm cool with her. I know her, she's not going to snake me.'

'You just don't understand, Jacob!' I picked up my phone and searched for a picture before holding it up to his face.

'Before this headline was front page of *The Sun*, my ex thought he knew the mother of his child.'

He took the phone and looked at it. It was the front page of *The Sun* from nearly two years ago when I'd got with my ex-boyfriend Danny Simpson: 'TULISA IS A HOME WRECKER'.

'That is what happened last time, and it nearly ruined

my career! I am currently on a drugs charge! There are only so many public catastrophes I can come back from, and that's if I can ever come back from the one I'm in now!'

'What happened?' he asked quietly.

'What happened is the guy told the mother of his child about me. He wasn't with her, but they were still sleeping together before we got together, the last time being the week before we met. At the time I didn't even know about that, and he didn't want her to feel hurt when it came out that he was now with me, so he told her. She then went mental and went to *The Sun* "claiming" to be pregnant with his second child and still in a relationship with him. She also claimed I knew all about it, and that I had stolen him from her. She got paid a nice big lump sum too! It almost ruined me and I'm still in the process of suing them now, two years later. And guess what? The baby she claimed to be having still isn't here! And the positive pregnancy test picture she sent him was identical to the second image on Google when you type in "pregnancy test". I can't afford to be dragged into this again. This could be a set-up, it could all be lies – *The Sun* could be paying her to do this!' I yelled. I couldn't believe he'd been so naïve.

'Not everything is a set-up, babe. Calm down. I understand why you're feeling the way you are, but I need you to trust me. Everything is going to be fine, I've got it under control!'

'You just don't get it, do you? You don't get how serious this is!'

'Listen, I'm just going to take her to the appointment and it's done. That's it, then we can all move on!'

'Well, she hasn't moved on by the sound of it! And how do you feel about her?'

'Babe, it's not like that, trust me! If I wanted to be with her, I could have. Even when I saw her, I didn't feel anything. She came all done up as well and I didn't even think to try anything.'

'What do you mean *to try anything?*'

'Babe, come on, this is me! A fit girl I was seeing comes to see me, looking stunning, that's still in love with me. And I knew I didn't have to tell you anything and usually I would have acted in a certain way in that situation, but I didn't! Because of you! I don't want to! Not with her, not with anyone!'

'Oh my God, have you heard yourself? You're making it sound like you're doing me a favour. That's fucking standard, Jacob! That's how it's supposed to be! Talk about narcissism 101,' I scoffed.

'But I'm being honest! I'm being honest like you asked! I haven't lied about who I am and who I've been, and I'm trying! More than trying, I'm doing it. It's a big fucking deal to me! I'm actually doing it! I thought you would respect it, and now you're getting mad and throwing it back in my face. Maybe I've got it wrong. Maybe I forget that you're not just my friend so there's certain things I don't need to say because then I'm just hurting you. I dunno what to say anymore.'

'I'm not angry because you're being honest. I'm angry

at the way you handled the situation and then had the audacity to remind me that you can't keep your dick in your pants.'

'Babe, please, man, help me out here. What do you want me to say? I feel like I can't win.' He reached out and tried to pull me towards him for a hug.

'No – stop it, Jacob! I need to think!' I sunk back into the sofa and closed my eyes. *Why did this always happen to me? Why couldn't I just be happy for a second? Why did everything that went up so high always have to come crashing down so hard?*

I just wanted a simple life, and as usual I was way off.

Chapter 17:

TU BE OR NOT TU BE

I gave a hard knock on my apartment door. 'It's me, I forgot my keys,' I mumbled.

Gareth opened the door and paused as he saw my face. 'Oh, I can already tell what kind of night this is going to be. I've seen that look before. Go upstairs, put on your PJs. I'll be up in a tick with a coffee, and you can tell me all about it.'

Half an hour later, me and G were curled up on the sofa, having a good old intense chinwag. I had explained the situation to him, and his reaction was just as I had expected.

'Oh well! Isn't that just a lovely bit of news you brought home? So shocking, yet not surprising in the slightest! Never a dull day in the life of Tulisa, is there? So, what are you going to do?' he asked.

'I'm going to end it,' I sighed, feeling heavy.

'Hmmm, OK. A bit hasty maybe?'

'What, coming from you? You're not exactly his biggest fan,' I frowned.

'I never said I didn't like him, I just feel like he doesn't always understand your situation. But to be honest, I like the way you are around him. It's the most yourself I've ever seen you since you were with Fazer. And I have to give him credit, he's making you happy at a really shit time. I'm just saying it's not really his fault, is it? And sometimes I think you look for excuses to push people away.'

'It's not just that though, it's everything. I can see where this is going with him. There's too many red flags, I'm asking for it, and I don't need this shit right now.'

'Well, why don't you sleep on it?'

'I suppose,' I grunted,

'I'm going to make another coffee. Aunty Maz is coming round, she should be here soon. In the meantime, don't do anything too hasty,' he said sternly, before heading downstairs. He knew me too well; I had already made my decision.

I sat fiddling with my phone, thinking long and hard about what I was going to say and how I would put it. I know it seemed childish putting it in a text, but it was the only way I could say everything I wanted to say, and clearly. I also knew if I spoke to him, he would try and find a way to convince me otherwise:

T: Jacob, this isn't easy for me in the slightest. I care about you a lot and I have loved our time together. But I just can't do this. Taking into account everything that's gone on and certain things you've done and said, I just don't think you're capable of making me happy and giving me the security I need. Your commitment phobias, you wanting to be the leader in the relationship, your past lack of ability to stay loyal, the arguments. I can see where this is going and I would rather end it now than let it end in tears later. I don't have any bad feelings towards you whatsoever and I hope in the future we can be friends. But I think for the next couple of months it's best we don't contact each other in order for us to move on. Take care for now and I wish you all the best. X

My heart raced as I pressed send. Was I running again? I didn't want to end it, but it felt like the right thing to do. But it hurt, really hurt. To the point I didn't realise how much I now actually felt for him. But I needed to use my head over my heart, I couldn't make the same mistakes again. My phone began to ring: it was Jacob. I stared down at it.

No, don't call me, I thought, *you're going to make it worse!*

Why couldn't he just text back? I didn't want to hear his voice, or see his face. I was afraid I'd change my mind.

I texted him again:

T: Please, Jacob, just leave it, we don't need to speak to each other right now. It's just gunna make it harder, just leave it for a while x

J: T, please just answer the phone, I just wanna talk to you

The phone continued to ring and I continued to stare at it. He sent more texts:

J: just 5 minutes

J: you can't just not talk to me after everything

J: answer the phone!

I sat there, just watching it ring out. I got another text:

J: I can't believe I am sat in the park on my own with Prince and I feel like I've just lost my new best friend and got back my old one. It's fucked up. I'm not even gunna front. I'm actually hurt right now. I didn't even think I'd feel like this, but I do. After everything we've been through and you can't even talk to me? Just let me come round and talk to you and say my bit. Just hear me out, and whatever you wanna do then, you can do. But at least hear me out first. X

My attention was suddenly drawn elsewhere as I heard my front door open: it was my Aunty Maz. She was talking to Gareth and saying hello to Narla. She called up the stairs to me.

'Hello, little one! I'm just gunna take Narla out for a walk because she looks like she needs a wee!'

'OK, cool! See you in a bit!' I shouted. The phone started ringing again. What the hell was I going to do? This was killing me. I got another text:

J: Fuck it, I'm gunna swallow my pride, I'm coming round, I'll be there in 5, make sure you open the door.

My heart jumped in my chest! He's what? He must be bluffing! There's no way he would just turn up without a response? Or would he? I began flapping about in my pyjamas.

'Gareeeeth!' I screamed.

'What?' he shouted from his room.

'Helppppp!' I whined, tripping up over my pyjama bottoms as I ran to my room to get changed. He came running up the stairs.

'What's happened?'

'It's fucking Jacob!' I whined, frantically rummaging through my chill clothes for a plain pair of PJs while pulling off the ones I was wearing that were covered in My Little Pony, 'He's bloody coming round! I ended it, via text, and he's bloody coming round!'

'Well, tell him not to then!'

'I can't! He's very persistent!' I shouted, hopping about on one leg. 'I'm hoping he's bluffing but it doesn't sound like it.'

'Well, just don't answer the door. He'll go away eventually!'

'That's a good idea, I didn't think of that. I could have gone out for all he knows...'

'Exactly, just chill!'

I exhaled loudly. 'OK, OK, I'm calm, I just won't answer.'

The phone began to ring again, and my heart thumped even harder. *Please go away*, I thought. I got another text:

J: I'm outside, open the door

My eyes widened and I rushed to the window. I peeked slyly through the side of the curtain. Shit! He really was here! I jumped back from the window and ran to the sofa and sat down. I turned the phone over and took it off vibrate so I didn't have to feel it ring. I took a deep breath, trying to slow my pacing heart. All of a sudden, I jumped as I heard the door go.

I could hear my aunty's voice: 'She must have her phone on silent or something, sorry about that. She's upstairs. Nice to finally meet you, by the way!'

'You too, Maria, it's a pleasure.' I heard footsteps coming up the front stairs and the door opened. I stood up and froze.

Jacob flung open the door, stopped dead in the doorway and stared at me. I looked back at him nervously, unsure of what to say. He stood with his phone in his hand and a look of utter disappointment. His eyes felt like they were piercing into me. I looked away and sat down.

'Jacob,' I nodded. He walked towards me.

'What, you weren't gunna let me in, no? You couldn't even answer the phone?' He looked at me, waiting for a response as I kept my head down sheepishly. He shook his head. 'Imagine that. You weren't even gunna let me in. I was about to start ringing your neighbours' doorbells, and then your aunty turned up. Don't you think that's weird? Strange, no? Like I was supposed to come in.'

Another one of our strange little coincidences, I thought. He sat down next to me on the sofa, sparking himself a cigarette and taking a few lugs in silence, like he was preparing himself for whatever he was going to say next.

'OK, first of all, let me make it very clear that I don't do this. I'm not this guy, I don't chase and ring down phones or turn up on doorsteps. This is a first for me. I'm not quite sure why I'm doing it, but I am, so I obviously care about you, a lot. I don't normally click with people the way I click with you. I don't know about you, but this is different for me, in a good way. Is it not for you? Do you feel like this with every guy you've been with?'

I shook my head and looked down again. He looked at me and frowned. 'Or yes?' he enquired.

I took a breath and sighed. 'Obviously I've been in love before so I have felt very strongly for someone. Relationships aren't as new to me as they are to you, but every person is different and the feelings you have for them are different. I haven't felt like this before, because what I have with you isn't the same as what I've had with anyone else. I just think maybe because you don't really get close to women, it's a bit more of a shock to your system than it is to mine. Does that make sense?'

'I get it. Why do you have to be so clever with your words all the time instead of just answering the question? My point is, if I feel like this, I can't just let it go without a good reason. And when it comes to your reasons, I don't understand them. I haven't done anything wrong. I didn't know this would happen, I never said I wasn't shagging anyone before you, and I was honest.'

'Well, you could have told me you hadn't used protection,' I glared at him.

'Trust me, I've been to the clinic, babe. Don't even worry about that.'

'Yes, I bloody will worry! How am I ever supposed to trust you? You can't help yourself! I know what you're like!'

'But I haven't done anything to you though?'

'So you say,' I muttered.

'Babe, don't be stupid. I'm with you every day! The most we're apart is a few hours!'

'Yeah, well you had time to meet her, so a few hours is all it takes,' I pointed out.

'I'm happy right now, I'm content, I don't want to fuck anyone else. I like what we have, it's real, I don't want to spoil it. And you're right! In the future it could happen, just like anything could happen – you could shag someone else!'

'Oh, shut up, Jacob,' I snapped.

'You know what I mean though,' he said.

'You're basically saying because you're happy, you're not gunna go out and shag someone, but what happens if you become unhappy?' I said.

'You are killing me, man. What do you want from me? Do you want me to pour my guts out? Get on my knees and talk a load of shit to you? I'm being real with you! You don't even know how I've changed for you, I'm trying here! You say I don't make you happy, but I know that's a lie! Look at me in my eyes and tell me I don't make you happy, and I'll walk out that door and you'll never have to see me again. Go on!' he glared at me.

I put my head down and looked at the floor.

'I haven't lied to you, I haven't got with anyone else. I know we argue a lot, but we are working on that.'

'What about your little mind games and control issues? Always playing games, tryna make me feel insecure so you have the power.'

'I don't know why I do that. We're both just very fiery, we seem to get a kick out of pushing each other's buttons. And *you* can talk about mind games, you're always threatening to leave! "If you keep pissing me off, I'll leave, this is all too much for me, I can't hack it, meh meh meh",' he mimicked me.

I glared at him again. 'Well, you threaten to leave me just to get a reaction. Like the fear of losing you will make me give you more. I see everything you try and do, it's just mind games. You can't play with me, I'm too clued up for you.'

'So, you know what it is! When we argue it's bullshit! Don't act like you're not just as bad as me, sometimes worse.'

'I only play with you 'cause you play with me, it's as simple as that! I don't like to play, but if you wanna play, I'll fucking play.'

'I don't wanna play anymore, it's draining,' he sighed, searching my eyes for some inkling of what I was thinking, as I stared at him blankly.

Then his mouth cracked into a wide grin. 'Can I have a hug, please? I really want a hug right now. Come on, just a hug. It's me!' He moved forward, trying to wrap his arms around me.

'No! I know what you're trying to do! Stop it!' I slapped his hands off me. 'You must be used to absolute melts! That shit doesn't work with me, pal! Listen to me!' I sat up and faced him, looking him straight in the eyes.

'Are you a snake?' I asked.

'What?' he frowned.

'Would you fuck over your mates, you know, one of your boys? Would you snake them?'

'No, obviously not! What kind of question is that?'

'So, when you're with someone, what is that person supposed to be to you if it's real?'

'Your lover?' he said questioningly.

'Yes, your lover and your...friend! In fact, when you're truly solid with someone they are supposed to be your best friend, closer than anyone. So they are really due even more loyalty than someone that's just your friend. So, if you wouldn't fuck over one of your friends, what makes you think it's OK to do it to the woman you're with? Because she's a woman and you have sexual feelings towards her as well, does that make it OK? You say you're not a snake and you could never snake your friends. But is your woman not your friend? Technically, cheating on a woman that is your friend and your lover is even worse than snaking one of your mates.'

'Woah, woah, woah, are we talking about you here or just women in general? 'Cause, as you know, most of the time women are my lovers not my friends, and I'm honest with them about the fact I'm not looking for monogamy.'

'I hear that, I also understand it, so let me put it to you like this. Am I your friend?'

'Yeah, you are, but when I'm...'

'Ah, wait! I haven't finished, we're talking about me and you now, not you and other women! Earlier, you said in a text you felt like I was your best friend. Right or wrong?'

'Yeah, I did.'

'So, are you the kind of person that would fuck over your best friend?'

'No, of course not. I see where you're going with this. Very clever, you little fucker,' he chuckled.

'Hey! Look at me in my eyes while I'm saying this! I want you to promise me, as your mate and swear to God, that no matter what happens, if you ever feel like you want to get with someone else, I don't care when or how, you will end it first. Literally, you do not have to say why, just end it.'

'Fuuuuck me, you are intense! Do you wanna bite my neck and take my blood while we're here?'

'Good! I'm glad you're feeling under pressure, I hope you snap and run away! Go for it! Because I'm good. I was happy to move on right now, but if you want it to continue, then you need to recognise the seriousness of this situation! I want you to feel it like a ton of bricks. And if you're not ready for it, there's the door. You need to realise this is a commitment, not a joke, and I am telling you from now, I'm not that woman who will sit back and think what I don't know won't hurt me. I wanna know everything! And I will dig to find out everything! And if

I get the slightest inkling that you are fucking me over or that you have disrespected me in any way, I will be straight out that door quicker than you can blink, and I will never come back. And that, my friend, is a promise. That is a threat. Loud and clear. Remember it.'

'Fair enough, I respect that,' he nodded.

'Well, like I said, you know where the door is, but if you wanna stay, you look your "friend" in the eyes right now and swear to God you won't lie to me.'

He put his hands on his head and sighed. 'You are hard work, mate. Why are you bringing religion into this?'

'Because I know that you worry more about what God thinks than what I do, and if you make a promise to God, you're taking it a lot more seriously. So go on, if you're being honest and you mean what you say, say it to God and look me in the eyes while you do it!'

'This doesn't even leave me room for a fuck-up, and I can't predict the future!'

'Well then, leave,' I shrugged. He sighed again and rubbed his hands over his face.

'OK, OK,' he sighed.

'Look at me, please,' I said sharply. He looked up into my eyes.

'OK, I swear to God.'

'Swear what?' I frowned.

'That I won't lie to you!' he bellowed.

'Good, now know this. If you ever do, you're a snake! You've fucked over your friend and lied to the Lord Himself and you'll have to live with that for the rest of your life.'

'You're actually mad, that is some deep shit you just pulled. You have a next-level way with words, you should have been a politician,' he laughed. I looked at him and grinned finally.

'Vote Little Mix!' I shouted, banging on the coffee table.

'You what?' he said, confused.

'You don't watch enough television, never mind,' I sighed, rolling my eyes at him.

'Shut up and give me a hug now, please,' he said, pulling me into his arms and smothering me. 'I actually thought I'd lost you for a minute then, didn't feel nice at all.'

'You're on a trial period, mate.'

'What? Shut up, man, you know you're happy I'm here right now, and that I came knocking on your door! Go on, lap it up, bighead!'

I giggled into his chest as he tickled me. 'Come on, come and meet my Aunty Maz properly. Time to meet the family and give you some more of that commitment pressure! Do you feel sick yet?' He pretended to barf all over me. 'You're not gunna last five minutes, mate.'

He glared at me before pinning me down and nuzzling his face into my chest, where he began kissing me slowly and seductively all the way up to my ear. I felt a tingle down my spine as I took in his familiar scent and felt his warm mouth and cool breath against my neck. He paused for a moment, leaving me in suspense before giving me a hard playful bite and whispering in my ear, 'I think we both know I last way longer than that.'

Chapter 18:

IT WAS ALL A DREAM

THE CELL DOOR clinked open, and the female officer looked at me sadly and shook her head.

'How the hell did you end up in here, ey, love? Your type just ain't built for it,' she sighed.

I looked up at her in silence, with a blank expression. I felt numb. Numb, and cold to the bone.

'Come on then, missy, lunchtime,' she smiled.

I stood up and looked down at my grey jumper and jogging bottoms – at least it was normal to wear comfortable clothes now. I followed the officer through the long corridors and past the other cells. Some of the doors were open and some closed. The other female inmates were scattered down the hall. Every head turned to look at me as I walked past, whispering and talking to each other, some laughing as they did. One of them called out to me.

'Nananiiii! I used to love you back in the N-Dubz days!

What the fuck happened, mate? Who would have thought you'd end up in here?'

I looked at her and raised my eyebrows sarcastically. 'Fish!' I called back to her.

'You what, love?' she said.

'Fuck it, shit happens,' I said. I held my head up and stared back at everyone that was staring at me before continuing to walk. I saw another face in front of me, not like the others. This face was glaring at me, angrily. It was a bigger girl, surrounded by a group of smaller girls. They all stared a hard cold stare as I got closer to them. The bigger girl was the one that stood out. She was the leader of the pack and I could tell she wanted trouble. I glanced at her and gave her a stern look before I carried on walking.

'Oi!' she shouted. 'You know my cousin Chantelle, innit! From back in the day! When you was about 17, you had a fight with her!' The female officer slowed her walking so she was stood by my side.

'Just carry on walking,' she whispered. I turned to look at the big girl.

'I remember her, she tried to jump me with six other birds,' I said.

'That's the one! A couple of your mates fucked her up afterwards,' she snapped.

'Well, it's a dog-eat-dog world, isn't it?' I replied.

She pulled her head back and laughed. 'This fucking bitch thinks she's the dog's bollocks!' She stood up from the wall she was leaning on and walked up to me till her face was close to mine. The female officer put her arm out in between us.

'Eeer, that's enough, thank you very much,' she said.

The big girl kept her stance and glared at me. I squared up to her and leaned my face forward, glaring back in silence. I could smell the Golden Virginia tobacco on her breath as she spoke.

'You ain't the fucking Female Boss in here, bitch! You're mine!' she spat at me.

I stood still and held my ground, looking back at her grimly and staying calm. She lifted her hand up to her neck and ran a finger across her throat, as if to slit it.

'Right, playtime is over, girls,' the prison officer said. 'Keep moving, please, as you were.' She pushed the big girl back towards the wall and grabbed my arm, pulling me along as she began to walk.

'You ain't gunna get far in here like that, girl. I tell you, pipe down, take the shit, and do your time. We can't protect you all the time.'

I pulled my arm out of her grip. 'Why? They're gunna fuck me up anyway? I might as well take it with pride,' I said.

'There's a difference between a beating and a razor in your back! Carry on and that's what you'll get.'

We entered the cafeteria and I quickly scanned the room.

'Go and get your food, I'll be standing in that corner till you're done,' said the officer.

I nodded and walked over to the queue and picked up a tray. The whole room stared at me and began talking about me amongst themselves. I moved down the queue and heard a loud slapping noise in front of me and jumped. I looked down to see a sloppy substance on my plate that had been placed there by a woman behind the counter. I stared at her blankly while she placed a small cake on the side of my tray and smiled at me before nodding to the left, gesturing for me to move on. I walked down to where I saw a drinks section to grab myself some water. All of a sudden, the big girl I had been in the confrontation with earlier appeared beside me. She towered over me, grinning evilly.

'I'll take that!' she said, snatching my cake. I stared down at my tray, before looking back up at her.

'Give me back my fucking cake,' I growled, and she took a step towards me.

'Why, what you gunna do about it, bitch?' she snarled. I locked my eyes onto hers.

'I said, give me back my fucking cake, now!'

I noticed her hand slip out from behind her back and I spotted the sharp silver blade. The moment felt like it went into slow motion as I watched her hand rise up and swing back. The light from the ceiling glistened against the blade as it reached its highest point. I jumped backwards with the tray still in my hands. As the blade came flying back down towards my face and missed, the big girl flew forward. I swung the tray up in the air, scattering the food everywhere. Then I crashed the tray down hard on her head with full force, watching her fall hard and flat to the floor with the blade glistening in her hand. I lifted up the tray and smashed it over her head again, harder this time, again and again, until she lay still. I looked around, coming back to my senses.

'Does anyone else fucking want some?' I screamed.

All of a sudden I was rushed and thrown down to the ground by a load of police officers that came out of nowhere. The side of my face hit the floor, next to where the big girl still lay. Both our heads were in the same position, facing each other. I felt the cuffs click hard and tight around my wrists, and I stared into her eyes as all the people around us rushed to her aid. It was like she was looking at me, but she wasn't, she was looking through me. I saw a thick layer of blood begin to spread across the floor from around her head, spreading further and further until it surrounded my face. I could feel it, smell it, practically taste it. I looked into her eyes one last time before the officers pulled me up from the floor. Her face was cold and lifeless, her pupils dilated.

She was dead.

The officers dragged me through the cafeteria and down the corridors back to my cell while I kicked and screamed. Everyone turned to look at me in horror and disgust this time. My body hit the hard cold floor of the small cell as the policemen threw me back inside. I looked up helplessly at the officer that was stood in the doorway glaring at me.

'You killed that woman!' he growled

'NO!' I screamed 'She was going to kill *me!*'

He shook his head and laughed. 'You better get used to this, darling, 'cause you're gunna be in here for a long time.'

I watched his face until the cell door slammed shut. The sound of metal hitting metal clanged in my ears. Crawling backwards into the corner and lifting my head back, I screamed a loud scream that turned into a cry. A piercing painful wailing noise that echoed past the four walls of the cell and throughout the prison. I felt as if every bit of hope I had in me was gone, and it was never coming back.

'Tulisa! Babe! Babe! Wake up!' I jumped out of my sleep, gasping for air. I felt the salty tears dripping into my mouth. 'Babe! You were crying in your sleep again!'

I recognised Jacob's voice. It took me a few seconds to realise it was a dream. The tears continued to drip down my face as I cried even harder. I felt his arms wrapped around me tightly.

'Sshhhh, it's alright, you're alright. It was just another dream, you're safe! I've got you,' he whispered, as I cried into his chest. Eventually I began to calm and the cries turned to whimpers and snivels.

'I'm sorry, I'm scared,' I whispered back.

'Ssshhh, I got you. I'm not going to let anything happen to you ever again.' He kissed my head and pulled me tighter into his chest. I took a deep breath and exhaled. I lay there still and silent but wide awake as Jacob fell back to sleep.

I looked at his fingers that were slid between mine as he held my hand to his chest, savouring the moment. He had saved me during one of the darkest times of my life. But now the darkest hours of all were fast approaching, and those I would have to face alone. Because in that courtroom (and in that cell, if it came to it), no one was going to hold my hand anymore.

It would just be me, against the world, and face it I would.

Chapter 19:

WHEN TU BECOME ONE

'COME ON, BABE, we're gunna be late,' I yelled up the stairs to Jacob. I could hear him still in the bathroom, spraying himself with the finest aftershave and God knows what else. 'It's never a good sign when a man takes longer than a woman to get ready, you know!'

'Oh, shut it, you mug!' he hollered back down the stairs.

I glanced outside through the huge floor-to-ceiling windows in the kitchen before returning my gaze to the mirror to fiddle with my new, very fancy and posh top hat for the day's special occasion. The sun was beaming, and it was a beautiful day outside! *Perfect day for a wedding,* I thought, *lucky buggers.*

It was a family friend's wedding, and Jacob was my plus one. I loved the fact he was coming with me and going to meet the whole family. It made me feel like we were solid. I was a little giddy and excited about it, but I also had a slightly unnerved feeling about the whole day. My trial was imminent at this point, but for once, the feeling didn't revolve around the trial. The night before, I'd had a strange feeling that I had mentioned to Cat. Randomly at around 12pm, sat with Cat on my sofa, it became so overwhelming I had turned to her out of the blue.

'I don't want him to come, Cat,' I said. She frowned, confused.

'Why not? What do you mean you don't want him to come? Of course you do, it's a big deal!' I shook my head at her.

'I'm telling you, I have a feeling, psychic glitch, a big one. It's fucking overpowering.'

'Oh, for fuck's sake, T, not one of them! How powerful are we talking? What is it? What are you sensing?'

'I don't know, like something really bad is going to happen, and whatever it is, it's going to be really bad. What if it involves me and Jacob?'

'What? But how? You're the happiest you've ever been with him. He's just asked to take you on holiday and he's going to a fucking wedding with you! Are you sure it's not the trial? It's getting close now.'

'No, it's not the trial. I mean of course I'm stressed about the trial but I'm always stressed about the trial. I don't know, Cat, this is something else. I'm just telling you what I sense. You mark my words, something's going to happen, I just know.'

'Well, what are you going to do?'

'I think I'm going to tell him not to come.'

'What? You can't do that! He'll be furious. He's gunna think something's wrong!'

'I don't know what else to do, Cat, it's really strong! I feel physically sick from it, I could literally heave! He doesn't wanna do all that family shit anyway, you know what he's like! I'm gunna text him and give him an excuse to get out of it. Hopefully, he takes it!'

I sat quietly for about two minutes before pulling out my phone and typing away:

T: Babe, thinking about tomorrow, it's all a bit
of a hassle. Probably easier if I just go on my own,
you're just gunna get hounded and draw more
attention. You really don't have to come, you
know, it's cool. x

J: What? What the fuck are you talking about?
You wanted me to come and I'm coming! What's
your problem now?

T: Nothing, babe, it's just a lot of hassle, I'm just
saying it's cool you don't have to x

J: shut up, I'm coming, see you tomorrow at 9 x

It didn't quite go to plan, obviously.

* * *

'Babe! Hurry up! Drew's gonna be outside soon to drive us! We're gunna be late!' I shouted up, agitated now.

I sighed before heading over to my laptop on the kitchen

counter to do a bit of writing and keep myself occupied while I waited.

The book, which had started off as a diary when all of this began, to document this inconceivable part of my life, had begun to take a more structured form. While reading it back, I noticed that my writing jumped between two different styles. At times it was more like a diary slash autobiography, and at other times it was more like a novel, from a first-person perspective. When I was reading the parts that were written in the more novel style, I became engrossed in my own story, as if it wasn't even mine.

This is good stuff, I thought.

I then began sharing my writing with friends, who were equally engrossed and became weekly subscribers to my latest chapters. And that's when I decided this wasn't going to be an autobiography about my year of love and hell. This was going to be a story. A story that anyone could read, not just a Tulisa fan or a lover of celebrity gossip. A story that could make people feel something. And the best part was, it was a real story, and it was mine.

I began tapping away eagerly, with the familiar intense frown that was my writing face when I was in the zone. I could do it for hours, sometimes through the night, and I would only realise how long I'd been going when I noticed the sunlight creeping through the curtains. It was a great and very much-needed escape during this time.

I heard heavy footsteps down the stairs that paused by the hallway mirror. 'Oh, here she goes! I can hear her typing away again on that book.' I heard Jacob's voice call from around the corner.

'Well, it's better than sitting here waiting for you and doing nothing,' I said sarcastically.

'And what's going in this book exactly?' he asked inquisitively.

'I told you, everything.'

'What... like... EVERYTHING, everything?'

'Yes, Jacob, EVERYTHING. I told you this when we first started dating. I'm writing a book and everything that happens in my life this year is going in the book, so if you have a problem with that, you're going to need to vacate my life. Problem?'

'It's just a lot, isn't it? Everyone's going to know about us, every detail. It's not the life I would choose to live. But what can I say? You're worth it. And I understand that this is your story and you should tell it, and anything that benefits you and helps you, I support you with.'

I stopped typing and smiled. *Cute,* I thought. 'You've become quite the leading man in the story,' I grinned.

'Oh, have I now? You better be making me sound good!' he said jokingly but stern.

I laughed heartily. 'You will sound as good as you are, mate. Remember that the next time you piss me off, it's going in the book!'

He popped his head around the corner and grinned. 'Wow! Powerful, babe, you look stunning.'

I gushed and put on my best girly voice. 'Why, thank you, kind sir, you don't look so bad yourself.'

He walked towards me and pulled me into his strong warm arms. I stared up into his big brown eyes and smiled. He leaned in and gave me a loving kiss before staring back at me.

I smacked him on the side of his bum cheek cheekily and pulled back.

'Come on, we've got to go! We're late!' I said. He grinned and slapped me back on the arse twice as hard.

'Come on then, bighead! Ladies first!'

When we arrived at the church, the ceremony had already started. I was mortified. Fashionably late, as usual. I tried to walk as quietly as possible to our seats but my big stilettos clonked against the hard church floor. Everyone turned to look at us.

'OMG, sit the fuck down quickly, I'm going to die,' I whispered. Jacob sniggered and jumped quickly into his seat before everyone eventually turned back around.

I sat quietly, trying to be serious, watching the bride and groom. Although I loved the idea of getting married myself one day, I found serious situations like this rather comical. The more serious something is supposed to be, the funnier I find it. Maybe it's a nervous thing. I felt a poke in my ribs and turned to Jacob and glared. He chuckled to himself quietly. I faced back towards the altar until I felt another poke.

'Stop it! Behave!' I whispered. He looked at me and grinned before poking me again. I slapped his hand away, trying not to laugh. We both faced forward with big grins on our faces, then we glanced back at each other again, bursting into a silent raspberry. I shook my head vigorously and punched him hard in the leg.

'Stop it! Why can't we just enjoy a wedding like normal people? Look around at everyone else and look at us! Behave! You're making me worse!' I whisper-shouted.

'I'm sorry, I can't help it. I know we're thinking the same thing, it's funny,' he giggled quietly.

'Stop it, or I'm not taking you anywhere ever again. Can't we be a nice normal couple for five minutes, at a wedding, enjoying the ceremony?' I said, trying to be serious.

'OK, babe, sorry.' He wrapped his arm around me and held my hand and placed a kiss on my cheek. As he did, the bride began to cry.

'Do you think you'd cry if we got married?' he whispered. 'No, I'd probably be laughing like I am now,' I whispered back.

'You bitch, I'd probably do the same,' he grinned. Then he leaned into my ear and whispered to me, 'Well, this is very romantic.' I burst into a silent fit of laughter until I had tears rolling down my eyes. He pressed his head into my neck, trying to hide his own amusement.

'You bastard! I hate you! Thank God we're sitting at the back.'

Once the ceremony was over, we all headed to the reception. Jacob was back to his best behaviour, being the ultimate gentleman, chatting away and entertaining my whole family. At one point a drink was spilt over my grandfather and he was quick to jump in to see if he was OK, helping him out of his wheelchair and getting him cleaned up. It was rather a cute moment, to be fair. But the person he was most impressive with was, of course, my mother.

My mum has suffered with schizoaffective disorder since I was born. It's a mental health disorder that consists of psychotic symptoms, hallucinations and delusions, as well as mood disorder which in my mother's case is bipolar. It's essentially a combination of schizophrenia and bipolar. Throughout my childhood there were a lot of episodes, breakdowns and hospitalisations. She was also misdiagnosed till I was about 17, which didn't help, as she was always on the wrong medication. Needless to say, my childhood wasn't exactly a walk in the park.

Jacob had gone to her side and stayed there from the moment we were allowed out of our seats in the church. I was still unsure what to make of it. I sat in the outside seating area with Jacob and my mum, sipping on a glass of champagne. It was a lovely reception, and everyone was in great spirits.

Jacob turned to my mother. 'Are you OK, Anne? Do you need anything?' My mum gave her usual sweet smile when she was in a good mood.

'No, sweetie, I'm OK, thank you.' My mother had a real air of innocence about her, very childlike and sweet when she was stable. I definitely got my soppy side from my mum, but I had always felt like I had to be the strong one and she was the child. I think a lot about the fact that our relationship isn't a typical mother-daughter scenario, and that I don't have those kind of 'every child needs their mother' feelings. I know she knows that, and that she longs for me to feel that way. At times I find it heart-breaking that I don't.

Jacob sat with his arm resting around her chair, like he was protecting her. I watched them intently. When Jacob was around her, it took the pressure off me. I felt relaxed.

'How's the house coming along, Anne?' Jacob asked. She'd recently had some decorators in.

'Oh yeah, do you need anything, Mum? New washing machine, dishwasher? Anything like that?' I chimed in.

'No, I'm fine, sweetie. The house is lovely! Though I did have a problem with the plumbing the other day,' she replied softly.

'What's wrong with it? Who do you call when you have problems in the house and need something done, Anne?' asked Jacob. She paused for a moment. Sometimes she would take a while to register a question.

'Eeerm, I don't really know,' she said, looking a little glazed. This was something some of her carers would deal with, but she was struggling to remember. I went to repeat the question for her to understand but Jacob gently lifted a hand down by his leg to stop me. I felt like he'd already completely got the gist of her behaviours and I found it fascinating to watch, considering it wasn't anything I had ever witnessed with anyone else I'd brought around her.

'Anne, where's your phone?' he asked.

'Oh, it's here, sweetie,' she said, while continuing to stare into the distance for a moment before shakily pulling it out of her pocket to show him.

'I'm going to put my number in here under Tula/Jacob, and whenever you have any problems at home, any time or day, no matter how often, from plumbing to a lift shopping, I want you to call me, and I will come round or send someone round straight away. Do you understand, Anne? Any problems at all,' he said to her softly. My mum's eyes lit up.

'Really? Oh, that's lovely, Jacob! Are you sure?' She smiled widely.

'Of course I'm sure, Anne. Tulisa is with me, I take care of her, and you are her mother so I will take care of you as well.' He smiled at her.

'Oh, you're so kind, Jacob. Thank you ever so much, that's lovely to know.' She gave him a big kiss and a hug. I'd never seen her like a boyfriend of mine so much. Hardly surprising though, was it? I gave him a look, a mixture of confusion and appreciation. He pinched my cheek and smiled.

'I'm going to get us some more drinks, Anne. T, what would you like?'

'Usual for me, babe,' I said.

'I'll have another diet coke please, Jacob,' said my mum.

'Are you sure you don't want a little glass of champagne, Anne?' he said.

'Oh no, no, not for me, I don't drink.'

'That's very good, Anne – it's terrible stuff,' he grinned. He leaned over to kiss me on the cheek and whispered in my ear 'opposite to her daughter then'. He stood up and winked. I gave him a sly middle finger under the table while smiling sweetly so my mum couldn't see. As he walked off, she turned to me.

'Oh, isn't he lovely, Tula?! I love him, oh I hope you stay together. Do you think you could get married?' she asked sweetly. I laughed loudly.

'Oh, Mum, we're a long way from that. Let's see if we get past the six-month mark first, ey?' She looked at me with a little sadness in her eyes now.

'It's nice seeing someone taking care of you for a change. You're always looking after yourself, so stern all the time. It's OK to need someone you know, sweetie, someone to love you and rely on.' I smiled at her and sighed.

'I know, Mum, but no one will take care of me better than me. You have to have your own back before anyone else can, trust me! Anyway, I haven't done so bad, have I?' I said with a little wink.

'No, you've done amazing. My little girl is a superstar! I'm so proud and happy for you, sweetie!'

My mum wasn't really aware of the trial and what was going on. It was too much for her to comprehend and her short-term memory would make her forget, so I didn't plan to tell her until just before the week it would actually start.

She continued, 'I just mean I want you to be happy, with a man, to protect you. You've always been on your own, always.'

'Don't you worry, Mum, I'll be just fine. We don't need a man – girl power, remember? The Spice Girls!'

'Oh yes, of course – they were your favourite! Remember

"Mumma I Love You"! I loved that song.' I smiled at her and gave her a little hug and a kiss.

'Of course I do, Mum! Mine too, kiddo! Mine too.'

A few hours later and the party was in full swing. Jacob was sat inside with my mum, keeping her entertained, and I went outside for a quick cigarette. As I got outside, I saw a group of guys from the wedding in the seating area. They clocked me straight away.

'Tulisa! Mind if we have a picture?' one of the guys called over to me.

'Yeah, course, Hun!' I said, making my way towards them. 'You want individuals, or a group shot?' I asked.

'Nah, I want one on my own, mate. Forget this lot,' one said, and they all laughed. I did the rounds and took a picture with all of them, one by one.

'All sorted!' I exclaimed.

'Nah, actually I was wondering if you could do one sitting on my lap or giving me a kiss on the cheek,' said one of the guys cheekily.

'Ooh, I don't know about that, mate. I don't think my fella would be too happy if he walked round the corner and saw me on a stranger's lap, kissing him on the cheek!' I laughed.

'Oh go on, it's just a photo. We're your fans, he should understand that,' he moaned.

'Nah, mate, I don't think so. It's not really appropriate. Either way, nice to meet you all though, enjoy your night,' I replied.

'Fair enough,' the guy frowned. His mates all chuckled.

I began walking away towards the field behind the reception area to finish my smoke. I looked out towards the forest in the distance at the end of the field. If Jacob hadn't been inside, I'd probably have taken a little stroll with my drink and popped my headphones in for some tunes. Whenever I had a drink I would usually at some point during the night get the urge to wander off on my own and find a nice spot so I could listen to some music. I was a typical INFJ (Introverted, Intuitive, Feeling and Judging) personality type. I looked across the field at the forest and the sun setting behind it. This was my kind of setting for a serious iPod session. I could've quite happily disappeared for an hour into that field for some chill time and then headed back inside, but I couldn't leave Jacob.

I zoned into the quiet and peaceful sound of nature in front of me, trying to ignore the hustle and bustle of the reception in the background. I could make out an owl calling in the forest. In my family it was Greek superstition that the call of an owl was a bad omen that you should avoid listening to. I've always been a little superstitious on a minor level but not with things like that. I couldn't understand how such a beautiful creature could represent something bad, but Grandmother's words still somehow made it feel spooky. I felt a shiver run down my spine. *There's that funny feeling again*, I thought. All of a sudden, I felt two hands quickly grab me with extreme strength from behind. I jumped and gasped for air as I tried to spin around.

'Boo!' yelled Jacob. I let out a big sigh of relief.

'You fucking dickhead! Don't do that to me! You know I hate things that make me jump! I can't take it with these bloody heart palpitations!'

He cackled in amusement. 'Well, you shouldn't be walking out here all by yourself then, should you?! You never know what's lurking in those woods!'

'A few owls and some fresh greenery! My kind of place,' I said.

'Yeah alright, Mother Earth! Hug a few trees while you were out here, did ya?'

'No, but I'd like to hug you right now.' I wrapped my arms around him and looked into his eyes. He looked very tipsy, with that red eye-glazed look.

'Thank you for what you did earlier for my mum. That was really kind of you. Honestly, I really appreciate it.' I kissed him on the lips.

He pulled back and smiled. 'Listen, it's standard. You're with me so she's with me. I got you.' He kissed me again. I nuzzled my head into his chest and squeezed him. I stayed there for a moment, taking in his scent as he rested his head against my neck and pulled me into him tightly.

'See, you can be nice,' he whispered.

'What do you mean? I *am* nice,' I replied.

'No, you know what I mean. Soft, feminine, a woman!'

'I *am* a woman, I just need to feel secure to show you that,' I whispered back.

'I could do this forever, you know, this is me. When you're like this, I feel proper happy with you. I can just graft, stay focused, build a future, do my thing and come back to this, happily! When we're at our best there ain't nothing else out there for me. I don't need anything else, just don't let me down, man.' He kissed me on the forehead.

'Vice versa,' I said. We both remained staring into each other's eyes.

'Oi, Tula bula! What are you two doing out here?! Speeches are about to start – get inside, you little lovebirds! Save it for later,' called my Aunty Jill from a distance.

'Come on, my little stallion! Let's go inside!' I said.

'Stop saying little, you patronising little shit!' he frowned.

'Babe, you know I say little with everything – little walk, little bit of food, little drive, you little bastard!' I laughed.

'I know, my little lady. Now get your ass inside,' he said sternly, smacking me on the bum.

'Yes, sir,' I grinned.

'That's more like it,' he smiled.

Later on, I was stood by the bar getting some more drinks for me and Jacob. He had gone outside for a cigarette and I spotted him strolling back inside with another man. They seemed to be chatting away rather boisterously, and I could tell that Jacob was drunk now. I squinted to see who the other male was next to him. As they got closer, I realised it was the same guy I'd had a photo with outside earlier on, who had asked me to sit on his lap.

Jacob's eyes locked with mine as he came towards me, and I saw a familiar glare in them that I knew all too well now. If Jacob had too much to drink when he was around me, there was always going to be a problem. The strange thing was that he wasn't bad with a drink in him in general. I had known him as a friend before we got together and he had always carried himself well, but when he drank around me now, it seemed to do something to him. I was beginning to put it down to the fact that it was because he couldn't handle his emotions.

'Babe, why have you been bullying this young lad?' He glared at me, the turn was instant.

'What? What the fuck are you on about? Are you taking the piss right now?' I snapped.

'Nah, I ain't. What you hyping for, causing trouble, telling him you can't take a photo 'cause your fella will beat him up?! What's wrong with you and your fucking attitude, man?'

The guy stood next to him like he was having the time of his life and piped in, 'I don't wanna cause you two any drama. I was just telling him that there was a better way you could of gone about it. You were a little bit rude with it, no offence.'

Jacob slapped him hard on the back. 'Don't worry, son. She gets a bit lairy sometimes – she's a bit of a wild spark, she just needs reminding to rein it in,' he boomed.

I stood in silence, looking at the both of them, with my jaw nearly to the floor. I was mortified. I couldn't believe what I was seeing and hearing. Me and Jacob could argue and he could be an asshole at times, as could I. But this, this I had never seen before. He had taken the word of a guy he'd just met and used it to start an argument and humiliate me in front of a complete stranger. A guy who he clearly didn't give a shit about and was patronising, like he gave birth to him. Yet still he was pretending to defend him over me. I was flabbergasted. What the fuck was going on?

'Woah woah woah, stop right fucking there, right now! How dare you?! First of all, Mister!' I turned to the guy next to him. 'You don't go round asking women to kiss you on the cheek and sit on your lap! My response to your request was perfectly polite with a bit of banter, said in jest! I was laughing and smiling when I said it. I didn't make any threats or imply anything, so I don't know why you've now made yourself busy, going up to my boyfriend and starting trouble!' I said sternly.

Then I turned to Jacob. 'As for you, my fucking partner, the person who you already forgot after a few wines that you're meant to be a "team" with! You don't know this fucking guy from Adam! The guy was trying to get me to sit on his lap, so I politely told him where to go! I simply said, my boyfriend wouldn't like it! In a jokey way, and now you're standing here, practically ganging up on me with him, accusing me of something I didn't do, over this random guy's bullshit story!'

The guy tried to pipe in, 'Listen, I was just...'

I raised my hand at him. 'Stay the fuck out of this for a moment, please, I think you've done enough damage. Now I'm gunna end up being rude.'

'Watch your fucking mouth, man,' snapped Jacob. I stared at him and shook my head, I still couldn't believe it.

'What the fuck are you doing? Have you lost your fucking mind? Is this a joke? Is this a wind-up? Am I on camera right now? Are you actually registering what you're doing?' I yelled at him.

'Don't raise your voice in here, let's take this outside,' Jacob snapped.

'Outside? We're going home, mate!'

Chapter 20:

IT WOULD NEVER HAPPEN TU ME

AN HOUR LATER, after an awkward cab journey, we were back in our area.

'Take a left here please, boss,' I said to the cab driver.

'Where are you going?' snapped Jacob.

'Back to mine!' I snapped back.

'Don't listen to her, mate. Straight on and to the right,' he said to the driver.

'No, driver, left here please, I want to go...'

Jacob lifted his hand over my mouth. 'Don't listen to her. I'm the man in this car, this is my woman and I'm taking her home.' I pushed his hand away from my mouth.

'Fuck you, Jacob! I'll walk! Stop the car right now, driver!'

I felt the car come to a halt, and I jumped out of the taxi. I saw a local park I recognised and stormed towards the entrance. I'd never actually come here before, only driven past it, but I assumed I could somehow cut through the park and come out on a main road, where I could get a cab. I heard Jacob get out and slam the car door behind me as I reached the park. I could hear the sound of his stomping feet getting closer behind me, then I felt two hands land on my arms and spin me around.

'Stop running away all the time, expecting me to chase you! I have never chased a woman so much in my fucking life! I'm not doing it anymore. If you run off again, I'm not coming after you, and I can promise you that! Now sit on that bench and talk to me,' he glared.

I looked up at him with my blood boiling. He hadn't got over these mind games, he'd had a drink tonight and it was all coming out.

'Do you not see what happened back there? Are you delusional?' I yelled.

'No, I ain't fucking delusional! You're delusional! You got a big fucking mouth and an attitude problem and you need to pipe the fuck down before you get me into an argument 'cause of it!' he shouted.

'Oh, I think you can do that all by yourself, big bollocks! You were completely fooled by a stranger tonight! You sided with some random guy you had just met and attacked me with him for no reason! Do you know how fucked up that is? Do you think I'm a fucking liar? When he says I said one thing and I look at you and say I said another, you believe *me*! What happened to the fucking team? Do you know how weak we just looked? Like a pair of fucking twats! It's embarrassing! I can't fucking believe it!' My face was hot and bright red with anger now. I wanted to grab him and literally slap some sense into him, shake him into reality. Yet he was stood there looking at me like he wanted to do the same thing to me.

'Your fucking attitude is embarrassing! You just can't fucking help yourself! Why can't you just pipe the fuck down! Act like a fucking lady! You don't have a pair of bollocks! I do! I have the balls and I have the dick! Deal with it or fuck off!' he said furiously.

I looked at him, shaking my head. Who was this person? This wasn't my Jacob. There was no getting through to him, he was just on a mission to destroy our relationship. I felt the frustration building up inside me. I wasn't sad or angry, I was beyond both. I felt on the edge, like I couldn't take anymore – this was getting ridiculous.

'Why are you doing this?!' I screamed. 'This isn't even an argument! You've just started something for no reason! Because you're fucking drunk and you can't handle your emotions and you're taking it out on me! You wanna know what your fucking problem is?! I'll tell you what your fucking problem is! You're scared! You're fucking shitting yourself! Because you've finally got feelings for someone that you can't control! Because you're in love with me and you can't fucking admit it! To yourself, let alone me!' I shrieked.

He placed his hands on his hair and shook his head. 'So if you know that then why the fuck do we keep doing this?! Why can't you just act fucking proper?!' he yelled.

'Oh my God!' I screamed. 'What are you on about?! I *am* acting proper! I can't fucking do this anymore! I can't! You're fucking killing me here! It's too much!' I felt the tears from all the frustration begin to stream down my face. I started to sob, real heartfelt painful sobs; I wanted to scream.

'No fucking more, Jacob! No more! I am not letting you do this to me! I am done. I am fucking done with you! No more of this bullshit! Enough now. We are over! Stay the fuck away from me. No more games, no more calling me tomorrow and making up! That's it! We are through! Fuck off now!'

'Go! I'm not fucking chasing you this time!' he yelled.

I turned towards the park and stormed off in tears. I was done tonight, I had had enough, well and truly. He had pushed me too far. As far as I was concerned, we were finished. As I made my way sobbing through the dimly lit park, I noticed there was a large, high metal fence that surrounded the field and behind the fence was a pathway that led to the way out. *How the hell do you get to the pathway behind the fence?* I thought. I scanned the field and spotted a streetlamp right at the end of the field, next to the fence, where it met a line of trees. It looked as if there was an opening down there onto the path. My arms were crossed as I cried and stomped my way through the grass, deeper into the field. I could feel the heels of my Louboutins sinking into the mud with each step.

Great! Now I've fucked my new shoes as well! I knew bringing him to the wedding was a bad idea! I bloody knew it!

I'd been walking for a minute when I realised how dark and quiet it had got, all of a sudden. I glanced back at the entrance in the distance. I couldn't hear any cars anymore. I looked forward towards the streetlamp. I registered that I was alone in a dark park in the middle of the night in high heels and a pretty little dress. *This probably wasn't the best idea*, I thought, but the streetlamp didn't look too far now. If I could just get on that path, I was sure it would lead me to the main road on the other side of the park.

I went into my bag and pulled out my house keys, slipping a key in between each of my fingers, giving a knuckleduster effect. It was a trick I had been told to use by the lads when I was younger if I was ever in trouble or under attack to protect myself. I clenched my fist tightly with the keys poking out. *Better safe than sorry*, I thought, as I continued to stagger through the field. The grass had got high and the mud was thick. I could just about step through it without falling over.

When I eventually reached the streetlamp, I squinted as I thought I could see what looked like a wall behind the trees. I walked a little closer until I could see it clearly. It was a dead end! No opening! Bollocks! Now what was I going to do? I'd have to go back, there was no way out. I felt the tears begin to sting my eyes again as I whimpered in distress. *Please, God, help me out. Can this night get any worse?* I wanted to slump to the floor and cry my eyes out, but I couldn't because of all the mud. So, I just stood there, in the middle of a field, with only a dim street light, crying in the dark.

All of a sudden I jumped out of my emotional state as I heard a snap. It sounded like a stick breaking in the bushes, as if someone had stepped on it. I froze, quickly scanning the bushes and trees. What the fuck was that? I listened and watched intently as my heart began to thump harder in my chest. Was there somebody else here? I jumped again as I heard a rustle in the bushes. I felt the fear taking me over. *Please, Lord, let that be an animal,* I thought. My eyes locked on to the bushes where the noise came from.

I spotted movement, there was something inside them.

My eyes widened with fear as I saw the dark figure in the shadows. Then, to my horror, it dashed out from behind one bush and into another, revealing its true form for only seconds in the dim light. It was a tall dark figure, hunched over and creeping like an animal through the trees, but it wasn't an animal. It was a man.

My heart almost stopped in my chest as every woman's worst nightmare became my reality. I felt no emotion other than pure fear surging through my bones. I couldn't move and I couldn't breathe. I watched the figure continue to shuffle around in the bushes as it watched me from the shadows. It slowly began to creep to the edge of the bush till eventually, it sprung out into the light.

The streetlamp was behind him so the front of him was in shadow, but I could just about make out his face. He was slightly crouched with his arms out and hands spread by his sides, like an animal ready to pounce. He was a big guy, not wide, but very tall, and he looked very strong.

He was dressed in a black tracksuit with a rucksack on his back. He looked middle-aged with tanned skin, dark eyes and a shaven head, but the thing that stood out the most was his smile. He was grinning at me evilly, showing his teeth. He stayed crouched and still, watching me with his evil eyes glistening through the shadows. I was frozen in shock and fear, when all of a sudden he made a loud sound. 'Hssssssssssss,' he hissed like a snake.

I jumped. My mouth dropped open in pure horror and my body began to shake. His smile and eyes widened even more at my reaction, as if he'd become even more excited by my fear. He began to creep towards me slowly, still smiling, with the look of pure thrill on his face. Reality began to kick in as I switched into survival mode and my brain began working again. I couldn't run – he would be faster than me. He was stronger with longer legs and he was wearing flat shoes. Even if I kicked off my heels and ran with bare feet he would have the advantage, plus I would probably slip in this mud.

I also didn't want to turn my back on him.

I visualised a knife stabbing me from behind. He could have had anything in that rucksack or in his pockets. I couldn't turn my back on him, I was better off facing him head on. Either way there was about to be a struggle and it would be me or him going down. I clenched the keys in my fist. *He probably doesn't know I'm holding them,* I thought. *I look like a weak vulnerable girl crying in a field, let him think that.* I slipped the hand with the keys behind my back. *When he gets within reach, stay looking scared and wait till he gets close, then kick him in the nuts full throttle*, I thought.

I visualised myself doing the forward karate kick that my Uncle B had taught me when I was a child. You have to step into the kick and push out with the base of your foot, pushing your attacker away from you. If I could get him in the nuts and injure him, I could lay into him with my fist of keys. Then, run. Run for my fucking life. I had one shot at taking him out. If he got me in his grip, I knew I was fucked. My thoughts raced as I tried to conjure up my escape strategy within seconds as my attacker was creeping closer all the while.

I stepped to the left, slightly moving away from him but to the side, so I stayed facing him. He pounced to the left as if to make me jump and hissed loudly again. *Fuck fuck fuck*, I thought. *Help me, Lord, please help me!* My eyes locked with his, still terrified and shaking, trying to prepare myself for a counter-attack. How the fuck was I going to do this? This wasn't a play fight, this wasn't a fucking computer game! I'm five foot six and eight stone against a six-foot hissing psychopath. *This could be it, this could be how it all ends!* My whole life felt like it was flashing before me. I pictured myself lying dead in a ditch and the reactions of my loved ones. He was about six feet away from me now, his evil eyes and grin looking even more sinister up close. I felt the panic rise up in me and I gritted my teeth, trying to find strength through my tears. He looked at my face and cackled like he was getting off on it.

He's nearly here, I thought. *Get ready!*

He spread his fingers out wider and twiddled them, hissing at me loudly again. It sent chills down my spine. *You sick evil fuck,* I thought. *You can't fucking have me! I'll fucking have you first, you bastard!*

I leaned back and lifted my leg slightly, getting ready for the kick. He reached his hands forward as if he was about to go for my arm. I held my breath in my throat, my heart beating a hundred miles an hour, like the adrenaline was the only thing stopping me from passing out from the sheer terror of the situation. *Help me, Lord, please!* I screamed in my head one last time.

All of a sudden, out of nowhere, I heard a deep booming voice in the distance behind me

'OOOOOIIIIIII! Don't you fucking touch her!' roared the male voice.

The words echoed through the field. The man in front of me froze and his eyes widened, his evil grin dropped into a look of fear. He looked behind me and then looked at me again.

'OOOOOIIIIIII! Get the fuck away from her!' The angry voice boomed from behind me. The voice was getting closer, they were running, and fast. A feeling of pure euphoria and relief came over me as I recognised the voice. It was as if the clouds had opened up and God Himself had answered my prayers!

It was Jacob!

I looked at the man before me who was now in a state of panic, like he didn't know what to do. He was still glancing at me and then behind me, his eyes going back and forth. *Run!* I thought. *Turn around and run to Jacob, now!* Before I could even think twice, I spun around and began dashing through the mud towards his voice, high heels still on, slipping and sliding through the field – there was no time to take them off.

'Jacob!' I screamed at the top of my lungs. 'Jaaaaacob! Help me! Pleeeeaase!' I shrieked.

'Tulisaaaa!' he shrieked back at me. I spotted his white shirt in the distance, he was running towards me at full speed. My heart pounded even harder at the sight of him and I began to sob uncontrollably.

'Jaaacob!' I shrieked again. I was barely running now, it was more of a drag.

I was giving Laura Dern in *Jurassic Park* vibes, 'ALAAAAAN, RUN, RUN'.

He sprinted towards me until he caught me, as I fell into his arms, bursting into a fit of tears and wailing loudly. 'The... there was a man,' I gasped through my sobs, 'a... a man in the bushes!'

He grabbed me and pulled my head into his chest with both hands, panting loudly, out of breath. 'I know, I know, I saw him, shhhhhhh, he's gone, he ran, it's OK, I got you, you're safe, sshhhhhh.'

I was shaking uncontrollably in his arms in complete shock as he held on to me tightly, catching his breath.

'Oh my God, my poor baby, what the fuck was he gunna do to you? I'm never letting you out of my sight again. I'm so sorry, I can't believe it. Look at me, I'm shaking – I feel sick at the thought,' he panted.

I looked up at him into his eyes. I saw the fear in them, the fear of the thought of what could have happened.

'You saved me,' I whimpered, 'you came after me, you saved me. Imagine if you hadn't. You saved me, Jacob.' I clung on to his shirt and cried to him. He kissed me on the head.

'That's it! Never again! You're not going anywhere without security, anywhere!' he shouted angrily.

'Please don't be mad, I'm safe now,' I sobbed.

'I feel sick, I feel fucking sick! Feel my heart, I can't bear the thought.' He shook his head and squeezed me tightly, kissing me again on the head. 'Come on, I'm taking you home, right now.'

He lifted me up into his arms and began carrying me through the muddy grass.

I lay my head on his chest, still in tears.

Imagine if he hadn't come after me, I thought. I'd had a feeling about today! But I hadn't expected anything like this. But then again, in my crazy world, did it really surprise me?

At least there would be one positive out of it – what a chapter for the book!

Chapter 21:

HAPPY BIRTHDAY TU YOU

I WOKE UP groggily in my bedroom and lay still, looking up at the ceiling. It was July 13th, and it was my birthday. Tomorrow would be the first day of the trial, and I was not a happy bunny. Last night I had gone out with Daz, and Michelle who was down for the weekend, and we'd had a big blow-out. When every day feels like one of your last possible days of freedom, it's difficult to set yourself healthy limits. I was absolutely hanging out of my asshole.

I had told everyone that I didn't want any cards or presents, no trying to chirp me up and most definitely no singing! This was my second birthday I would spend on a drugs charge. I was now closer to 30 than 20, and I had wasted the last year closer to my teens with this massive weight on my shoulders. I was 24 when this had started and the feeling of turning 26 and still going through it was grating on me. *They should have left me in remand*, I thought.

I could have done half the time by now or even be out and it would have been over with.

Compared to how my life used to be, the year running up to the trial might as well have been spent in prison. Not being able to work, tarnished, stagnant, trapped, and as far as most people were concerned, guilty before charged. As far as I was concerned, this wasn't a life. I wasn't living, I was just plodding along and waiting. I wanted today to be over with. I didn't even want to acknowledge the fact that it was my birthday. The thought of people being happy around me, and me blowing out candles made me feel sick. This was no time for celebrations. From tomorrow, shit was about to get real. To make matters worse, Jacob was abroad for work that he couldn't cancel for the weekend. He would arrive back tomorrow while I was in court, not that he could come to court anyway. We'd managed to hide from the press so far, and this was definitely not the time for our relationship to become public. But I was upset that he couldn't be with me today and tonight.

My phone began to ring, it was Jacob: 'Happy birthday, Princess! How you feeling?'

'Like shit,' I grunted.

'Oi! Remember what we said! Positive thinking! Stop all that! It's your birthday! Go out with your friends and enjoy yourself!'

'Meeeeeh,' I made my silly noise. 'I don't want to enjoy myself. I could be going to prison in three weeks, I need to get in the right frame of mind to prepare for the worst.'

'Shut up, man, you're not going anywhere. But I hear you, just do what makes you happy today.'

'Cool, I'll speak to you in a bit,' I said moodily.

'Alright,' he sighed. I hung up.

I could hear Michelle's chirpy booming voice heading up the stairs, she must have heard I was awake. The door burst open and she ran into the room with arms open wide.

'Haaaaappy birthdaaaaay to youu!' she began to sing loudly.

I grabbed the covers over my head and buried myself under them. 'Nooo!' I yelled 'Stop! Not today! Please!'

I had always hated my birthday because something bad always seemed to happen on it, ever since I was a child, like some kind of weird birthday curse. And they always made me super-emotional and anxious. I was the same around Christmas and New Year. My friends nicknamed me the Grinch. I pulled my head back out from the covers and saw Gareth running in after her and signalling to her to cut it out. I looked up at him as if in pain.

'I tried to tell her,' he said, trying not to laugh. Michelle continued to belt it out until she finished and plonked herself happily on the end of my bed.

'Mate! What do you mean, not today! I can't fucking sing happy birthday any other day can I, ya twat?' She laughed her usual loud hearty laugh. Me and G looked at each other, shaking our heads, and I chuckled.

'Alright, alright, I won't be a misery guts and stay in bed all day. I'll get up, but I do have one birthday request in exchange.'

'What's that?' asked Michelle.

'I'm dying for a coffee,' I grinned. Gareth looked at me and frowned.

'Bitch! Don't even go there, you get one of those every day! How about today I won't spit in it, just 'cause it's your birthday, maybe even pop some cream in as well for the special occasion!'

Michelle burst into a raging fit of laughter, rolling around at the end of the bed, followed by Gareth. I tried to hold it in, but it was no use, I burst out laughing too. I smiled to myself. At least I could still have a laugh.

I managed to manoeuvre my drained hungover body from the bed to the sofa in the upstairs lounge, where I put on the telly and spent the day lounging with Michelle. My head was pounding, and I felt really ill. The thought of going to court tomorrow was making me feel a lot worse. It didn't feel like my birthday, it felt like the worst day ever.

Later on, Daz came round to chill with us and brought us some food from a local Greek restaurant he'd found, as my favourite one was closed. When he arrived, it was like the clouds opened up and an angel walked in bearing gifts! I was actually starving for once. I hadn't been eating and my weight had plummeted to seven stone ten pounds. We laid out all the food on the table and got stuck in. But we instantly looked at each other in dismay as we took our first bites.

'That's absolutely minging, mate,' said Daz. Michelle pulled a funny face as she nibbled on her piece of chicken.

'I would expect nothing less today. Don't worry, Daz, it ain't your fault!' I sighed.

'Sorry, kids, favourite's not open! Chinese, anyone?' he said. Michelle nodded her head.

'Yes, please. I can't eat that, tastes like shit on a plate,' she said. They both looked at me for agreement.

'I don't mind, guys, whatever you want, I've lost my appetite.'

Michelle instantly piped up. 'No fucking way, mate, you need to eat! I'm sorry, T, but you're starting to look ill! If you get any smaller, I'm gunna report you missing!' She chuckled.

'She's right, T, you have lost a lot of weight. You're the skinniest bird I know, to be fair, and that ain't a compliment,' said Daz. I looked up from my phone where I was texting Jacob.

'Alright I'll eat, chill out.' We had been texting all day as normal, but in the past hour the texts had taken a strange turn. They had become snide, like he was digging at me for something, and I had no idea why.

'Brilliant!' I turned to Daz. 'It's my fucking birthday, I've got court tomorrow and your mate's gone on the turn for no reason! Absolutely charming! I'm not even entertaining this shit today, I'm not in the mood. He wants me to snap and give him a reaction, I can tell.'

'What's wrong with the old fella?! What have you done to piss him off now? You two are just sumin else, I don't even have any words for it anymore. You're the girl and boy version of each other, absolute power trips.'

'I haven't done anything this time, he's just got the hump for some reason, he's acting weird.'

Daz shook his head and shrugged. 'I dunno with you two anymore. Anyway, where's Gareth?' he asked.

'He's downstairs, locked in his room as usual, doing his detective work.'

'Detective work?' enquired Michelle.

'Inspector G, mate! Trust me, he's obsessed!' I said, shaking my head.

She laughed.

'Tell him to come and eat with us. What's wrong with him?' said Daz.

'Trust me, he won't leave his room. The trial starts tomorrow, these are his last precious moments to do his digging.'

'Digging for what?' Daz asked, confused.

'It's literally all he does. I'm with Jacob most of the time, and he stays locked in his bedroom studying Mahzer Mahmood and the case. He's bloody brilliant at it, to be fair though. I told him he should become a private detective, he's discovered a hell of a lot,' I exclaimed.

'What's he looking for?'

'Everything he can find. He's trying to find links between every single person we've met in the past three years to the sting. He wants to find out who was sent in, who was real, who's not, and most of all, he wants to find the source, the person they are claiming gave them the information that kick-started their investigation. We know that either someone's lied or the source doesn't even exist.

And without the source or some evidence to prove that I was a drug dealer, and that's what led them to set me up, their whole case becomes useless. But because of a legal technicality called journalistic privilege, the prosecution doesn't have to declare who or what the source is.

'They obviously have no source and only did this for a story, but I can never prove that because they don't have to reveal where it came from. They planned this from the start – they know the system and they are using the legal loopholes to their advantage. I can't even tell my side of the story because I'd have to bring Nish the PA into it, and I'm legally not allowed to because of journalistic privilege. It's so fucked up, from them to the courts, to the CPS, the whole thing is rigged. They know what's happening and they're just letting it happen because of a legal loophole.

'Gareth's currently looking for potential witnesses that could dish the dirt on Mahmood. People that have worked with him in the past. He's studied all of his cases and probably knows everything there is to know about the guy, how he operates, and who with. He's uncovering his team, who he's set up and how, his illegal movements during his stings and how he covers them up. Anything that can help my case and solidify my defence.'

'I can't get my head around it all!' said Daz.

'Me neither, Daz, me neither,' I sighed. Then I got up and headed to the toilet with my phone in my hand.

As I got into the bedroom, I saw a text from Jacob. My heart felt like it stopped in my chest as I read it. I started to feel dizzy as I took in the words. I staggered backwards towards my wardrobes, rested my back against them and slid down till I was sat on the floor. I felt a heavy weight in my chest and my heart began to pump hard, a lump rose in my throat and I felt like I was going to puke. *Just breathe*, I thought, *breathe*! I heard Michelle call to me as she headed towards my room.

'T! Do you know where the...' She stopped in my doorway and noticed me on the floor.

'T?' Her facial expression instantly changed as she rushed down to me, concerned. 'T? What's happened? Are you alright?'

My breathing was heavy, like I was having another one of my panic attacks that Michelle had witnessed many times before.

'It's alright, baby, just tell me what's wrong,' she said, stroking me. I looked up at her and shook my head. I couldn't speak. I lifted up the phone and handed it to her as I began to cry. She took the phone from my hand and looked at it. She paused for a second, as I watched her face begin to turn bright red with anger.

'You fucking what?' she yelled. 'You fucking what? Is this a fucking joke?' she bellowed in her thick Manchester accent. Her piercing blue eyes turned devilish with fury. Michelle was one scary bitch when she was angry.

'DAAAAAZ!' she roared. She got up and stormed out of the bedroom and into the living room with the phone. I could hear her raging voice boom throughout the house. 'Does someone want their fucking bollocks chopping off? Does he think he can mess with my girl like that? Does he

244

know who he's fucking dealing with?!' I sat on the floor still crying, relaying the words of the message in my head. The text had read:

> J: I know it's your birthday, and I know you have court tomorrow, but I made you a promise, and I'm letting you know I'm about to break our promise as soon as I send this text. You told me to tell you if it ever came to it, so I am. I'm sorry x

Michelle came storming back into the room and looked at me, still crying on the floor. 'Oh no, you don't! Don't you dare cry another tear over that sick twisted evil bastard! He's not even worth it! He's a horrible manipulating evil bastard! I don't even believe him! He's not sitting there about to fuck another bird and texting you all night! He's had a drink and he's tried to wind you up and get a reaction 'cause he can't stand the thought that you might be having a good time away from him on your birthday, and he doesn't know for sure what you're doing or who you're with! He's been digging at you all night so you can spend the night texting him, unhappy instead of enjoying yourself, and when he hasn't got what he wanted and you haven't snapped, he's sent you that!

Do not let that little fucker get in your head! These sick games between you two have gone too far! Yes, in the past you have been just as bad as him, but this is another level! That is pure fucking evil! It's like kicking a dog while it's down! I will knock his fucking block off! He wants to fuck with my fucking mate like that on her birthday when she's got court the next day and could be going to prison, yeah? I'll put him in the back of the fucking mini, mate!' she shouted.

Michelle putting people in her boot was an ongoing joke, due to her temper when provoked. 'They need to be careful, or they will end up in Shelly's boot' the saying goes. I lay slumped against the wardrobe, looking at the floor, all cried out. As the tears stopped, all of a sudden I felt myself begin to turn. My initial reaction was of course sadness, but it was about to transform into something else. In 0.5 seconds, he had awoken the Female Boss. My entire demeanour changed instantly. I looked up from the floor at Michelle. I saw her notice the change as she spotted the familiar fierce twinkle in my eyes, like the weak quivering little girl on the floor had now become possessed by someone else. My head was lowered as I glared up at her.

'Pass me the phone.' My voice was calm but full of bass. She looked at me nervously; she knew what time it was.

'Nah, mate, what do you want the phone for? What are you gunna do? I know that look, mate, you're doing that calm psycho face you do. Where are your car keys?'

The calm psycho face she was referring to was a familiar trait to everyone that knew me, one of the very few traits I had inherited from my dad. Whenever a family member saw it, they would always say it reminded them of my father.

'Don't worry,' I said, with my facial expression still blank. 'I won't put a brick through his Ferrari, pass me the phone.' She gritted her teeth and handed me the phone hesitantly.

'Spark us a fag please, Shell,' I said, as I began writing a text to Jacob.

She handed me a lit cigarette. 'I don't fucking like ya like this, man. I think I preferred it when you were crying.'

'Oh, there will be no more crying. You can forget about that,' I said.

'What are you saying to him?' she asked. I finished typing the text and pressed send before sliding the phone over to her in silence. She gave me worried eyes before reading. She was calm now. My anger had counteracted hers. She no longer felt she needed to protect me from him, but more so me from myself.

The text read:

T: Let's hope she's worth it, and she's a good shag!

I'll give your grandmother's icon to Daz.

'That's my fucking girl, there she is! Don't even give him what he wants. Kill him with silence!' she said. I smiled at her.

'Always, he's messing with the wrong bitch,' I declared.

'But T, honestly, do you know what the joke is? I seriously don't believe it. There's no fucking way that text was sent just to hurt you. If he was about to fuck a bird, he wouldn't be sat there texting you beforehand. Something fishy's going on. Come on, let's go and sit in the living room with Daz.'

I followed her into the lounge. I fully got what she was

saying, something just wasn't right about it. He could be a bastard at times, but not like this. This was next level, I struggled to find him capable of something so evil and cold. But it had happened nonetheless, and I had to take it at face value. I pulled out the icon from my handbag and passed it to Daz.

'There you go, you give that to your friend.' He looked at me and shook his head.

'I don't know what to say, T, something ain't right. I can't see him doing this to you without a reason, I know him.'

'Well, it's too late for that now, isn't it, Daz? The damage is done.' I sat down on the sofa next to them both, grabbed the PlayStation control and went to press play on the DVD like everything was normal. They looked at each other, baffled, and looked back at me. I frowned at them both.

'Listen, what's done is done. Fuck him! He better stay the fuck away from me from now on! It's my fucking birthday and I start court tomorrow, so let's all just chill the fuck out and watch the film.'

My phone went off, as I received another text:

J: You fucking horrible bitch! I can't believe you gave my grandmother's icon to Daz!

I looked at Daz. 'Did you tell him I gave you the icon?'

'Yeah, I did, he texted me and asked.'

'Why the fuck is he sat there texting us if he's about to shag another bird? Tell him to F off!'

'Mate, please! This is a lot, I feel stuck in the middle right now! He isn't saying anything about shagging another bird, he just sounds like he's in a bad way!'

'Oh, does he now?! Well, serves him right!' I grabbed my phone and began texting Jacob back:

T: Why the fuck are you still texting me? Put down the phone and get back to your slut! Give her a kiss from me! I hope she's worth it!

I pressed send and went into contact settings and blocked him from contacting me in any way. I was done. The only thought I had in my mind right now was that life's a bitch and I just had to accept it. It seemed no matter where life took me, it would still find a way to surprise me at times. I was sat there fully taking it in my stride, but inside, I was taken aback, I hadn't seen this coming. But that seemed to be the case with everything at the moment.

If there was one good thing to come out of it, it had drained me of all my soft emotions. All the things that made me weak, all the things that I wanted deep down and had still hoped for, were gone. Love, trust and happiness, something real. It all disintegrated because of one text. I felt cold inside. The only hope I still had was that everything in these past two years was happening for a reason. It was a lesson to be learned, a teaching that would help me to grow and make a difference. Everything I knew, everything I felt, everything that had led me to this moment, my entire life, couldn't be for nothing. That this was all somehow bigger than me.

I lay on the sofa watching *The Hunger Games*, a movie

I had watched many times and had become slightly obsessed with. I could relate to Katniss, I felt like I was watching another version of myself. I looked at Daz and Michelle, who were asleep on the sofa fifteen minutes into the film. Gareth had probably passed out on his laptop by now. I smiled to myself. I was completely alone, just how it was meant to be right now. As much as the night's events had upset me, they had made me ready, brought me back from the distraction that had kept me going through the motions up until now. But I no longer needed a distraction. Now I needed to focus... to fight! All the things I yearned for in my heart wouldn't help me right now, I had to face this by myself. This was my journey, my path, and mine alone. It was time to embrace it. It had gone too far and I had to try and take something from it no matter what the outcome, rise or fall. After all, when it comes down to it, there really are no winners, only survivors.

Chapter 22:

DAY ONE OF TU-RIAL

I STARED THROUGH the front window of the car at the mass of press and paparazzi waiting for my arrival outside the court. Gareth placed a hand on my shoulder and leaned towards me. 'Head up and stand straight,' he whispered in my ear. I nodded at him anxiously before he got out the other side of the car to walk around and greet me.

As the door opened, I was blinded by the camera flashes that came flooding into the vehicle. I could hear my name being shouted from every direction, by what sounded like a hundred voices at once. I slowly stepped out of the car and waited for my eyes to adapt so I could find my bearings. I tried my best to look forward and walk as firmly as possible in my high heels through the blinding lights. As I got to the security entrance of the court, I saw the female officer I had warmed to during the previous court dates. She gave me a warm smile.

'Hello, love, how are you feeling?' she asked softly.

'I'm alright, not shaved me head yet,' I said, smiling back at her. Behind the security detectors waited Kev, my escort, provided by the court. A short stocky man with shaven white hair. He had a stern face at first glance, the look of someone you wouldn't want to mess with. But as soon as he cracked a smile, he was like a teddy bear. I really liked Kev. He was a sound guy, and he gave the impression that he knew what was happening was wrong.

He led me, Gareth and Simon towards a private room, where my legal team were waiting. After a short meeting we were called into the courtroom. I took a deep breath and downed the espresso I had gripped tightly in my hand. This was going to be a long day.

I stood in the dock, anxiously trying to take in all the information. I was about to find out whether or not the prosecution would have to reveal the identity of the woman that played the role of Nish during the sting. Mahmood was claiming she had played no part in convincing me to act a certain way throughout the set-up, even though she had conveniently taken off her recording device at the same moment I'd said in my defence that she took me to the toilet and told me to up the ante.

In fact, the key part of my defence all came down to Nish and how she had been coaching and manipulating me and Gareth throughout the sting, which had led me to put on an act. But I could only bring her into my defence if she was cross-examined on the stand and given the chance to either defend herself or admit that my accusations were true. She had so far requested that her identity remained hidden, and supposedly told Mahmood she did not want to appear in court.

Unless the judge now ordered her to do so, she would not have to be cross- examined, and I would not be able to mention her in my defence. Considering she was pretty much ninety per cent of my defence, I'd be in big trouble if she didn't appear. It was already my word versus Mahmood's, and if I couldn't mention Nish, I wouldn't even be able to explain my side of the story. I sat listening intently, waiting for the judge to give his decision on bringing Nish forward. Everything depended on this. If I couldn't tell the jury about Nish, I had no defence at all. My ears pricked up as the judge cleared his throat.

'Due to the laws on journalistic privileges, the person known to the courts as Nish may keep her identity hidden and will not have to attend trial...'

I shook my head furiously at his words. This couldn't be?! It wasn't fair! It wasn't right! Mahmood had known the loophole was there all along, to help him create his perfect set-up. It was exactly the same as the issue with the source. If we could prove the supposed source that made the original tip-off to the paper, which they claimed kicked off their sting, didn't actually exist or had lied, there wouldn't be a case. But again, because of journalistic privileges, Mr Mahmood and *The Sun on Sunday* did not have to reveal their source's identity. This wasn't about finding out the truth or if I was innocent, it was just a powerful man's game of chess. Rule vs rule, law vs law, and legal loopholes.

Regardless of the facts, the law was now legally overriding the truth and essentially ignoring right and wrong.

What kind of a legal system was this, and what kind of fucked-up world were we living in? It was day one, with three more weeks to go, and already I felt like my fate was sealed. I closed my eyes and saw the prison cell I had seen in my nightmares for the past thirteen months and shook my head in despair. I leaned my head towards the sky and held back my tears. I'd experienced what I deemed to be quite a few miracles in my time. I could only hope and pray the best was yet to come, because I definitely needed a miracle to get out of this one.

As I zoned out from the courtroom and my brain swirled with a million thoughts, I felt a familiar trickling sensation from my nose. I raised my hand under my neck and looked down to see the bright red blood begin to splatter across my palm. *Crap. Nosebleed*, I thought.

When I was around 20, I'd had a polyp growth removed from my left nostril as it was affecting my breathing, but the surgical wound had never seemed to heal properly. Whenever I became stressed or my blood pressure went up, it would start to bleed profusely. The room became eerily silent as I noticed all the eyes in the court turning towards me, one by one, with looks of shock and horror as the blood began to cover the bottom half of my face and splattered everywhere.

I looked up at the judge in silence, trying to catch as much blood in my hands as I could for what felt like the longest minute of my life, looking for some kind of signal as to what to do. A female police officer next to me finally ushered me out of the box and through a door out of the courtroom.

She handed me a tissue as I pulled my head back.

What a fucking day.

The next day, the headline on the front cover of *The Sun* was: 'TULISA'S NOSE BLEED AT HER FIRST DAY OF HER COCAINE TRIAL'. Boy, did they revel in it.

Chapter 23:

ONE FOR SORROW,
TU FOR JOY

I SAT IN the car on the way home, feeling disheartened but strong. There was no room for emotion right now. I felt my phone vibrating in my bag and reluctantly pulled it out to see Daz's name on the screen.

'You alright, mate? How was court?'

'Same old bollocks. I can't be bothered to go into it, mate, it's been a long day,' I mumbled.

'OK, well, listen...' He hesitated for a moment, and I knew what was coming.

'Go on,' I sighed.

'Listen, I've had Jacob on the phone and he's absolutely devo'd man. He's saying he's really sorry and it's not what you think. He really wants to see you. He said will you meet him at 6pm by the field? He said you'd know the place.'

He was referring to our little nature spot. I paused as memories of the previous night came flooding back.

'I don't want to meet him, Daz. I've got nothing to say to him. You saw that text, he's lost me, mate, end of.'

'T, you know I wouldn't lie to you. I know him and I'm telling you now, I can hear it in his voice he's telling the truth! I don't know what's happened. He won't tell me, says he wants to tell you himself. But whatever it is, he hasn't done nothing with another bird, I'm telling you now. You knew the whole thing was weird anyway.'

'Even if that's the case it's the utter disrespect of what he said and when he said it. I don't know, Daz, man, I really don't wanna see him right now.'

'T, please, the guy's in a bad way, man. He hasn't actually done anything, just hear what he's got to say... please.'

'I'll have to think about it, Daz, I really don't wanna see his face right now. I'll ring you in a bit,' I muttered. Daz sighed down the phone.

'Alright, make sure because he's on my line and you've blocked him so he can't even call you.'

'Alright, alright, cool, speak soon,' I said abruptly, before putting down the phone. Gareth frowned at me.

'I can only guess who that was about, shock!' He rolled his eyes sarcastically.

I got home and plonked myself on the bed. Why does it always have to be so bloody complicated? I decided not to ring Daz back. Jacob could wait and I hoped he was suffering while he did. So he should be, after how he made me feel. And when I had so much to deal with already.

I popped the telly on, I wasn't going to be making any calls today.

At 6pm my phone began to ring. It was a random number but I didn't pick up.

T: Who's this?

After I texted, the number started calling again – three missed calls later I got a text:

J: It's me, answer the phone. I'm at the spot.

Figures, I thought, watching the phone ring again:

2 MISSED CALLS

T: Allow your attitude, I don't know why you're there, I never told Daz I was coming.

3 MISSED CALLS

J: JUST COME PLEASE, JUST HEAR ME OUT, I BROUGHT THIS PHONE FOR YOU, SOMETHING HAPPENED THAT MADE ME DO THAT, I HAVEN'T BROKEN MY WORD

7 MISSED CALLS

I watched the phone ring out. I sensed he was telling the truth, but why the hell would he do that? I knew there was only one way to find out. I wanted to not talk to him and let him hurt the way I did, but by doing that I was going to make myself suffer. I wanted to know the truth.

T: I don't know why I'm really bothering, maybe I'm just intrigued to see what you could possibly come up with to explain your disgusting actions, but I will let you talk. Think very carefully about lying to me. The universe has a funny way of having my back. I will text you when I'm 5 min away, and I'm only coming there cos u don't deserve to set foot in my house.

2 MISSED CALLS

J: I CAN'T BELIEVE U DONT BELIEVE ME WITH THE LEVELS WE'RE AT!

2 MISSED CALLS

2 MISSED CALLS

T: You tell me u know it's my bday and ur about to fuck another bird when you get off the phone, knowing that I have court the next day. Don't take the moral fucking high ground with me, mate. How dare u! I shouldn't even be speaking to you right now! I'm leaving in 15. If u don't like it, lump it!

2 MISSED CALLS

J: I'VE DONE NOTHING TO LET U DOWN!

3 MISSED CALLS

T: I've told u I'm coming, pipe the fuck down and chill out.

2 MISSED CALLS

J: I WANT TO TELL YOU SOMETHING, ANSWER THE PHONE U MUG!

2 MISSED CALLS

T: Carry on and I won't turn up u inconsiderate bastard! You're lucky I don't smack your face in when I see u. Shut the fuck up and wait!

J: GET ONE THING IN YOUR HEAD, THE LAST GIRL I SLEPT WITH WAS U!

T: I'm about to start driving

J: DO U KNOW WHERE I AM ON THE FIELD? I'M AT THE SPOT WHERE WE ALWAYS CHILL

T: OBVIOUSLY!!!!

J: HAVE U LEFT?

T: I'm on my way! Chill your fucking beans!

J: ONLY U!

I put my phone in my pocket and headed to my car.

You're damn right only me, I thought, *and I'm about to bust your fucking balls!*

I arrived at the woods where we always walked Prince, from mornings to late-night walks. We had a particular spot where we would stop and sit, kind of like our special place. It was also our meeting place to talk whenever we'd had an argument. I strolled down the familiar footpath, taking in the late evening sunshine and the sound of the birds tweeting as if I would never see or hear them again. I felt like I was finally putting my life into perspective. Although I had very strong feelings for Jacob, I was done with stressing over the outcome of our relationship. With all that was going on, love was the least of my problems.

I stopped as I reached the gate at the end of the path and let out a deep breath as I turned the corner. I spotted Jacob with Prince at the end of the field. My heart thumped a little in my chest at the sight of him as I headed towards them. I sighed to myself, how did we get here? Prince spotted me when I got halfway and came running towards me. I was happy to see him at least. I petted and greeted him before turning my attention to Jacob with my arms folded and my facial expression blank.

He walked towards me with his arms open wide and a pleading look on his face.

'My baby! You, you don't even know!' he exclaimed as he tried to hold me in his arms. I threw his hands off me.

'Don't you fucking touch me! Get the hell away from me, you delusional madman! Get off! I'm here to listen so go on, talk!' I snapped, glaring at him. He put his hands on his head and then threw them in the air.

'I haven't done anything! Look at me! Look in my eyes! I haven't done anything! For once I actually haven't done anything!' he yelled.

'Well then fucking explain!' I yelled back.

'I will, I just want to hold you. This is all bullshit!' he said, trying to wrap his arms around me again as I pushed him off.

'You're not touching me! Now talk!'

'OK, sit down at least.'

'I don't want to sit down. You sit down and I'll stand! Talk!'

He looked at me and sighed. 'Alright, basically, first of all I had a drink after work, quite a few drinks.'

'Doesn't take a rocket scientist to figure that out, go on!'

'Basically, someone called me to say they'd seen you with some guy earlier in the day, as in like, *with* him with him.'

'Oh my *God*, not rumours again, go on!'

'I basically got really pissed off, but I didn't want to confront you till I spoke to the guy first. So I was waiting for someone to get his number, but they were taking ages, and I was talking to you and I was angry because I couldn't say anything yet. But I didn't want you to get upset if it wasn't true, so I thought no, let me just wait. So I did, and then I got drunker and drunker. And I was winding myself up, and I convinced myself it was true and then... basically, I just exploded and lost it, I wanted to hurt your feelings. It was stupid, and then I finally got the guy's number. And I called him 'cause I know him, and he told me it was a new bird he was seeing and sent me a picture of her, and the joke is, she actually does look like you.'

I shook my head and frowned at him. 'Wow, that's an epic concoction of a story! Did you think long and hard about that one?'

'Oh my God, this is ridiculous. I haven't done anything, I swear to God! Look at me! You know me! Come on, why

263

the fuck would I do that otherwise? Tell you I'm about to fuck another bird? That's crazy!'

'No, *you're* crazy! Even if you're telling the truth, you still shouldn't have sent the text! That was fucking evil! Absolutely disgusting! And you can't complain about the fact I don't believe you! You text me to tell me you're about to shag another bird. No matter why you said it, what the hell do you expect? You brought this upon yourself!'

'Baby!' He winced as he tried to grab me and hold me again.

'Get off of me!' I shouted.

'Tulisa, look at me! I'll show you the messages! I swear on my best friend's grave I haven't slept with anyone else!'

I looked into his eyes and I knew he hadn't slept with anyone that night, but I was still furious. There was a possibility that he was telling the truth, but another part of me believed it was all bullshit, and the real reason he'd sent it was to play games. A very sick game that a lack of control over me and too much alcohol had led him to.

Either way there was no excuse for his actions, but for some fucked-up reason I understood him and the fucked-up psychology behind what he'd done. I knew because sometimes I did things like that too. I looked at him like a child and shook my head.

'Why does it always have to be so complicated with us?'

He stared at me longingly 'You know I'm telling the truth! I can see it in your eyes! You know me! You get me! I know you know!'

I put my head down, trying to hide my amusement

at the situation. I could see the longing in his eyes and I secretly loved it, but right now I wanted to stay angry. We were toxic as fuck.

'Tulisa, stop, man, please, don't give me a hard time. I know how shit that must have been for you, but I know you know I'm not that stupid. I fucked up but not on that level, and it was really bad timing, I know, and I'm so sorry. I'll make it up to you, just give me a hug, that's all I want.'

He went to approach me with arms open again, but slower this time. I frowned at him and sighed. There was no denying we had some serious issues, but with everything going on I just didn't have the energy to deal with them right now. I could be going to jail in a few weeks, and I felt like I needed him. Deep down, I just wanted him to hold me and tell me it was going to be alright. I unfolded my arms and placed them by my sides. He instantly wrapped himself around me.

'I'm so sorry, man, I should never have tried to hurt you like that, I thought I'd lost you there,' he whispered, squeezing me tightly and kissing my cheek repeatedly. I rested my head on his shoulder.

'You did lose me!' I snapped, before letting out another big sigh. 'What am I gunna do with you, Jacob?' I said. I rested my head on his shoulder – and spotted a magpie sitting alone in the field.

'Oh no, there's one magpie. We never see one magpie,' I whined sadly, as he turned his head to look.

'Just wait, there will be another somewhere. There's always another.'

'No, there won't, there's just one. What the fuck is that supposed to mean? I only see one on my own, we always see two,' I sighed, getting genuinely upset.

'Ssshhhhh! Look!' he whispered as he grabbed me and spun me around. My eyes widened and my jaw dropped as I saw another magpie fly down out of nowhere into the field and join the first.

'Ya see,' he smiled, squeezing me again,

'But... but how did you...'

'Because I'm a G,' he laughed.

'You little shit, I bet you saw it all along.'

'I didn't actually, it must be your psychic sense rubbing off on me,' he grinned.

I smiled with joy at the two magpies. 'There you are! Hello, Mr and Mrs Magpie,' I said. He shook his head and spun me back into him.

'Just be good to me and I'll be good to you. I've got you,' he said, looking deep into my eyes.

'No, you be good to me and I'll be good to you! Shithead! And I hope you know this is definitely going in the book!'

'No, it bloody ain't!' he exclaimed,

'Oh yes, it bloody is!' I snapped.

'I keep forgetting about this bloody book, I better start behaving myself,' he chuckled. I nodded at him and smiled sarcastically in agreement,

'I'm over halfway through, so now would be a good time to start.'

Chapter 24:

SAINT MARINA

I WAS WOKEN by Gareth gently shaking my shoulder. Unlike yesterday when I was dead as a door nail, I jumped out of my sleep with a sharp gasp. I had managed to get five hours' kip. I was constantly exhausted at the moment, I'd had insomnia since this whole saga had begun, but at least today it felt like I'd had enough sleep to function again. I squinted up at Gareth through my puffy eyes. He stood over me with a cup of coffee in his hand and his head tilted to the side. He was looking down at me, analysing what state I had woken up in.

'How do you feel?' he asked.

'Better than yesterday,' I replied.

I slowly pulled myself upright and looked down at Michelle sleeping peacefully next to me. Snug as a bug in the Land of Nod. I really wanted to be in her world right now. I clasped the hot coffee in my hands and took a sip. The hot sweet liquid sent a warm wave surging through my body, bringing me a little more to life. I reached over to the box of Silk Cut Purple and pulled out a cigarette. I took a deep lug and exhaled in preparation for my first phone check of the day. I pressed the button on my iPhone with a sick feeling in my stomach. God knows what I was going to wake up to. There was always a new drama or story to start the day in my world at the moment. I only had one text, it was from Jacob:

J: X

A simple kiss on its own, sent at 1am. I grunted grumpily. I was still a little off with him, since the birthday drama. I was now on day three of the trial and reality was really starting to hit me. It was clear from the vibe in the courtroom and the look on my lawyers' faces that things were not going well. It felt like the battle was lost before it had begun. The judge's rulings had made sure of that. An hour and a half later, I stood up straight, looking in the mirror and smoothing down my fresh suit jacket.

'Five minutes, T!' Gareth called.

'Cool.'

As I walked down to the car my phone popped off again, with another text from Jacob:

J: Good luck today. I'll be sending you good vibes. I'll be back on Sunday if you need me for anything, call me any time x

He had gone away for work again. As I walked down to the car, I thought about the added stress he'd brought to me at this dark time, yet at the same time it was weirdly a distraction.

I just needed to put him to the back of my mind right now and get on with what was important, fighting for my freedom. I went to put my phone back in my bag as I got in the car and I noticed a black LV wallet that wasn't mine. I opened it up and pulled out the cards. I looked at Jacob's face on the driver's licence. *Can't bloody get away from him,* I thought. I pulled my phone back out.

T: you left your wallet.

J: MY BBE X

T: bbe?

J: MY BABY! or is that too soft for you lol

T: Don't come soft unless you're coming solid

J: I am as solid as they come, that's why I have to mind how soft I go

I shook my head and put my phone back in my bag before popping in my headphones and blasting Eminem's 'Till I Collapse'. I stared down at the Greek icon of Saint Marina in my hand. Last night, my aunty had come round to my house to give it to me and reminded me that today, 17th of July, was the day of my baptism in Greece, and the day of Saint Marina, the saint of the church I was baptised in.

My Yia Yia (Greek grandmother) had also called me and told me that I should pray to her for help with my case and that I would see tomorrow that everything would be OK. I had sighed agitatedly and told her I had another three weeks to go before any outcome. 'OK, pray, you will see,' she'd said. I knew this nightmare wasn't going to end today or tomorrow, but I prayed either way.

After the past three days' events, and that horrid abuse trial, I was beginning to prepare myself for the worst. If I was found guilty this judge was definitely sending me to prison, I could feel it, and I really needed to start getting my head around that. I kept visualising myself sitting in a cell and what my routine would be inside. Laying in my bunk at night, eating my lunch, my first encounter with a bully, exercising in the gym. I thought about how I would deal with every moment and emotion. How I would survive.

There was no time for pity parties right now. It was too real. This was really happening. It was time to get into Female Boss mode. It was a risk, because if I put my defences up the jury might think I was a stern-faced bitch, but I could only be one way or the other right now. There were no half measures in this situation. I thought about that cell again. The Female Boss it was. Something had changed. I felt solid, serious and the strongest I'd ever felt. I had hit rock bottom, the lowest I could possibly go. I had been taken to the edge, and I wasn't willing to snap. No more tears on the bathroom floor, no more fear. What will be will be, and I was ready for it.

I arrived at the court and did the usual freakshow

catwalk, past the herd of paparazzi and press behind the barriers that had been put up for me. I was relieved to get to the end and see Kev waiting by the doors.

'You look a little better then yesterday, I'll tell you now,' he said.

'I feel it, funnily enough. I'm feeling strong.'

'Good! Don't let 'em get you down, babe. You're going to be just fine. I can feel it.'

'Cheers, Kev,' I said, cracking a smile. I called over to Simon and Gareth, who were standing by Costa Coffee. 'I'll meet you up there, guys.'

They smiled and gave me a nod as Kev led me to the lift. As we stood in silence Kev reached into his back pocket. 'I got you a little something,' he said, pulling out a card with my name on it.

'Aaaaaw, Kev! You didn't have to do that! Bless you!' I exclaimed, taking the envelope. I opened it up and began reading the card inside:

Tulisa,

I cannot imagine what you are going through at the moment, but I have been hit with the wrong end of the stick on more than one occasion in Bosnia and Afghanistan. These phrases might help or make you laugh.

'Tough times never last but tough people do'

'If you're going through hell, keep going'

'First they ignore you, then they ridicule you, then they fight you and then you win!'

Kind regards

Kev

A big smile stretched across my face. 'You're a good man, Kev. It's good to know there are still some good people left in the world,' I pulled him towards me, and gave him a big hug. 'You've got a good heart, I can't tell you how much that means,' I whispered.

He patted me gently on the back. 'I'm just glad I could put a smile on your face,' he said. I looked at him and smiled again.

'Well, you did. Couldn't think of a better way to start the day.'

I sat in the dock, waiting for Mazher Mahmood to step into the witness box. The large curtain in front of the box was drawn across at an angle so that the press and public couldn't see him. He was allowed witness protection because he had so many people that wanted revenge for what he had done to them. People even wanted him killed, and even though I didn't wish death upon anyone myself, I wasn't surprised. He had ruined so many people's lives with his deceit and lies. Once he took aim at you, he would stop at nothing to ensure your downfall, whether you were guilty or not.

My eyes locked onto his face as he came through the side door. I could see him making a conscious choice not to look around as usual, like he was avoiding eye contact with someone. I wonder who that would be. But it was too late for him. As he looked up for a second, his eyes looked directly into mine. I glared at him, a deep hard glare that felt like it went straight through him. He quickly looked away sheepishly.

I knew for a fact that he was proud of what he'd done, and that he felt no sympathy or remorse. He sees people like me, that were raised from 'the lower class', as scum. 'Scum' being his own word. Worthless pawns in his sick game of chess. He believed he was powerful and superior, yet he could not bring himself to look at the small 26-year-old female in the little pink dress sitting in the dock. What a coward he was.

Look at me! I thought. *Have the decency to look at me! Face me like a fucking man!* But he didn't. I knew that I had more balls in my little finger than the man before me. As the questioning began, I leaned forward into my glare to add some extra pressure, not that he had a problem with lying to people's faces.

I smirked and sniggered at his lies while he answered the questions. At times I was repulsed and I shook my head. I listened intently to the lies upon lies, watching him at work, enjoying himself as he covered up his tracks and wormed his way out of the tricky questions, laughing and smiling, making jokes and digs as he went along. I couldn't help but think this man was pure evil.

But as the day went on, my mood began to lighten and change. I felt calmer, more used to his presence and accepting of my possible fate. I began to feel bad about all the negative energy I had been feeling towards him. I was allowing him to make me stoop to his level, wasting my energy on him and disrupting my positivity like some kind of leech sucking the life from me. All of a sudden, I had a change of heart.

My perspective on life had changed since this whole thing began. I'd like to think, although I wasn't perfect, I'd always had a kind heart. I had begun to realise things, like how precious life is and how truly lucky I was to have got as far as I had. I also felt more empathetic towards others. I'd started to look past the surface with people and I realised how much their journey sculpts them into who they are. Most of all, I realised, hurt people end up hurting other people. I'd found a sense of peace within this knowing.

I felt like I was seeing the bigger picture of this thing called life, and I was seeing it a lot more clearly. I felt ENLIGHTENED. *Do the right thing, T,* I thought. *You can't preach if you don't do.* It's the man in the mirror scenario. In reality it's a lot harder to change other people than it is to change yourself. If everyone turned all their energy towards bettering themselves, rather than judging other people and trying to change them, I'm pretty sure the world would be a better place. That's not to say it's an easy thing to do because it's more work, but it's also a lot more productive.

I had to forgive him, I had to let go of the animosity before it ate me alive, I sighed to myself. I had said it to myself before and thought I meant it. But to have him sat there in my face so smug, while lying and trying to ensure he ended me, it was harder than I thought. I stared into his eyes, wondering what events had occurred in his past and what kind of life he'd had, to lead him to this point. We are all products of our environment to some extent. I had no idea of the life he'd lived or the experiences he'd had, so I couldn't know whether he was just pure evil or had been influenced to turn that way. Maybe he was hurting inside himself. He was not for me to judge. I didn't have to like him, but I didn't have to hate him either. I had a heart, I could empathise with my enemy. That's what made me different from him. I looked at him and said the words in my mind: 'Forgive him, Lord, for he knows not what he does. He is blind. Help him to see clearly, to see the light. Help him to become a better person. Teach him in whatever way you see fit. Take him out of the dark and into the light. Amen.'

I had tried to understand him, I had felt sympathy and prayed for him. I could do no more. I still didn't like the guy, but I felt better in myself. After I said the prayer, the court had taken a short break before Mahmood's questioning and evidence continued. I sat in the little room with my barrister, staring at him blankly. I felt like all the life had left me, all the hope I had for fighting this battle was drained from my body. It had left me numb and empty, preparing me for a new battle, the worst possible outcome. I sat slumped against the wall, feeling cold and dead inside. I looked Jeremy straight in the eye.

'I'm going to prison, aren't I?' It was a statement, not a question.

'Well... you know, we have to try and keep positive, T. I'm working on something, there's some hope. We just have to wait and see,' he sighed.

I could see it plain and simple in his face, I knew. I looked to my left and noticed Gareth's travel bag wide open and a pair of my trainers inside it, along with some other bits and bobs of mine. *Wow*, I thought, *they packed me a prison bag. They don't even think I'll make it to the end of the trial without being put on remand.*

'It's alright, Jeremy, I get it,' I said flatly.

He looked back at me in silence, like his heart was genuinely breaking. Ben popped his head around the door. 'We're going back in, guys.'

I looked at Jeremy one last time before I wiped down my suit.

'Do you believe in miracles, Jez?' I asked.

'I don't know, Tulisa, but we may need one at this stage,' he sighed.

'I believe in miracles, Jeremy. I've had a lot of miracles in my life, and I still believe one might happen. You never know, Jez. You might believe in miracles too by the end of this.' I held my head high and strutted back into the courtroom. I sat down in the dock again, listening intently to Jeremy as the questions began.

'Mr Mahmood, I want to ask you again about the incident that happened in the car after the restaurant, when your driver, Mr Smith, Miss Contostavlos, and her two friends were present.'

I sighed to myself in the dock. *Here we go, more lies*, I thought.

'We know that your driver, Mr Smith, originally made a statement saying that on that car journey he overheard a conversation that brought him to the belief that Miss

Contostavlos was completely anti-drugs, that she didn't like drugs, didn't take them, and didn't want anything to do with them, or drug dealers for that matter. Is that not correct?'

Mahmood frowned impatiently at being asked the same questions.

'I don't know the exact detail of what he said but there was something about her being anti-drugs, but then he later said he realised he couldn't remember if it was her or her friend that had said it.'

'Yes, Mr Mahmood, later when he changed his state-ment to say that it was Miss Contostavlos's friend that had had a conversation that was anti-drugs and not Miss Contostavlos herself. And can you just remind us of whether or not you spoke to him during the time he made the first statement and then changed it?'

'No! I definitely did not speak to him.'

'Aah yes, of course. In fact you told us in the abuse trial that you hadn't spoken to him for over a year since the sting, and that you knew nothing about him changing his statement. Is that right?'

'Yes. That is correct.'

'And you're standing by that statement you made?' asked Jeremy.

I watched Mahmood's face change as he became a little suspicious. He could see that Jeremy was getting at something, as could everyone else, including myself, but what exactly he was getting at, even I was unsure of.

'Yes, I do,' he said, as he fidgeted in his seat.

I looked over at the jury. I wondered if they could tell that he was lying. I squeezed the icon of Saint Marina in my hand again, hoping and praying they did. Jeremy pulled down his glasses, rested them on the tip of his nose and stared at Mr Mahmood.

'And you're sure about that, Mr Mahmood?' he asked again. Mahmood looked at him, frustrated.

'Yes, I'm sure!'

The judge looked at Jeremy as if even he was agitated now and sighed.

'I think we've established his answer to your question, Mr Dein. Please move on.'

'Yes, of course, Your Honour. I'm sorry, there is a point to all this, if you'll just bear with me for a moment. I'll get to it now, Your Honour.'

I leaned forward in my seat and frowned, waiting for the punchline. *What an earth was he doing?* I wondered.

'I'd like you all to take a look at the piece of paper I have in my hand.' Jeremy gestured to the usher to hand out multiple copies around the court.

'Can you read the piece of paper in your hand, Mr Mahmood?'

Mahmood looked down at the piece of paper and gulped uncomfortably.

'Yes,' he said.

'Good! As you can see, it's a statement from your driver, Mr Smith. Signed by him this week. The statement says that during the time he changed his statement from the original one he made, he did speak to you. And not only did he speak to you about it, but he actually emailed the statement over to you. And if you look at the other piece of paper that you've been given, you can see a copy of that email. Which means you've been lying, doesn't it, Mr Mahmood?'

His face looked as if it went a shade lighter and he'd seen a ghost. I watched as the reality hit him of what was happening. I then looked at all the faces around the courtroom. Everyone's expressions began changing as they took in what they'd heard. The jury frowned as if confused as they registered it, even the judge stopped what he was doing. He put down his piece of paper and tilted down his glasses, raising his eyebrows at Mahmood. The whole room was silent, waiting for his response. You could have heard a pin drop. I leaned forward even closer to the glass, my heart thumping in my chest. All I could hear was the sound of my own breathing.

'Oh, sorry... I totally forgot I... I did speak to him. Yes, sorry, it must have slipped my mind, it was a long time ago,' he stuttered. I could see him starting to sweat as he squirmed in his seat.

'Oh, you forgot, did you, Mr Mahmood? How convenient! Because a moment ago you said that you were quite sure, did you not?'

'I... I must have forgotten. I remember now, he had contacted me for advice because he realised he'd made a mistake and he didn't know how to go about correcting it.' Mahmood was looking down now, like he didn't know where to look.

'Mr Mahmood!' I looked up at the judge as I heard his stern booming voice burst through the court. 'Do you expect me to believe that five minutes ago you had completely forgotten this, and you have now just miraculously remembered?'

The prosecution began ploughing into him, and my jaw dropped as the entire energy in the room flipped on its head. Like I was no longer the criminal, but he was. *What does this mean?* I thought. *If he's been caught lying, does it mean that maybe now I'll be able to use my evidence and have a proper defence? Tell the jury what really happened?*

I looked at Jane Hickman, one of my lawyers, as she turned around in her seat to face me. She nodded with a smile and slipped a thumbs up behind her chair for me to see. *What's going on?* I thought. *I'm confused, have I missed something?*

The judge shuffled his papers, looking flustered and highly insulted. 'With this new information I'm going to adjourn today's court.' He got up from his seat. 'All rise.'

I stood up with everyone as he left the room. Once the door had slammed, I jumped up to the glass with my hands pressed against it. I whispered through the gap, 'Psssssst, Jane!' She hurried over to me.

'I'm ninety per cent sure it's thrown out, case finished. We've done it,' she whispered.

'What?' I said, louder this time.

'Ssshhhhh! I'll explain after,' she said, before heading back over to the rest of the team. I staggered back and almost fell into my seat. Could this be true? Was this really happening? Was it over? Just like that? That's it? I was free? I looked down at the icon of Saint Marina and kissed it. I didn't know what was going on. All I knew were the possibilities of the words Jane had just said. I pulled out the other icon from my pocket, Jacob's grandmother's icon, and kissed it as well.

He had given it back to me at the park. The biggest, most euphoric smile began to crack uncontrollably across my face. My eyes lit up in a way they hadn't done since before this whole ordeal had started. I closed them as I clenched both the icons in my hand and tilted my head towards the sky.

'Thank you,' I whispered.

For the first time in thirteen months, over a year since this had all begun when I was 24 in 2013, and now at 26 years old, I finally felt alive again. As if the heavy dark weight on my chest had finally lifted and drifted up into the sky. It was possible I was free, it was the miracle I'd been waiting for! Somehow I felt like I had known deep in my heart this would happen. This was the hope I'd been holding onto, and this was no coincidence.

I sat with Jeremy, Ben and Jane in the small lawyers' room – the court had been adjourned till the following Monday.

'I can't see how they couldn't throw it out, he just committed perjury on the stand! He's probably going to get arrested. They will drop out all his pending cases. He's an unreliable witness now. Did you see the judge's face? I mean, excuse my French but to be quite clear, that evil slimeball is absolutely "fucked".' Jane winced at her naughty words.

'Oh my, Jane! I've never heard you swear before! You haven't gotta worry about that around me! Fire away! I'd quite like to see you let rip!' I grinned.

Jeremy was still shaking his head in the corner. 'I know, but from what I've seen so far, I just don't trust it. Anything could happen,' he said.

'I know what you mean,' frowned Jane.

I smiled at them both.

'I hear what you're saying, and I agree. But I have a feeling God isn't going to let them worm their way out of this one. What you've just witnessed, guys, is a miracle.'

It felt like the beginning of the end, the end of this dark time I had suffered, and I was finally closer to the light at the end of the tunnel. So close, I could reach out and touch it. Everything I had felt in my heart, and deep down knew all along, was coming true.

I kept my face neutral as I walked out past the paps and got into the car, where the documentary crew were waiting. Nobody had any idea the case was likely to be thrown out. I looked at everyone as I walked past. The paps, the journos, all whispering amongst themselves, the members of the public holding up their camera phones. They didn't have a clue about what was about to come. I smiled inside. They would know soon enough. Everyone would know, and then the documentary would air, and then, just maybe, I could get my life back.

Me and Gareth looked at each other as the car door

slammed shut and Drew drove off. There was a look of utter shock mixed with pure joy on both our faces. We shook our heads at each other. 'I think you've done it,' said Gareth, shaking with emotion. I looked at him with my eyes wide and a huge smile across my face.

'I think we might have, G.'

'I don't want to be happy yet, I'm scared,' he whispered back.

'I know, me too. Monday, Monday, we'll celebrate. Let's just try and keep our cool for now.'

Chapter 25:

TU GOOD TU BE TRUE

AS I HEADED down the pathway through the woods to me and Jacob's spot, I practically skipped my way along. I embraced the sunshine and the sound of the birds tweeting like I was in a scene from *The Sound of Music*. I was doing all sorts of weird shit, from saying hello to butterflies to stopping and placing my hand on a tree as if I was going to feel the earth's heartbeat. I was like Snow White with a tan and a Chanel bag. I felt so happy and strong, like I had this new lease of life. I felt my best, but more grown-up, more humble and more enlightened.

I'd gone for the 'peace and love' hippy look, wearing a cream and beige long floral dress and brown sandals. My hair was down and wavy, blowing around wildly in the summer breeze and I had hardly any make-up on, apart from a bit of cover-up over the dark circles from the sleepless nights and a little mascara to make my eyes look as alive as I felt. I bounced towards Jacob and Prince when I saw them.

'Hello, my little muffin! Did you miss your mummy?' I squealed in my baby voice, grabbing Prince as he jumped on me and we fell to the floor. I giggled and squeezed his cheeks while kissing the side of his soft squidgy face. I got up and turned to face Jacob.

'Hello, fuckface! How's tricks?' I grinned.

He looked at me suspiciously.

'You're very perky today, good to see,' he half-smiled.

'Well, life's too short for stressing over bullshit, so why the fuck not?' I grinned.

'Something's different with you, I can feel it,' he said, laying on the grass as I joined him.

'Is that so?' I grinned. He frowned at me, intrigued. I was afraid of what I was about to say, as if I was about to jinx it.

'I think it's over, babe, I think I'm free,' I smiled.

He shook his head, confused.

'What are you talking about? You don't know that for sure, babe, you've still got weeks to go,' he said, as if I was being delusional. I shook my head back at him.

'He got caught lying in court today. Unless they find some miraculous way of going against the only righteous laws that actually apply to my case that they've created, it's over, I'm free. My lawyers confirmed it to me.'

His eyes widened as he registered my words and his jaw dropped. 'Baby, you're free? It's over? Are you telling me it's over?' I nodded at him and smiled joyfully.

'My baby, you did it! You actually did it!' He lifted his hands to his head in disbelief as my smile grew even wider.

'I told you someone up there has my back.'

He looked at me, still shaking his head. 'How the fuck did that happen?'

His eyes were wide with shock.

'I thought you said you knew all along it would end this way,' I said. He looked at me, filled with happiness and confusion.

'Yeah, but not like this! Now the guy could be bloody prosecuted and you're free as a bird, you've fucking ended him! This is a miracle! You jammy little dodger! How the fuck do you do it? It ain't normal! Oh my days!' He reached out and grabbed me and squeezed me so tight I felt all the air leave my lungs.

'Babe, I can't breathe,' I whimpered.

'You did it! You fucking did it! I can't even tell you how happy I am right now! I knew it! But now it's happening and like this, I just can't believe it! Powerful! Absolutely powerful! You! Only fucking you!' He was yelling now. I felt his strong heart beating fast against my chest as he squeezed me again, he was practically shaking.

Prince jumped up and licked both of our faces, trying to squeeze in between us. The three of us huddled up on the grass. Me and Jacob kept staring into each other's eyes, full of joy. When it came to the spiritual side of things, no one got me more than Jacob.

'Oh my God! Look! It's your little mates!' he exclaimed.

I looked over and spotted the two magpies sat in the field, side by side, and smiled.

'Hello, Mr and Mrs Magpie,' I said, giving them both a salute.

'It's a sign, babe, you made it,' Jacob grinned.

'And you helped me get through it. Thank you for being there for me, babe, honestly,' I said seriously, staring into his eyes.

'I told you, I've got you, always,' he said leaning in to kiss me and resting his hand on my face. I pressed my lips against his and paused, enjoying the moment with the sun beaming down on us and the cool breeze on my skin. We'd come a long way from our first kiss to Duke Dumont's 'I Got U' and Jacob's cheeky arse grab.

'I've got you too,' I whispered.

Chapter 26.

TU-DAY'S A NEW DAY

MONDAY WAS FINALLY here! I stretched out my body
in Jacob's arms and yawned before relaxing back into his
embrace and snuggling into him as he awoke. Today was
the big day, this was it! It was possibly the first day of the
rest of my life as a free woman.

Two hours later, I headed to court with my team in full
force – Aunty Maz, Cat, Gareth, Drew, Jonathan Levi and
the camera crew. We had called the doc people immediately.
Simon Jones (my press manager) and my cousin Spiros
(Dappy's brother) met me there.

I touched the two icons in my pocket for comfort as I got
out the car, a Saint Christopher chain that I got from the
mum of my other ex-boyfriend, Jack O'Connell, was also
tucked in around my neck. I was still very close to her and
she had been in touch the whole way through it all. There
was an even bigger herd of paparazzi and press today, more

so than ever before. The press had clocked that something was going on, but they were unsure exactly what. Simon Jones had told me they thought there was going to be a jury change after Friday's events. I managed to keep my composure and hide my excitement over what could actually be about to happen.

When we first went into court, the judge started off by dismissing the jury from the case and then we were told we'd be taking an immediate short break, so I decided to go for a quick cigarette outside with Maz, Simon and Gareth.

The paps and press didn't realise I'd be out so early so they'd all gone for breakfast. I went and sat on a wall outside the court, stared up at the surrounding trees and breathed in the air. I was feeling very spiritual today.

This was it, I thought. *When I walked back in that court-room, I would get my verdict.*

I suddenly spotted my Mr Magpie flying down from one of the trees, but this time he flew straight down on to the wall and sat next to me.

'Well hello, Mr Magpie,' I smiled.

'Even your little feathery pal has come down for the big day,' laughed Gareth.

'He's solid, Mr Magpie, a true friend. He wouldn't miss it for the world, would you, Mr Magpie?' He tilted his little head at me before flying off, back up into the tree.

Simon clapped his hands with excitement. 'OK! Are we ready? Ready to get your life back? Look at them all! They have no idea! It's hilarious! I can't wait! This is the best day ever!' he said joyfully. Simon had been a true friend to me throughout the trial and had gone way beyond work duties.

'It hasn't happened yet, Si. Anything could happen in my world,' I said jokingly.

'Oh, come on, Tulisa, positive thinking! You know this is all meant to be! The start of the bigger picture! The return of Tulisa! Ta da! She's baaaack!' He threw his arms in the air dramatically and we all laughed.

'Let's go inside,' said G.

I was overwhelmed with emotion as I walked back into the court. I didn't know what to think, what to feel, it was all too surreal. I didn't really want to register any of the emotions properly until I heard the words with my own ears. I let out a big breath I didn't even realise I was holding in and gasped. I looked down at the floor in shock and sat down nervously in the dock. They had called my friend Mike in today and they had him sat next to me. Mike had been going through a whole different case for dealing the drugs, but the two cases were still connected. I had felt terrible: not only was I fucked off the back of it, but Mike was fucked too, and the worst part was that he wasn't even a drug dealer.

He had started off as a rapper but moved into acting and writing scripts. I had actually been trying to do him a favour by connecting him with Mahmood, which had obviously turned out terribly. I didn't know what was going to happen, but I still felt responsible. Not surprisingly, Mike was distraught since he found out and was arrested. I had been paying his legal bills but we hadn't spoken much – it was a very awkward and shit situation.

We'd had a couple of conversations though, and one in particular that very much sparked my interest. He told me that he'd been offered a deal – if he testified against me and told everyone that I told him to go and deliver the drugs, he'd been told he could walk free. I had found this extremely disturbing, from the justice system's perspective. Like something a lot bigger had been going on here. *They really are out to get me*, I thought. He had told me he had turned the deal down, which crushed my heart even more. If what he was saying was true, what a fucking guy! He was as solid as they come. I prayed that today he would be rewarded for that decision.

The judge entered the courtroom and we all did the usual stand up and sit down routine. The atmosphere was so tense, you could have cut it with a knife. The judge looked stern as usual, so it was hard to read where this was going.

I took a deep breath and held it in as he began to speak.

The judge told the jury the case 'cannot go any further' because there were 'strong grounds to believe' that Mr Mahmood had 'lied' at a hearing before the trial started.

Explaining his decision, Judge McCreath said: 'Where there has been some aspect of the investigation or prosecution of a crime which is tainted in some way by serious misconduct to the point that the integrity of the court would be compromised by allowing the trial to go ahead, in the sense that the court would be seen to be sanctioning or colluding in that sort of behaviour, then the court has no alternative but to say "This case must go no further".'

It's over, I cried in my head, *it's actually over!* It didn't feel real! I looked at Mike and saw tears rolling down his face, tears of joy.

I grabbed him and hugged him. 'It's over!' I said. I turned and looked around the room. All my friends were hugging each other and crying with joy. I looked at Gareth, who was staring right at me, looking very emotional. Tears began to roll down my cheeks as I looked back at him. 'We did it,' I mouthed. 'I know,' he mouthed back. I looked at Cat, who had her face to the ground, trying to disguise the fact that she was balling her eyes out, wiping her face profusely. I chuckled to myself, *even the ice queen is crying.* Everyone I knew was crying. The court was in uproar. All the press were in a state of hustle and bustle, on their phones, making calls, sending emails. It was all so loud and chaotic. Some members of the press and paps were trying to catch my eye.

As soon as I was let out the dock, I ran to Gareth and squeezed him, both of us shaking from head to toe. I turned to face a hysterically blubbering Aunty Maz. She could barely breathe. She grabbed me frantically as if I'd just been spared from death and cried in my arms, thanking God and all the saints in heaven for their mercy. She made the sign of the cross over my face.

'Saint Marina!' she cried. 'You've been blessed! I knew it!'

Her motherly emotion sent me over the edge as I burst into floods of tears on her shoulder, letting it all out. I saw the press watching me, all of them actually smiling now. I couldn't believe it.

'Come on, let's go to the room,' said Simon Jones tearfully.

'Thank you for standing by me, Simon.' I grabbed him and hugged him as I walked out of the courtroom, a free woman.

I spent about half an hour hugging and crying with everyone, even my legal team had tears in their eyes. Cat pulled back from a cuddle. 'OK, OK, enough for a moment, all these emotions are going to give me a heart attack, my brain isn't used to it! This is one of the most emotional journeys I've ever seen,' she snivelled. I smiled at her through my tears.

'After all these years, who woulda thought you were right? A man would never be the one to melt you, it was me!' She burst into a half-laugh, half-cry.

'Let's get the hell out of here! Finally! Are you ready to face the press and show the world you're innocent?' asked Simon.

'I'm shitting it, Si! I know I've gotta read my statement, I fucking hate reading statements.'

'Well, this is the happiest one you will ever read!'

'Yeah, I know. I just wish I didn't have to do it in these bloody high heels! I might throw them into the crowd afterwards,' I laughed.

'You will be fine! This is one statement you can enjoy!

Take your time and embrace it. All the press and paps are waiting for you. Now straighten that fantastic suit, fix your face and let's not disappoint!'

I waited and watched behind the glass doors for the all-clear. A female officer grabbed me and gave me a hug. 'I'm so happy for you, love! We were all rooting for ya!' She smiled. I took a deep breath and exhaled as I watched the huge crowd outside behind the barriers. It felt like I was going out to give some kind of performance.

'Are you ready?' said Simon.

'Yes,' I let out another big breath.

'Ready?' whispered G, looking in my eyes to make sure. I nodded at him. 'Good! Now remember, stand up straight, head up, read slowly and clearly like you mean what you say. Now strut out there like Kate Moss and show them Tulisa's back!' he said.

I smiled and nodded, taking deep breaths. I didn't feel fierce right now, because I wasn't fighting – the fight was over. I just felt grateful to be free, but I would give it my best shot. The two doors were opened for me as I walked out with the team. Everything felt like it went into slow motion. The camera lights flashed in unison, creating a blinding light. I struggled to see the mic stand in front of the news crews. The crowd was shouting things out, I could barely make out what I was hearing amongst so many loud voices. Once I reached the microphone, the lights calmed for a second and everyone waited for me to speak. I looked around at the massive audience. The printed statement was shaking in my hands. *Just be calm,*

I thought, *you've got this. Take as long as you want, just get all the words out clearly.*

So many people, paps, news crews, journos, bystanders, fans, even the jury had stuck around. I saw members of the public holding up their camera phones patiently, waiting for me to say something. When the fuck did this happen? Who the fuck am I? How did I cause so much hysteria? I'm just me.

I took another deep breath and let it out before I leaned forward towards the microphone.

'Let me be perfectly clear. I have never dealt drugs and never been involved in taking or dealing cocaine. This whole case was a horrific and disgusting entrapment by Mazher Mahmood and *The Sun on Sunday* newspaper. Mahmood has now been exposed by my lawyers, openly lying to the judge and jury. These lies were told to stop crucial evidence going before the jury.

'This evidence shows that I told Mahmood's long-standing driver that I disapproved of drugs, which is the truth. It is clear that the driver was pressured to change his statement to strengthen Mahmood's evidence and to damage mine. Thankfully the lies have been uncovered, and justice has been done.

'This case only happened because Mahmood and his team tricked me into believing I was auditioning for a major movie role. They targeted me at a time when things were going badly for me and they had no mercy. Mahmood got me and my team completely intoxicated and persuaded me to act the part of a bad, rough, ghetto girl.

They recorded this and produced this as evidence when I thought it was an audition. It was a terrible thing to do. As my lawyer said at the outset, we have now succeeded in exposing the real culprits and, most importantly, the real liar.

'As someone who has had my life ruined for the last year, I strongly believe that this type of entrapment should not be allowed to happen to anyone. I urge both the police and News UK to investigate Mazher Mahmood and his team and to put an end to his deceit in pursuit of sensational stories for commercial gain. I have not been able to work for a year and I am now looking forward to resuming my career. I will use these experiences to make me stronger. I would like to thank all the people who have supported me through this terrible ordeal, including my fans and, of course, my legal team.'

Once I finished speaking, I looked back up at the cameras one last time before I headed to the car. The lights roared up again, along with the voices. I could hear my name being called and shouted everywhere around me. As I walked towards the car, I recognised a particular member of the jury in the street. She stood watching the commotion and smiled at me, I smiled back. Then I fought my way through the paps and news crews to get into the car with the help of my team.

'Get out of the way!' I could hear police officers shouting.

As I got in the car I was immediately greeted by another bright light. It was the documentary camera. I instantly burst into tears again as soon as the car door shut. There was no room for holding back, all I could do was let it all out. I called my mum, who I had explained everything a little more to before the trial, and I called my grandmother and cried down the phone to both of them. I knew my Yia Yia would be happier than anyone that I was free.

Once I was all cried out and had calmed down, I checked my phone. There were so many messages. The news feed had gone everywhere and I was currently being replayed and blasted across the nation's news, along with the online press before it hit the papers tomorrow. Everyone now knew. I searched through text upon text of congratulations. There was only one person I wanted to speak to right now.

I opened the text from Jacob. I knew he had been watching and waiting:

5 TEXTS

J: you're free! Boooooooom! I felt it!

J: Love that, I'm so happy for you babe, you would not believe, I can see the happier you now, the less fiery one! lol

J: God's got us now babe, let's be clever

J: Call me!

J: I'm actually proper happy for you x

T: Thank you for holding my hand through the hardest time of my life... I will never forget that, no matter what, realer than all of them xxx

J: So you do get it lol, enjoy this day. You're special to me, don't let me down x

T: Vice versa x

J: hahahahahaha! Boooooom! Next chapter!

And the next chapter it certainly was.

When I arrived back at my apartment, my cousin Dappy was waiting outside to greet me. He had his usual emotional look in his eyes that he'd maintained since this had all begun. He gave me a big silent hug that lasted for about a minute and a half. I exhaled into it, taking in his familiar scent. We're more like brother and sister than cousins. We had grown up in the same household till the age of about three.

'I'm free, Daps,' I whispered.

'I know, sister sister. I'm so happy for you, I was so scared, man.'

'Everything is gunna be OK now, Daps, you'll see.'

'I know it will. Watch when we come back with N-Dubz, we're gunna smash it.'

'I know, love you, bro.'

'Love you, sis.

Not long after I arrived home, Jacob came over. Me, Dappy, Gareth and my Aunty Maz had all been drinking to celebrate. Needless to say, I was a little tipsy.

I hurried towards the knocking on my apartment door and flung it open with a big grin. Jacob paused, with a smile on his face, staring into my eyes. I stared back at him. What a moment.

'I'm free, I'm actually fucking free,' my voice was filled

with emotion. He lunged towards me and lifted me into the air with a big hug.

'Baby! I'm so fucking happy for you, man, you don't understand! I knew! I knew all along in my heart you would be OK! This is it now, don't ever forget this moment. No more bullshit. Watch your back and stay focused, we're gunna smash it!'

He placed me back down after spinning me around like a scene out of *Dirty Dancing*. I looked up into his big brown eyes and a tear fell from mine.

'No more tears now,' he whispered, wiping my eye. 'I've got you.'

He held my chin and placed a gentle kiss on my lips.

'And I've got you, babe.'

Me and Jacob were not perfect, far from it, but one thing was for certain, the love was real. I had never met anyone like him. We were so similar in so many ways. We had a soul tie, as if we'd known each other for many lifetimes, and probably many more to come. I loved him, with more fire and passion than I'd ever loved anyone. And I knew he loved me too. We still had a lot of issues that I knew we might not be able to overcome in this lifetime, but either way I was sure I'd still meet him in the next. We were meant to be together at this time, and he was meant to be by my side through all of this, as if it was destiny written in the stars. And for all the ups and downs, and no matter where we ended up, one thing was for sure.

He made one hell of a story.

Chapter 27:

FREEDOM

OVER THE NEXT 48 hours, my whole world was turned upside down, or you could say upright. The next day I did a media run with all the press. Finally, my side of the story was being told. I could feel the instant turn of energy, with the public and with the media. It was no longer about the fall of a popstar, it was about the rise of an underdog.

As the days passed after the trial, things took their time to sink in. I felt happy and positive about my life and the future most of the time, but it was as if I wasn't registering why. I'd become so accustomed to living on a charge for so long, I had to continuously remind myself that it was no longer happening, that the main weight off my shoulders was gone. I had to keep reminding myself of why I felt happy when I did, and why I should feel happy when I didn't. I was definitely dealing with the wreckage after the storm, but so far, I'd say I was coping rather well, and the only thing that was keeping me from being truly happy was the fear of losing my success and my income.

Me and Gareth had worked out a plan to start regaining my career. First, the documentary about my year of the sting had to air, then I would do a press run and interviews for the first time since it all began. Once the public saw the full truth behind it all, I had faith that they would be more accepting of my return and that more people, along with the press, would also get back on side, excluding *The Sun*, of course.

I also planned to finish and release my book. Then I would really tell my story, but not until I was a lot closer to getting my life back. I wanted a true happy ending, a real-life fairy tale, one that would give people hope! So, I could only hope that that's where my life was headed. I knew ultimately I would get there one day. I'd get my fairy tale ending one way or the other! After all, I'd got this far, hadn't I? But the problem is with me, you just never know what's around the corner, good or bad, and I knew there would be more madness to come. I just prayed there would at least be some good madness to make it all worthwhile. The only thing I could be sure of was that I would never be short of something to write about.

The world is a beautiful and dark place, and for all the bad in it, there is also good. For every struggle there is prospering, for every death there is a birth, and for every tear there is a smile! Life is a rollercoaster of cycles, give and take, the bad times with the good. And if I hadn't had the bad times, I might have forgotten how good the good times really were, and I might not have remembered how important it is to appreciate and give back, from the smaller things to the bigger things, depending on what you're capable of. From saving a life to just putting a smile on a friend in need's face. No matter how little a thing, it all counts. It would be impossible for one person to change the world, but imagine if everyone in the world changed themselves, just a little, the world could be a much better place.

I made a promise to the universe that, after my year of enlightenment that I had asked and prayed for, I would try to be a better person whenever I could, to be kinder, more understanding, caring, thoughtful, helpful, honest, grateful and forgiving towards others. I'm never going to be perfect, that's not what life is about, but I could definitely do better, we all could. We've gotta go through it, to grow through it.

I didn't know what was next for me. I mean, I had plans, don't get me wrong. The world was my oyster, I had the ability to dream again and try and make those dreams come true. But one thing I have come to know in my world is 'always expect the unexpected'. Either way, I believed the universe had my back, and a plan. So I could only do my best, and sit back and enjoy the ride.

SOME MONTHS LATER....

The wind blew my hair around furiously as I put pedal to the metal for my first spin in my brand new 458 Ferrari Spider.

'You fucking did it, T!' squealed Gareth. 'Just when I really believed it was all over, you fucking did it again, you jammy fucking bitch!' he said, laughing hysterically.

All of a sudden, the music stopped, as Gareth turned it down and rested his hand on my shoulder.

'T! It's Simon Jones. He just texted me, saying call me immediately! Exclamation mark! It's either spectacular or devastating news... Shit, feel my heart!'

'I can't, I'm bloody driving! What the fuck's going on? Put my phone on charge and get Simon on loudspeaker!' G quickly did as I asked. My heart raced with anticipation as I listened to the ringing tone over the sound of my deep breathing.

The trial had literally given me PTSD. Every time I saw Simon's name come up on my phone or the start of any headline, I felt like I was going to have a heart attack.

'Hello? Gareth?' said Simon Jones on the other end of the line.

'Yeah, I'm here, what's up? T can hear you too, you're on loudspeaker,' said G nervously.

'Are you two alone?' he asked.

'Yes,' we both said in unison.

'Good, I hope you're ready for what I'm about to tell you...'

TU BE CONTINUED...

EPILOGUE

APRIL 2025

I STARED OUT my living window peacefully at the green Cheshire hills and fields that stretched across the horizon as far as the eyes could see. I took in a deep breath and exhaled.

Finally, everything is as it should be, peaceful, I thought.

I was distracted by a sharp little knock on the window from outside and brought my eyes down to see the familiar cheeky grin of my goddaughter, Nevaeh, staring up at me. Her big blue eyes and golden curly locks glistened in the warm summer sunlight.

'I can see you in her more each day,' I said, turning around to Michelle, who was sat by the kitchen counter with her husband, Daniel, chomping down on the rice and lamb chops I'd cooked for them. She flashed me a warm hearty smile that felt like home while trying to contain the large bite of lamb chop she had just consumed.

Me and Michelle had come a long way. She had been there for me through thick and thin.

After the trial, over time, we had become more like sisters than friends. She was my family now, as was Daniel. I had known him through Dappy and Fazer for as long as I'd known Michelle. I had always had a big brother dynamic with him and he had always looked out for me, so when Michelle met him at a party seven years ago and they both felt a spark, I had happily given her the thumbs up and encouraged the relationship, which later lead to the birth of my beautiful god-daughter, Nevaeh.

The three of us, all Cancerians – Daniel's birthday being the day after mine – have become a very tight trio. We have created our own little family. Michelle and Daniel are like my brother and sister, and I am the happily adopted third wheel. It is such the family dynamic that I moved all the way to Cheshire to be closer to them. I had always loved Manchester and it had always felt like a second home to me. I had spent pretty much ninety per cent of my leisure time there over the years while staying with Michelle, it made sense for me to make the move.

I had also built another sister dynamic with my friend Percy, who I had known since I was 17. She had been around during the trial, but it was only really afterwards, as I reevaluated my life after everything that happened, that we really began to get super close and solidify our friendship. Percy was already at a distance from me at

306

that time, with her living in East London and me up in Hertfordshire, so due to that, her work commitments and her son, Pason my other godchild (total clever clogs), we would only get to meet up once every six weeks to two months. So, it has all worked out pretty perfectly because, after I moved, Percy would use her weekends as an opportunity to get away from London and come up North to let her hair down and relax. In between that we are each other's phone buddies and speak every day, the kind of friends that leave the phone on FaceTime in the corner of the room and go about their business.

Through our bond, Percy has in turn become very close with Michelle and Dan, and together we have become the fantastic four. Or as I like to call us, the soul family. True love is a beautiful thing; I feel extremely blessed to have it and I cherish it dearly. I have become the kind of person that would do anything for their soul family, as they would for me.

A year ago, I bought my dream home, only 20 minutes away from Michelle and Daniel and had spent 6 months doing it all up to perfection. It was the first time I'd lived anywhere that felt like home. I hadn't settled anywhere in my life. After the trial, I constantly rented, moving from apartment to apartment, never settling or making it my own. I had lived alone for seven years after I stopped living with Gareth, who I eventually grew apart from as people do in a world where we are constantly growing and evolving and trying to find ourselves.

I had learned to love living alone to the point where I

couldn't imagine ever living with anyone. It even made me dread settling down with a future partner. My home was my sanctuary, my peace.

My harrowing experiences in 2013 still affected me though and I had kitted out the house with alarms and cameras both inside and out, as well as large electric blackout gates. I also had two security guard dogs in training, though my little Narla was still rocking. In 2023 I was told that she had cancer and only had around 6 weeks to live, yet she is still here going strong, just like her mum.

I now live in a quiet countrified area in the middle of nowhere, which is exactly how I like it. My life journey has turned me into more of an introvert these days and I am pretty much a shadow of my old extrovert, sociable, party self. In my spare time I embrace the quiet life now. Don't get me wrong, I still love the odd blowout and fun sociable holiday now and then, but it is all very much few and far between.

Most of the time I remain focused on my health, fitness and mental wellbeing, eating well, training, meditation, routine and structure, as well as being very focused on taking the leap into the property game that I've got planned for the end of this year. Honestly, I'm a bit of nerd in my spare time. I've gone back to being an avid reader like I was in my teens. I'm obsessed with Ancient History and Ancient Alien theories. I'm currently on my fifth read of *The Emerald Tablets of Thoth the Atlantean.* I watch all things fantasy, play PlayStation and of course I still love to cook, especially in my new kitchen.

But most of all I love spending quality time with the people I love. I have always been quite a detached individual, a lone wolf so to speak. I was the kind of person that had a certain level of love for everyone and had a lot of friends, but I didn't really zone in on building healthy and strong bonds with any particular individual. But since the trial, that has all changed. Yes, I've got fewer friends but I've got quality relationships with the ones I have. Relationships that consist of love, support, respect, safety and loyalty. I can honestly say that, through the experience of the trial, I have learned love.

I have come a long way, not just in love, but in all areas of my life.

* * *

I proudly scanned my eyes around the open-plan living space that quite literally had me written all over it. From the Sumerian and Egyptian deities carved into the stone wall around the fire place to the large white, yellow and gold N-Dubz plaque I'd had customised to perfectly match the living room colours.

In 2022, after six years of planning with blood, sweat and tears trying to reunite the group, we had finally made an epic return to the spotlight. We had announced a brand-new arena tour as well as new music that had gauged a response more gratifying than I could ever imagine in my wildest dreams. The arena tour sold out in three minutes and went on to sell out three more times over that week, also selling out the London 02 arena four times over. Our new album went into the Top 10, and was our highest charting album in its first week.

It was only really in that moment that I felt a true sense of redemption and justice since the trial, as well as a sense of retribution towards my enemies.

I had always known the power of N-Dubz and the group had always been in my plans after the trial, knowing I would never truly feel like I had taken back my power until we came back together again. I would have to bring it back to where it all started. It was the only way, I knew that much.

Since the trial I had done my far share of dipping in and out of the industry. After the trial the documentary that I had filmed – *The Price of Fame* – had been released on BBC 3. Despite everything, I also immediately returned to *The X Factor* as a guest judge on 'Judges' Houses' and I was also on the panel during the Final, which felt like a nice touch of redemption at the time. I had also won a court case for writing a song called 'Scream & Shout' that had been number one worldwide for Britney Spears after will.i.am and the producer of the beat decided to release it without my clearance.

The pay-out for that had turned out to be pretty nice in the end and it has continued to pay me nicely to this day, so it worked out fairly well in the end. I dropped a few solo songs over the years too and would appear back on TV and radio for the 'promo runs' for a few months, utilising the press power that remained relatively strong whenever I decided to rear my head, only to disappear back into the safety of isolation and a quiet life once the promo was done, avoiding any type of camera and attention at all. I actually deactivated my Instagram for about two years, but I've come to enjoy it again.

My relationship with fame had become a paradox. Sometimes I had the urge to get out there and attempt to take over the world, to try and fight to get back to my glory days. But most days I just felt physically sick at the thought. It all seemed so meaningless to me now, fame, validation and approval from others, people that don't even know you and never truly will. It all felt so shallow and fickle. I had already had a dodgy relationship with fame and the industry before all the drama happened, feeling like a black sheep in the game. But now it all felt like absolute nonsense to me, quite literally straight-up bullshit. This idea that people are worshipped and put up on pedestals – sometimes for a real talent, noted, but a lot of the time, mostly for being attractive, well-connected and rich. Where was the fame for the people saving lives every day through great and hard work? The humanitarians trying to solve world hunger or the scientists dedicating their lives to saving the planet from global warming?

This was a life I had always wanted to live and was still living, but I was conflicted about it, and sometimes it grated on my soul. Some days I would still crave that kick of success and glory. Other days I wanted to buy a piece of fenced-off land, grow my own fruit and veg and convert to Buddhism.

And that is the journey of life, I suppose. A series of paths and questions, decisions and outcomes. Forever changing, growing and evolving like everything else in this wondrous universe, figuring out who we are and who we want to be. I had come to the conclusion that life was simply the school of knowledge through experience, and I was still learning and would continue to do so. I'm not supposed to know all the answers.

To live is to learn, and to remain comfortable and stagnant is nothing but a slow death.

This life had all but nearly completely destroyed me, and in many ways it had, only to rebirth a new evolved version of myself that I am now grateful for. I can see clearer now, I have a strong sense of inner peace and an internal happiness that comes from within. It wasn't easy, but I'm proud of myself. I've managed to successfully return with N-Dubz and had a fun little stint on *I'm a Celebrity*... though it has confirmed my feelings of wanting to remain a little less in the spotlight. I can't say I enjoyed eating lamb bollocks and being pissed on with rain during the rainiest season ever, but I am grateful for the experience because it's only by getting uncomfortable that we can grow. Mostly I was very grateful for the opportunity to show people my true self after so many years of such giant misconception of who I truly was, and I've certainly felt a change for the better in people's energy towards me since. All is finally well, but there were certainly moments along the way to get to this point where my hope was short...

After Mazher Mahmood's lies were exposed in court, he became the one facing prison and I became the key witness in the case against him. What a turn of events! But it also meant an even lengthier road for my 'sting' journey to go down. I felt as if that part of my life was never going to end. The whole thing had lasted years. The surveillance I was seemingly under at the time worsened and strange things started to happen, with men in Range Rovers following me round whenever I went out. Even my friends were being approached by strange individuals and some of Gareth's emails started to go missing, as if they had been deleted. I became paranoid to leave the house unattended and always wanted to make sure either me, Gareth or Narla was always home. Narla was just a Staffy, but she was a ferocious one when under threat.

One day after moving into a new apartment to try and escape the surveillance and press, I risked a walk around the block with Narla when Gareth was out. When I returned, my front door was not only wide open, but one of my moving boxes had been placed against it to keep it open. I felt as if someone was trying to send me a message, one that said, 'it's this easy'. I began feeling like my life was in danger. But after all the shit I'd been through, I also had strangely opposed emotions towards death. I didn't really fear it anymore. I only feared being made to feel helpless, small and broken by others. I feared fear itself, I suppose. And to avoid it, I would be willing to burn it all down, myself included.

Things took a dark turn between the period of my trial and Mahmood's trial, during which time, I made a much more definitive suicide attempt. I felt as if my life would never be the same; I felt empty inside as if all the joy had been sucked out of me and would never return. So I took a cocktail of sleeping tablets in a bid to never wake up. But I hadn't taken into account that I sometimes had a strange tendency to sleepwalk on one of the tablets I'd taken – it was mostly sleep eating, other times walking around and being extremely talkative. I had discovered this one night when I woke up to find a terrified Gareth at the bottom of my bed, staring at me as if I was possessed. After checking I was fully coherent, he showed me a video he had taken of my bizarre behaviour. He'd thought I had finally gone mad, but after speaking to my aunt – who knew all too well the dangers of sleeping tablets and once caught me in the kitchen making a creamy chicken pasta and pouring Worcestershire sauce on top – we had realised it was down to the tablets.

And on the particular night of my suicide attempt, not only was it a sleepwalk night, but it felt like it had been turned up to 100 with the other tablets taking effect too, during which time I had sent a few strange messages to people I knew and also made a phone call to my friend, Cat. She knew instantly that something was wrong and somehow managed to get me to unlock the front door before I passed out so she could get in. She headed straight over and she later said when she found me that she thought I was already dead as I was seemingly blue from head to toe – she could see veins running up my neck and through my face – so she rang for an ambulance. I've never remembered much about that night since or what happened afterwards, it was a complete blur other than little flashes here and there. I don't even remember coming out of hospital. I only know what Cat told me a few years later when I finally asked, and how the ambulance crew were desperately trying to keep me alive and how Cat thought I was going to die. I was in hospital for three days and when I finally came around the first thing I said was, 'Why the fuck am I still here?!' That moment I did remember.

Like I said, I don't remember much about that time afterwards but there is one memory that sticks out a while after, where I was sat in my bed and had a kind of epiphany. I decided it wasn't a coincidence that the sleeping tablet that had caused me to have such weird symptoms throughout my life had actually seemingly prevented my death, and that the 'universe' wasn't done with me yet in this lifetime. So, I decided to stick around and wait to see what was in store that could possibly be so important that some higher power had felt the need to keep me here and continue to suffer all this nonsense.

When it finally came to the time of Mahmood's trial, he decided on his first day of court that he would not put in any defence, therefore I wouldn't be called to be a witness. It was a relief as I certainly didn't want to step foot in a courtroom again. Mahmood was found guilty of conspiring to pervert the course of justice and was sentenced to 15 months in prison. He and his former driver, Alan Smith, were charged with the same offence following the investigation into 25 cases where Mahmood gave evidence. I'm glad a degree of justice was served, at least. I like to think that he had his year of enlightenment, just as I had mine.

But I heard through the grapevine that he only served a very small fraction of that time and that he went on to continue working with certain newspapers, behind the scenes and off the books of course. How's that true justice, eh?

I can recall a day, after Mahmood had gone to prison, when I was once again pondering – as I often did – on the fact that the case had all fallen apart on the day of Saint Marina (in the Greek orthodox religion), who I had prayed to, just as my Yia Yia had told me to. Something in me spurred me on to find out more and what I discovered surprised even me....

Marina was a young girl from Antioch of Pisidia (in what is now the Anatolian region in Turkey), who had chosen to never marry and essentially become a Christian nun, despite receiving much attention from men. The Governor of her region was in awe of her beauty and publicly asked for her hand in marriage, which she gracefully declined, staying true to her faith. So the Governor threw her in prison and proceeded to physically torture her, driving nails into her body and burning her with fire to change her mind. He did this publicly too and then eventually killed her. The people spoke of witnessing great miracles from Saint Marina when she was brought before them, one of them being the fact that her wounds would miraculously heal when they saw her.

She had told the people she had seen both Satan and God in her cell, and that she had prayed to God, who had in turn healed her. The people believed in her so much that they began converting to Christianity and the Governor became so enraged that he executed 15,000 people who he deemed to be her followers. It was a dark but fascinating story and I took comfort from her prayer that I found in my research. I'll leave you with a small part of that prayer that holds such significance for me – pay attention to the fifth line:

O God, who created heaven and earth, hear me. I ask You, my God, for every sinner who comes to

You repenting, erase all his sins. Everyone who comes to my alter praying, give him all what he asks for.

Anyone who is present in a scary court of law, and mentions my name in confidence, grant him victory over his foes. Anyone who builds a church in my name, or writes the story of my martyrdom, give him, my Lord, all what pleases his heart. All sick people who ask You wellness in my name, grant them soon, if You will, good physical and mental health.

Everyone who comes to my church or hears the story of my martyrdom, have compassion on him, O

Lord, by forgiving all his sins. Anyone who is afflicted or who falls in the hands of those who are cruel and unjust to him and he asks You in my name, give him deliverance and relief. Whosoever travels in an awful route, whether it be by land or by the sea, help him, O Lord, and return him to his home safely.

The believers who commemorate my martyrdom and those who present in Your Holy altar in remembrance of me, whether they be of the clergy or the laity; remember them, O Lord, in that Day when they stand in front of You. Judge them not, but rather give them comfort with Your saints.

When I first read those words, I knew in that moment that I would share the story of Saint Marina in my book. It always reminds me that for every hardship I have endured in this life, there was always a blessing.

And there were definitely more hardships – I had a few more court cases, which caused some financial issues, and there were a few more scandals, though obviously nothing that topped the experience of the trial. My depression was up and down, and I developed a dependency for sleeping tablets and benzodiazepines over the years that I finally managed to kick in 2024. Throughout it all, I remained determined to come out the other side and find my peace, with the faith that I would one day be in the place that I finally am now.

* * *

And what about love? My love life went on to be chaotic enough to write another ten books. Me and Jacob continued an on/off journey that in total lasted three years. It was mostly off really, but we'd always find our way back to each other. But, by the end the toxicity became absolutely unbearable on both sides. I don't think either of us had ever experienced anyone that triggered the other to such an extent, and I don't think either of us ever will. Still, it was an experience I have never regretted and I learned a lot from – about myself and others – in the game of love. Now, I look back fondly on our time together and believe it was most certainly meant to be during that time. Jacob was a really good guy with a good heart, we had just unfortunately brought out the worst in each other towards the end. I really do wish him nothing but love and blessings, and will always hold a special place for him in my heart. Jacob actually went on to marry and have children, and in 2016 I met a man (let's call him Miles) through Michelle that I went on to have an-almost ten-year journey with that still in a way continues to this day. Though I'll admit it has also been more off than on.

Miles is actually very similar to Jacob in character and looks, and they even have similar careers. But the biggest difference is in Miles' ability to handle me and communicate. He is definitely no angel and our journey has been extremely rocky, but one thing I will give him is that he has a way of not triggering and dare I say, even slightly taming 'The Female Boss' and he is less triggered by me and my ways than most men. I'm not sure if it's because he is a bit older than me, but he's the kind of man that will just walk over and quietly hug me if I'm shouting at him. He also communicates really well and always takes accountability for his actions. Most importantly though is he always gives me the sense that he'll always be there for me, and that he won't abandon me during tough times. He truly sees me as a person and, in many ways, he is very much the kind of man I need. But that hasn't stopped us from experiencing our fair share of drama, which ultimately has prevented us from settling down together. Miles has always been very keen on us having children and always said he'd want to get married, and during the happy times I had wanted the same, though I'd definitely been a little less keen on rushing into children.

After my last breakup with Miles, I went on a three-and-a-half-year celibacy stint. This might seem extreme but it wasn't unusual for me as I had always been more of a 'no sex before monogamy' type. And during this period I reconnected with an ex, let's call him Liam. Even though we dipped in and out of each other's lives, we have always had a strong connection. We even talked marriage and babies – our chats and intentions have always been intense. But like Jacob, I was wary because he was too similar to me. But that didn't stop a bit of a rollercoaster two years where I was pushing and pulling against the emotional connection I had with both Miles and Liam. When one of them would piss me off, I'd start speaking to the other, and so on. Fast forward to September 2024, when I bumped into Liam again. My feelings came back, and strong, and the energy just felt different, like it had stepped up a level. We started off a bit rocky but things got better and I ended up spending Christmas 2024 with Liam and finally put an end to my celibacy stint! I finally took the leap with Liam after all these years and at first, a part of me was really happy. It felt like the games had stopped on both sides and we connected like never before. It was extremely intense, emotional and passionate. We had also both been experiencing a lot of spiritual signs and synchronicities that made it feel as if the universe was pulling us together, and we were picking up those talks about the future, but the rockiness kicked back in once again soon after Christmas. The fear kicked in on my part and I had two freak-outs, where I wanted to do a runner. It was really confronting – I hadn't realised I was so unhealed. I was starting to recognise my own avoidant energy and toxic tendencies. And for the first time in my life, I decided that maybe it wasn't a coincidence that this connection had lasted so long and that this man was managing to light my fire more than ever after all these years.

Maybe there really was something more in this? Maybe my person had been right in front of me all along. I also finally realised that if I ever wanted something healthy and long-lasting, I couldn't keep repeating the same old patterns. So, for the first time in my life, I decided I wasn't going to run at the first sign of hardship and I wasn't going to play any mind games in relation to my own fears. I would stick at this and attempt to work through any problems to become a better version of myself, instead of cutting Liam off again. It had taken a lot of time, but I was becoming more self-aware and I was very slowly beginning to put aside the Female Boss... unless of course she was one hundred per cent necessary.

Then, at beginning of April 2025, just after we'd recovered from my last freak-out – which I had managed to pull us back from rather well, if I do say so myself – Liam pulled some shit that felt very much like our old toxic mind games, the same thing I was trying to overcome in myself. The big question for me was, was this who he still was or was this his trigger moment? Was it now just his turn to flip out and overcome, now we'd taken the big leap? We both played these games with each other because we felt a lot for each other, but we were equally terrified of being vulnerable. I felt as if I was ready and self-aware enough to try and change, but was he? Was this a part of the 'sticking at it' we'd resolved to do, something we could work through and come out of the other side? My heart asked these questions, but my ego wouldn't let the heart override. And so The Female Boss won and I pressed the block button yet again. I was starting to learn how to handle my own triggers, but I clearly hadn't been ready for his. And that was only a matter of weeks ago, dear reader, so you're right up to date. I know through friends that Liam wants to reconnect, but this time it's Liam's ego not mine that needs putting in check. So, in the name of Lady Gaga, how bad do you want me?

And now I've reconnected with Miles again. When will it ever end? I know you want some grand romantic conclusion but that wouldn't be real life. I don't know what to do with myself anymore. I felt as if I finally had every area of this thing called life pegged, as much as I possibly could at this point in my life. Everything was for the first time actually perfect. Except one thing: my love life.

The question is, was Mr Right already here? Had I already found my Mr Big? Or was it time to cut ties with all my exes and meet someone new?

Cut to now and I'm forcing myself to date again in a bid for a fresh start, but I have been reminded pretty quickly that I don't particularly enjoy dating, or 'courting' in my case, and I don't really want to get to know new people. I just want to skip all the small talk and uncover their deepest, darkest depths, their fears, their greatest beliefs and what really moves their soul. I wanted to fast forward to the comfortable silences, speaking to each other with only our eyes.

As you'll know from having read my book, I don't do well with surface and dating to me feels really surface, which in turn drains the life out of me and leads me to feeling bored really quickly. What can I say? My Venus is in Gemini. Some things you just can't change, however much soul-searching you do. I've always been a 'Think like a man, act like a woman' kind of gal. I've played the bachelorette for most of my life and at times it's been a lot of fun, but I'm now 36 with 37 fast approaching and all the games haven't brought me any real happiness, only temporary fleeting kicks of excitement and thrills. I know I'm tired of it all, but I am also still scared shitless of settling down.

I decided to freeze my eggs to take the pressure off and bide my time if needs be. All I know for sure is that everything I've been through has left deep scars, but I've also become a different person and it's time for a change. I'd say I'm finally open to finding someone to heal and grow with, and dare I say 'settle down'. I just need to make a bloody decision as to how I'm going to move forward and stick to it.

PING!

I reached down to grab my phone. My eyes widened at what I saw on the screen.

'Guys,' I said, faintly looking over to Michelle and Daniel, who were sat on my sofa while I wrote the ending to this book.

I strutted over to them both and lifted up the screen.

Michelle stared at it, eyes wide with her jaw slightly open.

'Jesus Christ, T. Your love life is like a fucking movie!'

Daniel just looked at me, shook his head and looked back at the screen before trying to contain a burst of laughter.

'I can't cope with you, T. I just can't cope,' he chuckled.

'What are you gonna do?' asked Michelle.

I looked at the message one more time before looking back at them both.

'Pour me a wine and ask me again in 10 minutes. I feel another book coming on...'

ACKNOWLEDGEMENTS

All books have a team behind them. I have to say thank you to Ciara Lloyd (Publisher), Lucy Tirahan (Assistant Editor), Natalia Cacciatore and Tamara Douthwaite (Marketing), Lucy Richardson, Eleanor Stammeijer, and Florence Philip (Publicity), Charlotte Brown and Niall Hegarty (Audio), Kelly Davis (Copyeditor) and Jane Donovan (Proof-reader). Thanks too to the YMU crew (Management) – Nader Dehdashti, Anna Dixon, Jess Titus and Sarah Namande. Thank you, all, for your belief in me and this project, and for all the comforting reminders of what a great story it is and that I can actually write... lol.

I can't tell you how much I appreciate your support and patience with my endless laptop meltdowns, lack of technical knowledge, as well as the fourteen-round battle over the cover design, and all the chaos and drama of a first-time author. You have literally turned my childhood dream into something real and allowed me to take the worst year of my life and turn it into something amazing and inspiring. Quite literally lemons into lemon cake!

Ever since I was a child, I was obsessed with storytelling, reading books and writing my own tales. I read mostly fantasy. I loved the excitement and escapism it brought me. I read more than anyone in my class and I'd always get straight As when it came to writing stories in my English lessons. Most teachers in my school disliked me due to my rebellious nature, but never my English teacher. I was always the English teacher's pet. Writing was always a huge passion for me, one that I was eventually blessed enough to use to my advantage through singing and songwriting. I became an avid storyteller through my music.

In 2012, after rising to even more fame having gone from music to television for *The X Factor*, I then became even luckier when I had the chance to release an actual novel. With the help of a writing partner, I was writing a story about a young successful actress called Sky who accidentally gets caught up in a drugs scandal and goes to prison. Everything was in place and ready to go. I couldn't wait! Releasing my own book was literally a dream come true. But as you've just read in this book, in 2013, I was arrested for selling £800 worth of cocaine. I found myself waiting to be charged and go to trial, where I would face up to four years in prison, and my life as I knew it was instantly destroyed. I was Sky, living a story I'd already written. I felt as if I was in a film or a great crime drama.

I instantly felt the overwhelming urge to start writing everything down. The madness inside was surging to the pen, just bursting to get out. At first, it was chaos. Bundles of information filled with dismay. At times it would turn into epic movie moments where I was telling the story exactly as it was happening through a first-person narrative and then I'd be jumping back to the past tense and sheer anarchy.

After a month or so went by and I began reading back everything I wrote, I realised that there was something in those epic movie moments. One thing I had longed to do as I grew up was write an incredible book myself from start to finish. A creation that was all mine. If I was ever going to write an amazing book, what better or easier story to tell than my own? I was living a real-life story that felt like a novel. The time was right. I knew that one day, if I ended up in prison, this book could be the only way of telling my truth. I always loved Martina Cole (I had my twenty-strong book collection signed by the legend herself), and I was also prone to the odd Katie Price book – I loved the juicy gossip, sexy romance and insights into the world of celebrity when I was a teenager. Two very different genres, that in my book would be combined.

I thought people would be intrigued by the criminal aspect, but they would also want the goss. It would be an insight into the world of celebrity, as well as a juicy love story and a courtroom drama. At that time, I was entering into a new relationship that was full of excitement and a lot of spice. So, I decided to tell it all. The love, the trial and all the tribulations that came with it. Warts and all.

Flash forward to 2014 when it was all over, and I was a changed and free woman. I wasn't sure how I felt about giving so much of myself. After all, I had given so much already. I was offered a deal, but I just couldn't bring myself to do it. I really didn't want any more spotlight then.

In recent times, life has changed. I came back with my band N-Dubz and had a top 5 album as well as a sold-out arena tour. We had managed to sell out the O2 Arena four times over, and in three minutes! I was financially stable again, and I didn't feel like I had anything to prove.

I had always worried that the book might feel like some desperate attempt to redeem myself, to be liked and to be understood. But that wasn't something I needed anymore. Now it's more personal. It will be my own closure. The first and final time I'll tell it all exactly how it was and rid myself of the anxiety that made me shy away from the world of showbiz for so long. Hopefully now my book can be read with a level of respect instead of just intrigue. I want it to be read as my truth through the form of my art. Most of all, I want it to be ENJOYED! Because I believe in it. It's a story like no other, told like no other, and I believe in my heart of hearts that it's a story that can excite, inspire and touch those who read it. The year 2025 is a big year for me, and I figured if I was ever going to do this, it needed to be now.

My father figure growing up was Uncle B, who sadly passed away when I was eighteen. He always used to say to me, 'It's not just your voice or your looks that will make you a star, T, it's your story. Your story is what will be the making of you.'

I felt the time was finally right to tell it.

To everyone involved: I am eternally grateful. Now let's bloody drink.

So a couple of weeks ago
I had a dream that I bought a
diary and began writing all my
thoughts in it, before and after
the dream I was also thinking
about it, I used to write in a diary
when I was younger. I have a
2-13 diary and a 16-18 diary,
pretty long time ago but not since, so why now? I guess back
than they felt like the most event-
ful years of my life... little did I k
so far in my 25 years on this
planet, this definitely feels like
worst 2013, 13 being a suppos